PEOPLE MANAGEMENT

PERSPECTIVES AND PRACTICES

Edited by

Bharti Thaker

2010

Icfai Books
The Icfai University Press

PEOPLE MANAGEMENT: PERSPECTIVES AND PRACTICES

Editor: Bharti Thaker

First Edition: 2010
Printed in India

Published by

The Icfai University Press
52, Nagarjuna Hills, Punjagutta
Hyderabad, India – 500 082
Phone: (+91) (040) 23430–368, 369, 370, 372, 373, 374
Fax: (+91) (040) 23352521, 23435386
E-mail: info@icfaibooks.com, icfaibooks@icfai.org, ssd@icfai.org

ISBN: 9788131407677

Editorial Team: Smitha Ramachandran and S Sreedar
Quality Support: K Prabhakar and Ch Ramesh

People Management

Contents

Overview

People management is an integral part of progress; as centuries have evolved from the Stone Age when people left home in search of food, thereafter constructed monuments, to the present times known popularly as the knowledge age. Centuries before Christ the mobility of people caused changes to happen, the Great Wall of China was built, and the Pyramids were constructed. Changes continued even centuries after Christ, as evidenced by the building of Eiffel Tower and the construction of the Taj Mahal. The environmental and economic changes led to major changes in the profile of the employee. The industrial revolution and technological advancement brought a steady evolution. People management changed in its matter and manner from welfare to training to industrial relation, personnel management and human resource management and to the present customized practices. People management changed as per the circumstances and the needs of the times; from the employers' side as well as that of the employees. The journey has been an extensive, beautiful phenomenon in itself. The very first article written by *Bharti*

Thakar titled **"Advancement of People Management: A Review"** is the curtain raiser explaining this phenomenon.

The book has three sections which explain the various dimensions of people management; they are **I) Evolution, II) Studies** and **III) Experiences.**

It presents issues which will take the reader on the evolution journey toward the future with various studies on fundamental theories on people management and is reinforced with the experiences of people management in certain industries like the IT industry, Police department, etc.

Section I – Evolution

The first article in the section **"Evolution"**, as already mentioned, describes the evolution of the journey. **"The Global Evolution of Industrial Relations: Events, Ideas, and the IIRA"** by *Bruce E Kaufman,* is the next article, which is an outcome of a review symposium which has scrutinized the above book and comments of *John T Delaney* and *Howell John Harris* are presented here. It examines the field of industrial relations from its early origins as a 'strategy and set of tactics developed by social reformers' in the United States, to keep the labour problem 'from boiling over into destructive class struggle' through its globalization after the Second World War up to its present period of decline. It provides scope for debate on the industrial relations area of people management.

The third article **"Square Pegs and Round Holes"** by *Charlie Grantham* and *Jim Ware,* explains what makes people work and brings out the observation that, for governing or managing the people, it is essential to work out proper systems and understand why people work. It also narrates that managing human resources has to be changed according to the time; in these changing times it is no longer a matter of telling employees what to do. The only way to succeed today is to let them know what the management needs, give them reason to 'buy in' and then give them the independence to work and produce results.

The fourth article in this section **"The Changing Face of Leadership – Defining Competencies for the 21st Century"** sourced from *enbConsulting,* shows the transition of leadership perspective from traditional leadership to the leadership perspective of the 21st century. The article lays emphasis on the leaders of future and leadership competencies of the future Global Leaders, Leaders in technology and Leaders in the New Economy. It also highlights those competencies which are considered building blocks for the future as a core cluster for an organization. The article explains the nature of the transactional leader (BC-1960) and the transition from transactional to transformational leader from 1960s to 1980s. It narrates how the period 1980-1990 saw the change leader as the transformational leadership which was gaining ground and it coincided with a period of intense change across all business sectors.

The fifth article **"The Seven Deadly Sins of Leadership Theory"** by *Mitch McCrimmon,* focuses on the development of a new leadership framework. This article describes in detail the seven deadly sins of leadership. It also highlights that there is a shift in focus of the industries, individuals and the working groups and the perceptions need to be changed to manage people in the organization. The author affirms the view that leadership is nothing other than promotion of new directions and is essentially associated with the senior organizational roles. Giving the example of Microsoft, it states how the group as a whole comprises better followers.

The final article in this section **"A Case Study: Changing Human Resource Management Education to Fit the Field"** by *Michael Bedell* and *Gary H Kritz* presents an effort that changed the HR educational model from a functional silos-focused model to an integrated outcome-based model. HR function as a strategic provider and a service provider is explained. The authors are of the view that Human Resource function is ideally positioned to help the organization manage the changes, that include capability awareness and development, change management, technology, employee lifecycle, etc. The article highlights the weakness in the traditional model and the logic for change.

Section II – Studies

Ample research has been conducted in this field. The second section titled "**Studies**" focuses on various such researches. The first article in this section "**The Validity and Usefulness of Management Theories: A Review**" by *J P Cornelissen* and *R Thorpe,* is a conceptual research which attempts to widen the scope of the debate about the relationship between management theory and managerial practice. It sheds light upon the solidity of the claim that academic management theories are validated by successful practical applications. The relationship between different management theories, academic research and practice is explained in detail. The need for the integration of academic research and practices is emphasized. The paper analyzes how far the management technology and practice is dependent on management science. It succeeds in clarifying the relationship between the management theory and practice. It opens a deeper avenue for research.

Organizations often assume that it is possible to 'design' an organization in the same way that engineers can design a new product. But, this is an erroneous assumption and the repeated failures of organizational restructuring provide significant evidence that a different approach is required. The second article "**Designing a New Organisation: A Complexity Approach**" by *Eve Mitleton-Kelly,* focuses on describing an alternative approach based on the logic of complexity with reference to a specific case. It describes the different qualitative and quantitative tools and methods used that help identify the social, cultural, technical and political conditions, that together lead to the co-creation of an enabling framework as the basis for the 'design' of a new organization.

The next article "**Corporate Rejuvenation: A Study of Indian Firms' Post-Economic Reforms**" by *Amita Mital,* studies the process of corporate rejuvenation in line with Indian deregulation and liberalization process. An in-depth analysis has been made of the external and internal factors contributing to the decline and strategies for turnaround/rejuvenation process. It points out that, in the rejuvenation process, amongst others, the information dissemination, commitment of employees, re-engineering processes of human resource management play an important role.

The succeeding article **"Change Management 101: A Primer"** by *Fred Nickols,* provides a broad overview of the concept of "change management" and is mainly written for people who are coming to grips with change management problems for the first time and for more experienced people, who wish to reflect upon their experience in a structured way.

The next article in this section **"Conflict During the Changing Process: Human Resources' Role in 2002 and in 2010"** by *A J du Plessis* is an outcome of an empirical study conducted in South Africa where 207 responses were studied. Primarily, the paper states that, in the absence of regulation mechanisms or insufficient mechanisms to countervail the influence of aggravators, conflict will escalate in size and intensity.

The last article in this section **"e-HRM: Innovation or Irritation?"** by *Huub Ruël, Tanya Bondarouk* and *Jan Kees Looise,* is an explorative empirical study in five large companies on Web-based HRM. Amongst other conclusions is the fact that e-HRM is an innovation in terms of the opportunities it creates to put employee-management relationships in the hands of the employees and line managers and the fast flow of communication. The same would prove to be an irritation, when goals are neither clear nor realistic to line managers and employees, when they do not fit the real needs of the line managers, employees and the HR departments.

Section III – Experiences

The third section "**Experiences**" consists of practices followed in the field of people management; these can prove to be stories for learning.

The first experience relates to the police department. "**Participative Management – A Case Study**" by *Janet M Emmet,* is a study of the participation management within the police department in California, USA. It studies the participation method as a way of community-oriented policing. It focuses on the PMT (participative management team), which has been successfully implemented and has helped the department to a great extent.

The next article "**Reform of Top Management Systems in Japan**" by *Aoki, Hidetaka* focuses on the Executive Officer System (EOS), being one of the top management reforms started in Japanese companies during the late 1990s and the reason behind the failure of this system to produce the expected result. The paper discusses the characteristics of Japanese type of board of directors which have a large number of directors. The internal hierarchy is strong and the percentage of outsiders is low; those promoted within the firm make up the majority. This governance provides the leadership to the organizations.

The third article in this section "**People Management in IT Industry: Issues and Imperatives**" by *Ravi Dasari,* analyses the HR trends and issues in the Indian IT industry. The paper is a consequence of a survey of the software and HR professionals working in the various software companies. The paper suggests the necessity for the firms to regularly screen software employees for computer-related injuries by hiring services of medical professionals concerned.

The last article in this section "**From People Success to Business Success**" by *Julie J Gebauer and Andrew S Cherkas,* focuses on the insurance industry and highlights the major elements that attract, retain and engage employees in it. The best practices in people management in the industry would help in developing a road map for success.

Section I

Evolution

1

Advancement of People Management: A Review

Bharti Thakar

People management is an integral part of progress. Centuries have evolved from the Stone Age, where people left home in search of food, and thereafter constructed monuments to the present times, popularly known as the Knowledge Age. Centuries before Christ, the mobility of people caused changes to happen—the Great Wall of China was built, the Eiffel Tower was constructed, the Taj Mahal was built and Pyramids were constructed. The environmental and economic changes led to major changes in the profile of the employee. The industrial revolution and technological advancement brought a steady evolution. People management changed in its matter and content from welfare to training to industrial relation, personnel management and human resource management and to the present customized practices. People management changed as per the circumstances and the needs of the times both from the employers side as well as the employees'. The journey has been an extensive, beautiful phenomenon in itself. The article researches and reviews the aspects in brief.

Slaves During the 'Feudal Age'

Organized endeavors in people management have existed for thousands of years. The function of directing, planning and controlling of the working people has been an integral part of progress. Since time immemorial, approaches with a 'unitarist view', which believe that the workplace is one happy family with a common goal or the 'pluralist view' that believes that there are people with a variety of views and beliefs and they all have to be driven towards the company goals, have been practiced and experimented with. The existence of the human being surrounds around work and movement and therefore the practices have been propelled by this important fact. The human being either works for himself or for another. During the Stone Age, he worked for food and as civilization crept in, he worked for clothing and thereafter for housing to escape the wrath of nature. This is the fundamental truth, which has not changed since the early history of mankind.

With the initiation of movement across the seas, there grew the distinct class of 'haves' (Lords) and 'have-nots' (Slaves). The slaves worked for the haves and suffered the life of a slave. Many of our monuments, which we consider our heritage today, have been constructed by such workers. The Great Wall of China has been constructed and reconstructed through many dynasties and thousands of people have been engaged in constructing the same. The first dynasty of China was the Qin dynasty which started the construction in 221 BC. The emperor was known to be a cruel and tyrannical man who sent scholars and other thinkers of the time to work on the great wall. The amazing and unbelievable fact which has been noted is that more than a million people died in building this wall.[1] The Pyramid was constructed by approximately 100,000 workers who worked for 20 years on it. Few of the workers were the permanent workers of the Pharaoh, while others were brought in from the nearby villages. There is evidence from the women skeletons, which have signs of wear and tear suggesting that they must have labored with heavy stones for long time. Some graffiti have been identified on the walls which indicate that at least some workers took pride in their work; calling their teams "Friends of Khufu" and "Drunkards of Menkaure,"[2] these names suggest allegiance to the pharaohs and a likelihood of some good relations between the workers and the kings. The Islamic architecture is epitomized by Taj Mahal, the construction of which started in 1631 and continued for almost

22 years. Workers were brought in from all over the country and Central Asia. The legend states that Shahjahan cut off the hands of the workers after the completion of the Taj Mahal[3] so that the construction is not copied by any other person. Rosa Lucas, a coalminer at Lamberhead Green in 1841 said "I go down between three and four in the morning and sometimes I have done by five o'clock in the afternoon and sometimes sooner"[4] this suggest that in those days women were made to work in the coal mines.

These few instances from the past are of significance in understanding the profile of the workers and also the activities of people management or the quality of people management. The haves ruled over the have-nots. The work was done through the supervision of the middle men trusted by the lords and the kings. That is how some of the great monuments and forts were built; that is how the ships sailed from one shore to another and consequently people movement happened. The relations between the slaves/workers and the owners were practically non-existent. They worked on the whims and wishes of the owners. Wars were fought, and kingdoms were won. People were directed, controlled and led. As the industrial revolution was advancing since the 1780s, people were brought into the factories and were directed to work under controls. This gives abundant cause to believe that organizational functions and people management have been with us since thousands of years.

Seeds are Sown for People Management

The industrial revolution started with the need for rapid manufacturing processes in the eighteenth century in Great Britain and it moved to many countries by the Atlantic to America by the end of the Civil War. Adam Smith published the classic in economics, *The Wealth of Nations* in 1776, in which he argued the economic advantages of the division of labor. This led to the development of specialization in the jobs done by the workers. However, the orientation of people management continued to be to the extent of increasing the productivity. Machine power combined with some of the people management issues, especially the division of labor, made it possible to have large efficient factories and progress in the process of industrialization. In 1789 Robert Owen worked on recognition of workers in the factories; he argued that money spent on improving labor was one of the best investments that business executives could make. He is remembered more for his management theory, courage and commitment to reducing the suffering of the working class than for his management success. The management of the people inclined to be welfare oriented; however, the plight of the workers continued. They were exploited, harassed, and used as chattel. The external environment kept the workers in the deprived and miserable state. This led to some external social thinkers to study the state of workers and help them mitigate their sufferings. Much focus on the welfare of the workers started during these times.

It is generally held that the first personnel officer, referred to at that time as an industrial welfare officer, was Miss Mary Wood who was appointed by the Rowntree's in York in 1896. She was appointed to be a type of social worker for the factory, with responsibility to ensure the well-being of women and children in the workforce and to keep a watch over their health and behavior.

Cadbury was another pioneering company which developed a totally different approach, believing that the well-being of the workforce was the responsibility of each member of the staff. In 1900 Edward Cadbury spoke about the need to 'develop the social and moral character of each worker', stating that the 'supreme principle has been that business efficiency and the welfare of employees are but different sides of the same problem'.[5] This led to the climate where people working in the industry were recognized and various labor legislations were evolved to protect the interest of the workers. This gave a fertile ground for the industrial relations to evolve. The industrial welfare officer became a sought-for profession at the time.

Early in 1900, Mary Parker Follet advocated organizations' functioning based on a group ethic rather than individualism. She argued that individual potential remained only potential until released through group association. Our present way of looking at teamwork, motivation, leadership, power, and authority reinforces these issues of people management. Max Weber developed a theory of authority structures and described organizational activity based on authority relations in the year 1900. He described an ideal type of organization that he called a bureaucracy. He suggested this would set a hierarchy line of control clarifying the role and responsibility.

Fredrick Winslow Taylor published *Principles of Scientific Management* in 1911. He spent more than two decades passionately pursuing the "one best way" for each job to be done. Taylor sought to create a mental revolution among both the workers and managers by defining clear guidelines for improving productivity. He defined four principles of management comprising scientific methods to get workers to be more productive. He argued that adhering to these principles would result in the prosperity of both managers and workers. Workers would earn more pay and managers would earn more profits. Taylor succeeded in getting the level of productivity he thought possible, by putting the right person on the job with the correct tools and equipment, by having the worker follow his instructions exactly, and by motivating the worker with an economic incentive of a significantly higher daily wage. He reaffirmed the role of managers to plan and control, and that of workers to perform as they were instructed. He also planted the seeds for the training and development aspect of people management when he said, "The search for better, far more competent men from the presidents of our great companies to our household servants was never more vigorous than it is now. And more than ever before is the demand for competent men in excess of the supply. What we are looking for, however, is the ready-made competent man; the man whom someone else has trained. It is only when we fully realize that our duty, as well as our opportunity, lies in systematically co-operating to train a competent man, instead of hunting for a man whom someone else has trained so that we are on the road to national efficiency."

Frank Bunker Gilbreth and Lillian Evelyn Moller were the associates of Taylor and in 1912 they studied the work arrangements to eliminate wasteful hand and body motions. They were among the first researchers to use motion pictures to study hand-and-body motions. Demand for trainers to train officers and workers according to need started growing.

Henry Gantt extended the ideas of Taylor and added the concept of incentives. Gantt devised an incentive system that gave workers a bonus for completing their jobs in less time than the allowed standard. He also introduced a bonus for foremen to be paid for each worker who made the standard, plus an extra bonus, if all the workers under the foreman made it. Concepts of motivation took birth and overall the seeds for human resource management were planted.

Hugo Munsterberg published "Psychology and Industrial Efficiency" in the year 1913. He argued the case of importance of industrial psychology in the success of organization. He suggested the use of psychological tests to improve employee selection. He related the scientific management to industrial psychology. Much of our current knowledge of selection techniques, employee training and job design is built on the work of Munsterberg.

The profession of the industrial welfare officers was growing all over the industrial sector and by 1913 the number of industrial welfare workers had grown sufficiently for a conference to be called in York by Seebohm Rowntree. Sixty people attended it. At this conference the Welfare Workers Association was formed and after many changes it is now known as the Institute of Personnel and Development. The Institute of Personnel and Development is the professional body for all those concerned with people management and development. It has over 128,000 members all over the world.[6]

The Journey of People Management

In this manner the work spread from welfare to recruitment and selection and then to training; improving morale and motivation; discipline; health and safety; joint consultation and often wages policies. This expansion of duties resulted in the establishment of an adequate personnel department with trained staff.

Welfare personnel continued as a force until the Second World War and later manifestations of it were the provision of canteens and company outings for workers. Even today it can be recognized that the welfare tradition has some significance in the practice of personnel management, for example, health schemes and crèches for the children of employees. Many of these provisions have found their route through labor legislations, which were, in turn, evolved as an outcome of the strong industrial relations climate. Industrial relations were a strong addition to people management dimension. The industrial relation professionals worked on the assumption that there will be basic conflict in the employment relationship, which can never be reconciled and therefore mutual accommodation is necessary. The grounds for trade unions were prepared and struggle for power became an important appendage to people management.

The emphasis on personnel administration was fast gaining importance. It amounted to support for management and was basically concerned with recruitment, discipline, time keeping, payment systems, training and keeping personnel records. The size of the organization and the growth thereof had a significant impact on the existence of this function and the department.

After the Second World War and up to the 1950s, personnel management incorporated wider range of services including salary administration, basic training and advice on industrial relations, but the main focus was at the systems rather than at the strategic level. Increasing organizational complexity was notable in activating certain changes in the industrial relations practices. For example, the movement from collective bargaining at industry level to the level of the company was apparent. This resulted in the advent of the industrial relations specialists within personnel management. Another significant reason for this was also the increase in the number of labor legislation.

The 1960s and the 1970s saw a significant increase in the number of staff engaged in industrial relations and personnel work. This area was seen as a career and professional advantage. The state of the economy had an important part to play. In conditions of high employment up to the 1970s, there was evidence of much recruitment, selection, training and payment system activities in the practice of personnel management. This was prompted to an extent by the need of skilled labor and was reflected in actions to retain them and increase the skill levels of the workforce in general.

The approach to training was systematic and planned in the whole industrial setup. It was heavily influenced by establishment of the training boards by governments which exacted a training levy from industry and offered grants to companies that conducted training to the acceptable standards. In turn, this spawned a rapid growth in the number of training specialists within the personnel function. This led to considerable changes in the profile of the worker. Activities such as performance appraisal and management development also assumed importance, as did forecasting manpower needs. This insight came from the behavioral sciences.

Simultaneously trade union movement had also gained momentum. The increase in the influence of the unions brought about another significant change in the role of the personnel professionals. The strength of the bargaining power of the trade unions at the workplace was conspicuous. The involvement of the personnel function in matters connected with industrial relations issues, and with productivity deals as well, elevated the concern to the strategic significance. This period brought the advent of the strategic role of the personnel profession. At a time when most of its activities could be considered as system oriented, the emphasis on industrial relations heralded a delicate role for the personnel specialist interacting with both management and workers. This signaled a need to develop negotiation skills and to learn more about various systems of remuneration, and there was also a tendency to identify the personnel function with management.

The 1980s saw personnel management entering the entrepreneurial phase, adapting itself to the market economy and enterprise culture. It was not uncommon to find senior personnel executives contributing to the debate within the company about the future direction, the relevance of existing business objective, and improved ways of achieving revised objectives. This era heralded a preoccupation with the management of change, the development of appropriate corporate culture, the acceptance of Japanese industrial relations practices, such as single unions to represent a company's workforce, and Japanese management practices in the form of quality circles and total quality management.

Hunt speculated about the personnel function shifting in its emphasis. It was during the 1980s that the rise in human resource management began to attract the attention of personnel practitioners. There was a move away from the traditionally reactive industrial relations of the 1970s towards an approach which sought to achieve excellence in the organization through a committed workforce,[7] this could only be achieved through proactive people management measures.

Futuristic Approach to People Management

Human resource management came to be perceived as an exciting new approach to people management. It pushed personnel management and industrial relations steadily into the background. Books and journals were printed and university curricula changed. To suit this demand practitioners started commanding fancy salaries. Human resource management became a career option as never before. The world of people management was transformed so fundamentally and irreversibly that this transformation is often described as a paradigm shift.

The new human resource management model composed of policies promoting mutuality—mutual goals, mutual influence, mutual respect, mutual rewards, and mutual responsibility. The theory is that policies of mutuality will elicit commitment, which, in turn, will yield both better economic performance and greater human development.[8] The major theme running through this model is the acknowledgement that employees are valued assets of the company, that there should be interplay between a strategy for human resource and the main strategy for the corporate culture. It should be managed so as to make it compatible with the requirements of the corporate strategy as a whole.[9]

There is a belief that commitment by employees to the organization is nurtured when the organization informs them of important matters such as the mission statement, the values it cherishes and future prospects of the company. This leads to clear implementation of the business strategy. In addition, it is considered wise to involve employees in decisions related to organizational job design and allow them to function in self-managing groups.

Organizational growth broke boundaries and competitiveness had new heights, which increased the need for the Total Quality Management (TQM) and Just In Time (JIT) approach. These depend heavily on employee co-operation and contribution. It is impossible to achieve it without incorporating some elements in the management system. For this reason, firms involved in the process of effective TQM spend a great deal of attention on employee training, empowerment, involvement and recognition. Training is crucial to the new organizations. Due to this, another impact shift occurred, whereby there is an increased emphasis upon 'individual' as opposed to 'collective' relations. Accordingly, there is the recent upsurge of interest in direct forms of communication and involvement—often taking the form of team briefings, quality circles and the like. Commensurate with this are the developments in integrated reward systems, and the linking of remuneration to performance. The renewed interests in coordination can also be seen as a logical extension of such initiatives.

New work patterns have developed and most notable are the various forms of flexibility.

Peter Drucker's phrase is most appropriate in explaining the growth of people management: "A business enterprise has a triple personality; it is at once an economic, a political and social institution. In the first of these personalities, it produces and distributes incomes by operating within a nexus of factor a product markets. In the second it embodies a system of government, in which managers not only collectively exercise authority over the managed, but are also involved in an intricate pattern of political relationships. Its third personality is revealed in the 'plant community' which evolves from below out of face-to-face relations based on shared interests, sentiments, beliefs and values among various groups of employees."[10]

Finally the present 21st century belongs to the virtual organizations and large corporate houses. A lot of these run operations of the size of some countries. This has led to an extreme change in the profile of the employees of the growth of the knowledge workers, freelance workers, die-hard professionals and globe-trotters. The people management issues have now found a need to be customized according to the individual need. People management has advanced as the 'slave' has outgrown the organization. In the present decade as attrition becomes a major challenge for organizations where they lose trained and talented people, it is the people who command the systems and likewise their own management. The journey thus continues and more changes will be incorporated with every change in the economy and the profile of the worker. Nomenclature is packaging on the systems but the underlying principle is the people management.

(Bharti Thakar is a faculty member at Icfai Business School, Ahmedabad.)

References

1. http://library.thinkquest.org
2. http://www.nationalgeographic.com/pyramids
3. http://www.bookrags.com/Taj_Mahal
4. http://www.wiganarchsoc.co.uk.

5. Niven, N.M. (1967) *Personnel Management*: 1913-1963, London, Institute of Personnel Management, pp: 23.

6. http://www.cipd.co.uk. IDP Mission Statement (1997).

7. Grunig J.E. & Hunt T. (1984) "*Managing Public Relations*". New York: Holt, Rinehart and Winston.

8. Walton, R.E.(1985) "From control to commitment in the workplace", *Harvard Business Review*, Vol 63, nos 2 march –April.

9. Beer, M. and Spector, B. (1985) "Corporatewide Transformation in Human Resource Management', in Walton, R.E and Lawrence, P.R. (eds), *Human Resource Management: Trends and Challenges*, Boston: Harvard Business School Press.

10. Peter Drucker (1954) *The Practice of Management*. Harper and Row, New York Evanston.

11. Keenoy (1990) "Human resource management: Rhetoric, reality and contradiction", *International Journal of Human Resource Management*. 1(3): 362-84.

12. Noon M. (1992) "Human resource management: A map, model or theory?" in P. Blyton and P. Turnbull (eds) *Reassessing Human Resource Management*, London: Sage.

13. John Storey J. (1995) *Human Resource Management: A Critical Text*, London: International Thompson.

14. Legge (1995) *Human Resource Management: Rhetoric and Realities*, Basingstoke: Macmillan pp:66-67.

15. Tyson S. and Fell, A.(1986) *Evaluating the Personnel Function*, London: Hutchinson.

16. Hendry C. and Pettigrew A. (1990) "Human resource management; An agenda for the 1990's", *International Journal of human resource management*, 1(3) pp. 17-43.

2

The Global Evolution of Industrial Relations: Events, Ideas, and the IIRA (Bruce E Kaufman)

John T Delaney and Howell John Harris

The article is an outcome of a review symposium, which has scrutinized the book written by Bruce E Kaufman. The book examines the field of industrial relations (IR) from its early century origins as a "strategy and set of tactics developed by social reformers". This book is an important addition to the small but growing literature on the history of the field of industrial relations. The article includes comments by John T Delaney who appreciates the quality of the book and mentions that it uses history to place IR key debates in perspective and says that there is a ray of hope for the IR but it has to adapt to the flat world or be flattened by the world. Comments by Howell John Harris are lucid in style and he gives credit to Kaufman for working through all the records of the ILO and IIRA and the interviews of a host of Grand Old Men of the business. A chapter-wise interpretation and comments on the book have been given and is considered as it a complete study on the subject of IR.

Source: Industrial & Labor Relations Review, Volume 59, Issue 3, 2006 Article 81.

Editor's Introduction by George R Boyer

The past century has seen the rise and, in the United States and several other industrialized nations, the decline of the field of industrial relations. "*The Global Evolution of Industrial Relations: Events, Ideas, and the IIRA*[1]," by Bruce E Kaufman, examines the field of industrial relations from its early twentieth century origins as "a strategy and set of tactics developed by social reformers" in the United States to keep the labour problem "from boiling over into destructive class struggle" through its globalization after the Second World War and up to its present period of decline. The study is comparative as well as historical, tracing the spread of industrial relations to the United Kingdom in the 1930s, to Australia, Canada, and New Zealand in the 1950s, and to continental Europe and the rest of the world after 1960. Along the way, Kaufman examines recent trends in industrial relations in North America, Europe, Asia, Africa, and Latin America, and the important roles played by the ILO and the International Industrial Relations Association (IIRA). Finally, he addresses the decline in industrial relations in many industrialized nations and its vitality in several countries within the European Union. Kaufman concludes that the field "must have a future" because, without a program of industrial relations to "humanize, professionalize, democratize, stabilize and balance the labour market process and employment relationship," global capitalism could "turn dysfunctional and quite possibly self-destruct."

The Global Evolution of Industrial Relations is an important addition to the small but growing literature on the history of the field of industrial relations. Because of the breadth of the book, the editors of the *ILR Review* believe that it should be reviewed both by an industrial relations scholar and by a labor historian. We therefore invited John T Delaney, Associate Dean for MBA Programs at the Eli Broad Graduate School of Management, Michigan State University, and Howell J Harris, Professor of History at Durham University, to contribute reviews of the book. We express our appreciation to these critics for their excellent commentaries on an important book.

---

1 Geneva: International Labour Office, 2004. xxv, 722 pp. ISBN 92-2-114153-5, $74.95 (cloth).

Comment by John T Delaney

The Flattening of Industrial Relations

In 1992, Francis Fukuyama created a stir with his book, *The End of History.* Time has shown that it was not the end. By contrast, Bruce Kaufman's book could have been titled *The End of Industrial Relations,* as the assessments, inferences, and conclusions suggest a bleak, if not dire, outlook for the future of the field.[2] To Kaufman's credit, he did not intend this, and even suggests some "rays of hope" (p. 629) for the field. But the facts speak for themselves, and Kaufman's comprehensive historical compilation and assessment of the field of industrial relations (IR) suggests that the end of the field as we have known it may be at hand.

My intention is not to attempt a close review of twelve chapters containing 631 pages of historical detail on the evolution and state of IR across the world. Moreover, readers familiar with Kaufman's work know that it tends to be dense—full of detail—and this book is no exception. Because the dense exposition defies succinct description, I provide a general overview of the book, outline some strengths and weaknesses, and offer observations about Kaufman's conclusions and the future of the field. Most of my discussion is concerned with the book's latter half, which focuses on IR's global expansion, current circumstances, and future prospects. The book provides an expansive history of the field, extending Kaufman's other recent writing. It contends that IR emerged in the United States as John R Commons and others articulated practical ideas for solving the vexing "labor problem" facing the country. In particular, the field's founders sought to identify ways to create decent jobs, promote industrial peace, and allow American industry to prosper. Kaufman regards the field's origination in America as surprising, given that "the field's most towering intellectual work" (p. 586), the Webbs' *Industrial Democracy,* was British. The field developed an American character and flourished for five decades before descending to its current state.

IR did emerge in Britain and many other countries, albeit at a later date. Whenever and wherever the field emerged, however, it seemed to follow the same "inverted V"-shaped trajectory of growth followed by decline. In the United States,

---

[2] Indeed, Robert Taylor (2005) titled his review of Kaufman's book "The End of Industrial Relations."

for example, after the field's early ideas were adopted as public policy and workers secured some protections at work—through laws and unions—difficulties and differences emerged. IR's hallmark "big tent" seemed no longer to cover important workplace subjects, such as Human Resource Management (HRM), Organizational Behavior (OB), and important new areas such as negotiation and conflict management outside of union settings. This, inadvertently or by design, caused the field to become focused on labor-management relations at a time when global markets were beginning to erode the union power forged in the organizing battles of the 1930s. The net result was that by the 1980s it had become obvious that IR was in serious trouble as a field. It was no longer on the cutting edge of academic research, public policy, or solutions to perceived national problems. It has no longer attracted the top university students. The field's leaders were decreasingly involved in major government reform efforts. As the union movement declined, IR followed in tandem. By the 1990s, IR programs began to close their doors and IR's professional organization in the United States was in serious decline. In such a setting, predictions of the field's death were unsurprisingly frequent (see Purcell 1993; Roche 2000). If, at best, as Wood (2000:2) noted, "the trends of the past twenty years need not amount to the 'end of industrial relations,' they do expose weaknesses in its foundation."

Kaufman, whose *Origins and Evolution of the Field of Industrial Relations in the United States* (1993) earned him a Dr. Doom reputation among some, is well aware of these dire predictions and the field's weaknesses. He brings to this new book the same diligent approach that served him so well in the earlier one. *The Global Evolution of Industrial Relations* has three clear strengths. First, it is comprehensive. There can be no doubt that Kaufman has read and internalized virtually all of the field's early literature (at least that written in English) and that he has provided an excellent synthesis of the work. Moreover, because the economic roots of IR are strong, Kaufman's formidable knowledge of institutional economics ensures an accurate and measured assessment of the literature.

Second, the book uses history to place IR's key debates in perspective. For example, does IR encompass all aspects of the work relationship, or does it refer only to things unionized? This seemingly esoteric question is especially relevant to scholars today as they decide what to study and where to submit their research for publication. Are the thriving fields of negotiations and workplace justice part of IR, for example, or do they belong to some other discipline? Kaufman also addresses the field's largely unsuccessful quest for theory and its apparent second-class citizenship in comparison with the field of economics. He uses historical facts to trump some of IR's urban legends. For example, he points out that IR as a field grew because of private support from wealthy industrialists, not the rise of unions (p. 626). He also uses history to suggest an interesting hypothesis as to why the field did not originate in Britain: Sidney Webb needed to emphasize other areas of study as he sought to secure donations from the business sector to build the London School of Economics (pp. 178-87). Interestingly, as Kaufman notes, "The central insight from the historical analysis in this volume is that the problem-solving approach of industrial relations narrowed both over time and as it moved outward to other countries" (p. 623). There is no single explanation for the narrowing, but its occurrence helped shape the current state of the field. A key implication of this, as articulated by Roche (2000), is that international descriptions of IR regimes are better characterized by contingency than convergence.

Third, Kaufman is true to the underlying values of the field. He is concerned about the role of equity at work and in society. He addresses the split between Institutional Labor Economics (ILE) and Personnel Management (PM). He deals with the partisan political debates that have captured the field over time. He pays due notice to the tensions and frictions characterizing a field that bridges the interests of labor and capital. Whether Kaufman is a strict IR constructionist is unclear. That he knows the field's nature and development is unquestionable.

The book has two main limitations. First, the level of detail Kaufman provides on the history of IR in the United States, Britain, and Canada is not matched in his assessments of the field in other countries. While this gap probably does not affect Kaufman's conclusions about the state of the field in other nations, it generates an uneasy feeling about the field's situation outside of the big western English-speaking countries. Admittedly, this may be due to the lack of literature (especially English language literature) on IR in these nations. Whatever the cause, however, a consequence is that it is difficult for readers to assess the nature of the role played by the IIRA in promoting the field across the globe. In addition, the unevenness complicates predictions about the direction and future of the field outside the United States.

Second, I wonder whether one of the book's strengths is also a weakness. Specifically, the historical focus used by Kaufman to analyze IR may have unnecessarily restricted the analysis. Kaufman frames IR issues in the classic manner used by the Wisconsin School, namely from the perspective of the "labor problem." This approach gave the field a broad wake at its inception, but may be limiting when used to understand the field in other nations or in contemporary times. Admittedly, this may be an unfair criticism given Kaufman is providing a history of the field. But the approach seems to lead the analysis to standard IR solutions despite the fact that some of the most critical "labor problems" facing the United States (and the world) today seem to be resistant to those solutions. For example, globalization threatens to reduce the living standards in many traditionally well-off nations, even as it raises living standards in other parts of the world. How will the newly impoverished workers and the newly enriched ones react? What will each group expect and demand? One of IR's problems is that the field has not tended to address these questions in anything other than standard ways—for example, by calling for collective action to level the playing field with employers. Perhaps because of familiarity with traditional IR approaches or sentimental attachment to unions, collective organization and bargaining are seen as *the* solution to every workplace problem. Although there is nothing wrong with collective bargaining, its ability to address problems is compromised in a global marketplace that keeps wages in competition. Industrial democracy may no longer be obtainable within plants or business units or firms operating in a competitive environment. Kaufman's adoption of the standard analysis prevents him from contemplating nonstandard answers, such as the possibility that unionization and bargaining offer workers less protection than ever before (more on this below).

Kaufman's book generates many ideas about the future. I hope it will stimulate a no-holds-barred debate. Partly as a result of its particular strengths and limitations, the book gives rise to at least four questions that need to be considered by the IR community. First, is the future of the field going to be determined by chance? One of Kaufman's insights was that IR advanced in no small part because of the idiosyncratic efforts of individuals—the great men and women of the field. If this is true, the field's future will depend on whether Andy Stern proves to be this generation's Walter Reuther and whether the titans of today's wealthy industries, such as Gates, Buffett, and the Waltons, will support efforts to identify and promote ways to improve workers' circumstances. Currently, the prospects for such positive developments appear remote. It may be that on this question, although the clock has not run out, the field's luck has.

Second, will IR's decline coincide with a result vindicating Karl Marx? Kaufman recognizes the important role that the writings of Marx played in the development of IR. Marx, he argues, along with the Webbs, had "unsurpassed influence" on the field of IR. But he views Marx's influence as having been on the dark side: "his great influence was to present a vision of capitalist society so compellingly dire and dark that it moved the defenders of capitalism to mount a major counter-response" (p. 586). With the fall of the Berlin Wall in 1989 and the general conclusion that communism failed, contemporary sentiment (academic and political) is that Marx was wrong. Ironically, the forces unleashed by globalization and technological advance may resurrect the question. Few have considered the possibility that today's global economic developments could precipitate class warfare. Widening class divisions could become especially noticeable to those US workers who, because of globalization, are made clearly and conspicuously less well off than were their parents and grandparents. This may not lead to an armed revolution, but it could lead to a political one. And it would be ironic indeed if a movement proving Marx right gathered force under the eyes of scholars and politicians who continued to discount him.

Third, does it matter that the number of IR scholars has sunk below critical mass and that remaining IR programs survive by emphasizing HRM? These are interrelated questions to the extent that student enrollments drive the demand for IR faculty. As interest in unions and collective bargaining has declined, IR programs have survived in part by educating students interested in HRM. This strategy faces challenges from two trends—one business and one academic.

Over time, businesses have increasingly asked HRM recruits to have an understanding of business fundamentals; such knowledge is essential as HRM is expected to show evidence of a positive contribution to the bottom line. This trend has caused some employers to seek MBA students for HRM jobs.

For IR programs to provide the education desired by recruiters, it is increasingly necessary to offer training in normal business subjects as well as specialized HRM courses. In turn, this blurs the line between IR programs and business programs. If universities choose to avoid redundancy in programs, it is more likely that an IR program will be sacrificed for the business school than the reverse. For IR programs to survive in this environment, they may need to operate as pseudo-business schools, with uncertain implications for the field. Will the field be affected, for example, if it is assumed some day that the School sponsoring this journal is Cornell's *de facto* undergraduate business school?

On the academic side, the field's cohort of scholars is breaking apart as job opportunities disappear. Jarley, Chandler, and Faulk (2001) examined publication patterns in leading IR journals and wondered whether "IR journals will continue to provide a venue for sustaining a coherent, cumulative literature that will distinguish the field from other areas" (p. 343). Essentially, "casual authorship" by individuals outside of IR appears to be coming to dominate IR journals. This both shapes and reflects the reduction of academic IR positions. As this occurs, IR becomes increasingly defined by non-IR scholars and the remaining bastions of the field become increasingly segregated. Shrinkage in the number of scholars dedicated specifically to IR cannot help the field, and reliance on HRM does not guarantee stabilization of that number.

Fourth, why is the field declining at a time when IR issues are growing in importance? The "labor problem" is at the heart of some of the most critical dilemmas facing the United States (and the world) today. For example, US workers' adjustment to globalization is hindered by the lack of portability of pensions and healthcare. Issues of this kind are similar to those stressed by John R Commons and his associates when the field of IR developed. Moreover, education and employment issues related to immigration are also important today and relevant to IR. Many factors can be cited as contributing to the current situation—the September 11, 2001 terrorist attacks; the priorities of the Bush administration and the leadership in Congress; indifference by some employer groups; partisanship—but it is still odd that the field declines as its subject matter becomes more important. To some extent, members of the field are complicit in this problem. We have not advanced the issues in a way that has captured the public's imagination.

To some extent, the traditional approach in IR may be losing relevance (for a contrasting view, see Kochan 2005). For example, one part of the problem is that working today is increasingly comprised "assignments" rather than "jobs." Long-term commitments between employers and employees are dwindling, in part because such commitments introduce more cost, friction, and bureaucracy into the global marketplace than organizations desire. As fewer and fewer firms are able to continue in finding adequate productivity enhancement in the traditional job structure, most of them are being forced to adapt an assignment approach. There is no doubt that, as this change occurs, it shifts potentially large new burdens and risks onto workers. Whether we like the result or not, however, the shift is going taking place and will be difficult to slow.

In an assignment world, workers' success depends not on having a great union representative but on having an unbeatable set of skills. Thomas Friedman (2005) has asserted that the world today is "flat" and competition in a flat world is no longer between nations or even companies—it is among individuals. In such a world, traditional workplace mediating institutions have less to offer workers or employers than they had before. To the extent that IR is tied to the belief that workplace equity can only be provided by the introduction of a third-party representative, the field is in an untenable position. And to the extent that unions focus on this specialty, they will generate lower support. For unions to thrive, they must emphasize as never before a function with which they already have some experience: identifying ways to help workers develop current and adaptable skills. In a flat world, the sets of skills workers acquire will, in the end, determine who in society (and which society) wins and who loses.

Although the fate of IR may already be determined, there are many rays of hope for a field that looks at today's critical work-related issues. The key to unlocking the hope is to move beyond IR's standard approach. This includes recognizing that competition among workers is going to increase just as competition among firms has increased. In such a situation, workers can achieve stability only when they possess top-of-the-line or adaptable skills. If IR's basic purposes are to "humanize, stabilize, professionalize, democratize, and balance the market system" (p. 631), then it must do so in a way that promotes individual skill building, flexibility, and efficiency. Kaufman's book shows us where the field has been.

Friedman's book indicates where the world is going. IR must adapt to the flat world or be flattened by that world.

Comment by Howell John Harris

Industrial Relations: A Field in Search of a Future? But Don't Worry, Bruce Kaufman Has Done the Past

This is an enormous book—hence the *ILR Review*'s decision is, that a division of labor was the only fair way of treating its chosen reviewers (and also the author, who could not expect to encounter any single reviewer whose knowledge of the field is as compendious as his own). It is also a curious work—a combination of history of ideas (though Kaufman is emphatically not an intellectual historian), institutional history, and commemorative volume—that would surely have acquired neither its bulk nor its hybrid character without its, presumably generous, ILO sponsorship. It cannot be said to be an easy read. Never lively—though, considering how much Kaufman writes, it is almost unreasonable to expect him to have style as well as content, or, for that matter, for the proofreading to have been perfect—at times it sags badly. Kaufman evidently likes lists, and his book often turns into a catalogue weighed down with potted plot-summaries of key texts in the history of industrial relations, narratives of institutional developments that can never have been especially compelling even to the key participants at the time, and lots of names of people and organizations associated with the early development of IR in countries outside its Anglo-American homelands, as if Kaufman is desperate to mention almost everybody. Much of the research on which it is based is synthetic, and most of the sources are journal articles, books, and official publications, to which Kaufman's work therefore provides a valuable bibliographical guide. He has also worked through ILO and IIRA records, and interviewed a whole host of the Grand Old Men of the business. Kaufman uses the Harvard system rather than proper footnoting to cite all this material, a quite unreasonable imposition on the reader of a text of these biblical proportions, especially as it permits Kaufman to refer to entire secondary works when he is summarizing their conclusions rather than to the particular sections he is actually drawing on; only when there is a direct quote do we get a helpful page reference. This technique may be acceptable in a social science journal article, where the reader needs to be helped along, not tripped up by brackets in almost every paragraph. Also ill-advised was the author's frequent use of the historic present when discussing past events or research. Consistent use of the simple past tense in such cases would have removed another bone from this reader's throat.

Cavils aside, this is a book worth reading. It requires patience and persistence: the first time I tried, the beginning almost put me to sleep. Chapter 1, "The Roots of Industrial Relations," stretching almost from the dawn of time (or at least the late eighteenth century) until the First World War, and concentrating on Britain and Europe, is dry and dull and really adds very little, except for a sense of completeness that seems to have satisfied Kaufman's zeal to cover everything, however sketchily. But perhaps this is just a historian's reaction; industrial relations practitioner may need to be reminded about something called the Industrial Revolution, which happened once upon a distant time (or so some people think), and they may value some rather rudimentary plot-summaries of the works of Adam Smith, Karl Marx ("Another classical economist," p. 47), and other intellectual contributors to the definition and discussion of the emerging "Labour Problem." A second reading of the chapter is more rewarding, because then one can begin to see the merits of Kaufman's approach: he is interested in "the intellectual and policy effort to defuse and contain the Labour Problem" (p. 35) and in answering the question why this produced what became the scholarly field of Industrial Relations in Britain and the United States rather than in Imperial Germany, given the vital intellectual contributions of German historical—social economics to it. His answer is essentially political: IR, with its pluralist, reformist, accommodationist, even managerialist vision, was a product of, and a natural fit within, the two most democratic of the advanced capitalist states, which developed their own strategies of incorporating their emerging working classes into the political culture and preventing industrial conflicts from generating larger social turbulence. This is entirely plausible, though hardly original.

In Chapter 2, "The Birth and Early Development of Industrial Relations: North America," Kaufman comes as near hitting a stride as his technique permits. There is the same catalogue feel to the text—bulletpointed lists (pp. 128–30), paragraphs started "First" to "Eighth" (by which time the reader is flagging; there is even a "Ninth, and finally," on p. 115). But, as one would expect of the author of *The Origins and Evolution of the Field of Industrial Relations in the United*

States (1993), Kaufman has something interesting and distinctive to say; though, to readers of his earlier book at least, not especially new. Kaufman's grasp of the historical background of America in the late Progressive Era, World War I and its aftermath, and the 1920s is sometimes a little shaky, and the unproblematic exceptionalism of his one-paragraph discussion of American culture and consciousness (p. 126) would probably make intellectual historians reach for their guns; but his understanding of the ideological and policy reaction to the industrial relations crises of the late teens is more confidence-inspiring. He provides a good narrative of developments in the study and teaching of industrial relations in some US universities, the practice of personnel management in a growing minority of large and progressive firms, and the intellectual outlooks and resulting policy advocacy of members of both of the schools of practitioners he identified in his earlier work—ILE (institutional labor economics) and PM (personnel management). Kaufman's background is in labor economics, and it shows: he is at his most original and fluent when discussing institutional economics as the intellectual core of the ILE school, in particular, in these early years (pp. 95–116). He also explains very well the ethical roots of their reformist commitments, which found practical expression in their problem-solving involvement with the real world of workers, unions, and management. Kaufman is probably more impressed by the practical achievements of his PM school in shaping corporate policy in the 1920s than he should be, but he is spot-on in identifying the cultural prestige of managerial progressivism at this time and, in one of his most original insights, demonstrating its impact on the outlook of labor relations scholars, starting with John R Commons himself. Kaufman has rediscovered two of Commons's neglected works, *Industrial Goodwill* (1916) and *Industrial Government* (1921), as well as an important summary of 1920s managerial progressivism, published when its tide had gone out—C. Canby Balderston's *Executive Guidance of Industrial Relations* (1935)—and the insight that results is that, in the 1920s, ILE scholars made their peace with corporate America, or at least with its liberal variant. Trade unionism and social regulation were for those parts of the labor market that an enlightened capitalism could not reach. The "labor problems" approach had always been merely reformist; its readiness to accommodate itself to the requirements of a dynamic capitalist economy and the defense of managerial rights and functions, and its preference for "private ordering, decentralized decision making, and voluntary agreement"

(p. 130), would prove to be very significant for its future, post-New Deal, incarnation.

Kaufman's history of this New Era coming-together between his two streams in the US industrial relations tradition serves an important purpose in the overall scheme of his book: the latter chapters, whose review is assigned to my colleague, reach grim conclusions about the present state and future prospects of the IR profession in its American homeland. The outline of his argument is probably familiar to many readers: in and after the 1930s, IR turned its back on much of its own history, and became narrowly defined as the study, operation, and defense of the post-New Deal system of "workplace contractualism," to use David Brody's term for "voluntarist" collective bargaining within an originally supportive, but increasingly restrictive, legal and administrative framework. After some decades in the doldrums, Kaufman's PM tradition reemerged as Organizational Behavior within the academy, and as positive human resource management within a corporate world freeing itself from the incubus of trade unionism. These, not old-fashioned IR, turned out to be the shapers of the future. What had seemed to be a sidetrack turns out to have had the locomotive of history running down it. The result is a growing crisis of intellectual respectability, self-confidence, and relevance for IR practitioners within the United States: the New Deal labor relations system that nurtured them has gone down the tubes; perhaps they are fated to do the same, joining other antiquated crafts (saggar-makers' bottom-knockers and others) in the dustbin of history, or at best lingering on in a sort of living museum or reservation. They are trying to reinvent or at least re-badge themselves, the IRRA turning itself into the Labor and Employment Relations Association, as if this will make a significant difference to its fate. Perhaps, Kaufman seems to be saying, they are paying the price for taking a wrong turning seventy years ago; the temporary fusion between his ILE and PM schools in the 1920s, largely on the latter's terms, offered, and perhaps still offers, a better way of making their recommendations relevant to a near union-free, business-dominated America than the tired repetition of homilies from IR's post-New Deal "Golden Age."

Chapter 3, "Early Industrial Relations in Europe: The United Kingdom, the ILO, and the IRI," takes Kaufman and his readers off into less familiar territory. His method is much the same, a focus on Sidney and Beatrice Webb taking the place of Chapter 2's extensive discussion of Commons. But nothing of importance is neglected—the birth of the LSE, the contributions of G D H Cole, the establishment of the first chairs in industrial relations at British universities. He also addresses, not altogether convincingly, the apparent paradox that the institutionalization of the study and practice of IR proceeded much more slowly in Britain despite the pioneering intellectual contributions of the Webbs and the presence of a labor movement much stronger than that in the United States. Kaufman is at his weakest when he indulges in culturalist explanations for difference, and at his best when he follows the money trail—the demand for IR professionals' services, the supply of corporate and foundation resources for capacity-building in universities—which better explains the outcome. The chapter also contains a useful introduction to the early history of the ILO, together with an explanation for its trade union orientation, and a brief account of the Industrial Relations Institute (IRI) at The Hague 1925-39, which brought an American "PM" perspective to the heart of Europe.

In Chapter 4, "American Industrial Relations in the Golden Age," Kaufman is back on home territory. He starts with the New Deal, whose labor reforms, "due to several ironic and unexpected twists and turns, ... irreparably split the industrial relations community and helped contribute to a gradual divorce between the PM school of progressive employers and the ILE school of institutional labour economists" (p. 222). The Wagner Act is Kaufman's "turning point" (p. 226), as it is for so many labor historians. It helped usher in the world in which the IR profession would prosper; but it also contained the seeds of their current crisis, because it encouraged them to put all their money on trade unions, collective bargaining, "voluntarist" dispute settlement, and "pluralist" labor law. For decades the bet paid off, but eventually the old nag ran out of steam, stumbled, and died. The essence of Kaufman's argument is one with which many labor and business historians would agree: the Wagner Act was an aberration within the American political economy, only explicable by the exceptional circumstances of the Great Depression; the growth of the post-New Deal labor movement further depended on unusually favorable conditions within war time and postwar labor and product markets. The tragedy, or at least error, of the American IR business was to come to think of these conditions as normal and permanent, when they were anything but. When circumstances changed, IR professionals would have no new or useful answers, simply a tool-kit of practices for which there was less and less demand, and hoary old policy recommendations commanding less and less of a respectful or even attentive audience. In dealing with this "Golden Age," Kaufman is as usual encyclopedic, discussing the Human Relations movement of the 1940s and 1950s, developments within labor economics, the growth of IR programs at American universities, and the founding of the IRRA as a leading professional body, in theory for all academics and practitioners with an interest in matters of labor and employment, in practice mostly for those wedded to the New Deal model. There is the usual competent summary of field-defining researchers' work, with John Dunlop and Clark Kerr filling the shoes earlier occupied by Commons and the Webbs.

Chapter 5, "The Institutionalization of Industrial Relations in Australasia, Canada, and the United Kingdom," really takes up where Chapter 3 left off and explains the rise to academic prominence and, for a while, in the 1960s and early 1970s, political influence of the "Oxford School" of British labor specialists. Here as elsewhere Kaufman is an informative guide—a good explainer, synthesizing the conventional wisdom. There is a sustained comparison (pp. 268-78) of the differences—in emphasis, outlook, class background, political commitments, and even readiness to incorporate a broader interdisciplinary research agenda—between the closely related worlds of British and American IR scholars during the overlapping periods when both were at the zenith of their self-confidence and importance. The sections on the smaller, less-studied Anglophone nations are interesting because readers (including this reviewer) are likely to know much less about them, but Kaufman's approach is more descriptive than analytical, almost genealogical indeed in digging up the provincial fathers of these small emerging communities of IR professionals. And here my commission from the editors ended. It is a curious challenge to review half a book, and not know what the other reviewer has made of the rest of it. I have to confess to cheating—by the time I reached page 299 of the above-mentioned book, I was hooked, and read the other 330 too. Other readers will probably do the same. What turns Kaufman's book into more than a compendium, and what will probably attract most attention from an American readership, is his sense of the historically grounded crisis of the modern American labor relations system and of those IR professionals most closely attached to it. American readers might not agree with his prescriptions and predictions, with which my colleague will deal; but they will find Chapters 2 and 4 a useful introduction to why the crisis came to pass.

(George R Boyer is Professor of Labor Economics, School of Industrial and Labor Relations, Cornell University, and an Associate Editor of the Industrial and Labor Relations Review.)

References

Friedman, Thomas L. 2005. *The World Is Flat: A Brief History of the Twenty-First Century.* New York: Farrar, Straus, & Giroux.

Fukuyama, Francis. 1992. *The End of History and the Last Man.* New York: Penguin.

Jarley, Paul, Timothy D. Chandler, and Larry Faulk. 2001. "Maintaining a Scholarly Community: Casual Authorship and the State of IR Research." *Industrial Relations,* Vol. 40, No. 2 (April), pp. 338–43.

Kaufman, Bruce E. 1993. *The Origins and Evolution of the Field of Industrial Relations in the United States.* Ithaca, N.Y.: ILR Press.

Kochan, Thomas A. 2005. *Restoring the American Dream: A Working Families' Agenda for America.* Cambridge: MIT Press.

Purcell, John. 1993. "The End of Institutional Industrial Relations." *Political Quarterly,* Vol. 64, No. 1 (January–March), pp. 6–23.

Roche, William K. 2000. "The End of New Industrial Relations?" *European Journal of Industrial Relations,* Vol. 6, No. 3, pp. 261–82.

Taylor, Robert. 2005. "The End of Industrial Relations." *IIRA Bulletin,* Vol. 70 (August), pp. 9–10.

Webb, Sidney, and Beatrice Webb. 1897. *Industrial Democracy.* London: Longmans, Green.

Wood, Stephen. 2000. "The BJIR and Industrial Relations in the New Millennium." *British Journal of Industrial Relations,* Vol. 38, No. 1 (March), pp. 1–5.

3

Square Pegs and Round Holes

Charlie Grantham and Jim Ware

This article explains what makes people work; one size cannot fit all. In governing the people or managing them it is essential to work out proper systems and understand the people and why they work. In the early days, the way of the corporate was with the challenge of controls and through strict tight procedures, policy manuals. Professionals are still being managed as if they were in factories, in organizations designed to keep everybody on toes. With changing times managing human resources too has to change. It's no longer a matter of telling employees what to do. The only way to succeed today is to let them know what the management needs, give them reason to 'buy in' and then get out of their way.

One size misfits all.

We've been complaining recently about our own sense of being overloaded, if not overwhelmed, with work (of course, as we always say, it sure beats the alternative). More importantly, we've been recalling some conversations from the *2005 World Congress on the Future of Work.* While we don't have literal quotes, a

Source: www.thefuturework.net, Reprinted from Future of Work Agenda, April 2006.

basic and recurring theme was that the way large corporations are operating today is injurious to our health (mental, physical, and spiritual).

What's going on?

Well, we may have figured something out. In the process of cleaning up a very messy workspace recently we rediscovered the October 3, 2005, issue of *BusinessWeek* that contained a very provocative cover story called "The Real Reasons You're Working So Hard..."

And that article got us thinking a whole lot more seriously about that "injurious to our health" perspective (unfortunately, thinking seriously about the workplace doesn't happen often enough these days, because, well, we're working too hard).

You know what it's like—catching up on voice mail during the morning and evening commutes; logging on to check email before breakfast and after dinner; responding to Instant Messages from colleagues on other continents and in weird time zones at all hours, and participating in global conference calls at midnight, 4 a.m., and just about every other hour of the day and night. And everyone we know complains about being too darned busy to think.

We've all got tools (PC's, PDA's, the Internet, WiFi, cell phones, Treos, Blackberries, iPods, etc., etc.) and software (Google, Yahoo, NetMeeting, WebEx, Skype, Groove, Mapquest, Google Earth, spreadsheets, word processors, etc., etc.) that allow us to reach out and touch just about anyone or grab any data we need, anywhere, any time. And we use those tools 24x7 to connect with colleagues, friends, and family no matter whereever on the planet they—or we—are. Weren't they supposed to *help* us be more productive?

Yet it feels as if we're just spinning our wheels—and fighting bureaucracy.

Here's a couple of disturbing facts from the *BusinessWeek* article:

- More than 31% of college educated males (in the United States) are logging 50 or more hours of work a week, up significantly since 1980 (but most people *we* know would love to slow down to just 50 hours a week).

- Forty percent of American adults on an average sleep less than seven hours of a night on weekdays.
- Twenty-five percent of executives at large companies report that their primary communication tools—email, voice mail, meetings—have become completely unmanageable.
- Nearly 40% of those executives also report spending a half-day to a full-day a week on meaningless communication.

There's something really strange about the cultural norms in the workplace (at least here in North America) that drive this kind of behavior. If we're so successful, how come we're not "taking" all the increased productivity of the last two decades and "investing" it in more leisure time? After all, the French and Germans take about six weeks of vacation a year; why can't we?

The core message in the *BusinessWeek* article is that the underlying cause of all this wheel-spinning is the gross misfit between current organizational structures and processes, on the one hand, and the way most of us actually work (and need to work), on the other. Read that sentence again, slowly; it's a really important insight.

Here's the point: large organizations—both businesses and public sector agencies—are just about as archaic and obsolete as the dinosaurs we often compare them to. And they get in our way—literally. We are convinced that the organizational, procedural, and process misfits that dominate our economy in 2006 are slowly but surely destroying our productivity, our effectiveness, and even our goodwill.

Peter Drucker, always ahead of his time, had this to say about the corporation way back in 2001:

"For most of the time since the corporation was invented around 1870, the following five basic points have been assumed to apply:

- The corporation is the "master," the employee is the "servant."...

- The great majority of employees work full-time for the corporation. The pay they get for the job is their only income and provides their livelihood.
- The most efficient way to produce anything is to bring together, under one management, as many as possible of the activities needed to turn out the product.
- Suppliers and especially manufacturers have market power because they have information about a product or a service that the customer does not and cannot have, and does not need, if he can trust the brand. This explains the profitability of brands.
- To any one particular technology pertains one and only one industry, and conversely, to any one particular industry pertains one and only one technology."

(Source: "Will the Corporation Survive?", The Economist, *November 1, 2001.)*

As we've already said, we all know in our guts that virtually none of that is true anymore.

Unfortunately, it's a whole lot easier to change individual and small group behaviors than it is to drag formal procedures, processes, and management practices into the 21st century.

As the BW article puts it:

"*The problem, in a nutshell-to-go is this: Succeeding in today's economy requires lightning-fast reflexes and the ability to communicate and collaborate across the globe. Coming up with innovative ideas, products, and services means getting people across different divisions and different companies to work together. 'More and more value is created through networks,' says John Helferich, a top executive and former head of research and development at Masterfoods USA, a division of Mars Inc. ...*"

In other words, we need to work horizontally across both internal and external organizational boundaries (to say nothing of physical geography). But our whole concept of how to organize work and staff projects is built around an outdated and very counterproductive view of the organization as a legal entity that you are either fully inside of (as an employee) or outside of (as a contractor, customer, supplier, or simply as a non-employee). And every organization chart we've ever seen highlights of all the vertical lines of authority while virtually ignoring the horizontal flows of information and work processes that actually make things happen and produce value.

The hierarchical model of organizational structure and functional authority is built on the premise that the world is stable and that the best way to improve productivity is to drive variations out of the process: do it the same way over and over, and over again. Fine-tune it, replicate it, master it through repetition, and don't let anything change.

That view of the world is after all what the whole Quality movement and it's successor, Six Sigma, was built on. And for some processes, that is a wholly appropriate way to manage.

The other core (and equally questionable) assumption that dominated the industrial model of organization was that the "higher" you were on the organization chart, the more you knew, and the more you should be consulted before any decisions are made and implemented.

We all know darn well that the world (at least a large and growing part of it) just doesn't work that any more. But dealing with those realities makes a lot of people very uncomfortable. So (we believe) many managers and even senior executives stubbornly cling to those old, and clearly inaccurate, assumptions that Drucker described, even when they too "know" in their hearts that those assumptions aren't valid any more. The trouble is, they just don't know what else to do.

Lowell Bryan, a McKinsey & Co. director, put it this way in the BW article:

"Professionals are still being managed as if they were in factories, in organizations designed to keep everybody siloed. At less well-run companies, you're struck by how frustrated people are. They work like dogs and are wasting time."

It's the need for review and approval that slows organizations down, and creates situations where front-line workers are just going ahead and making the decisions they know are required (and correct), in spite of the formal procedures they are expected to follow. But they also know they're doing the "wrong" thing by circumventing those formal processes and risking censure from above if things don't turn out of the way they are supposed to. Unfortunately, this new reality just makes cynics of us all.

For most of us, that's not really new. But no one we know, who has really figured out what to do about it (other than fleeing corporate life as fast as they can). How many times have you complained about working too many hours, spinning your wheels, going "around" the system, being stymied by the bureaucracy, and not knowing what "those guys" in the executive suite expect of you?

Even though WDC is a small business, we're also struggling and constantly feeling behind the 8-ball (why did it take us almost six months to read the darned article about why we are working so hard?). But at least we're beginning to understand just how profound this misfit between formal management practices and the way most of us need (and want) to work really is.

And while we don't know the answers yet, we're growing more and more confident that at least we understand what the important questions are.

Here's the most shocking factoid of all to emerge from the *BusinessWeek* article: in spite of all the organizational "flattening," business process reengineering, downsizing, and cost-cutting of the last two decades, managers today, in 2006, make up a bigger proportion of the workforce than they did fifteen years ago!

We've got to ask the question: what in blazes are all those so-called "managers" doing all day? With a higher and higher proportion of self-directed knowledge workers producing the innovation and intellectual property that drives our economy, and with more and more of those knowledge workers working remotely, what is there for managers to do (other than slow things down and gum them up)?

Well, the good news in all this is that most of the successful knowledge workers we know simply ignore the hierarchy and formal procedures and go get the job done. (The best definition we've ever heard of the difference between professionals and blue-collar workers is that blue-collar folks "do what they are told", while professionals "do what is needed." Maybe that's overly simplistic, but it makes an important point that too many middle managers still don't get. The awful truth is that most professionals today don't need a manager to "tell them what to do".)

And now we're seeing a virtual explosion of new hardware and software applications that help those professionals find the people and the information they need to be successful—without going through any formal channels, asking permission, or needing much training. Just think of the collaborative tools we are learning to rely on: wiki's, blogs, collaborative online databases, virtual meeting rooms and distributed editing tools, open-source software, and even open-source management philosophies.

And if you haven't gotten familiar with the open-source movement, you should. It's a powerful alternative way of getting things done, and we see it as far more aligned with the information economy than are the more hierarchical, traditional approaches we've been dumping on here.

As a way to get started, we heartily recommend reading Stephen Weber's excellent book, *The Success of Open-Source*, which we reviewed in these pages almost two years ago, in June 2004. And for another insightful and more current book see *The Power of Many*, by Christian Crumlish (reviewed in February 2005).

The open-source movement is a really important development because it is re-inventing the way knowledge gets created and shared in a meshed network, rather than a hierarchical, command-and-control context.

Randy MacDonald, senior vice president of human resources at IBM, said this recently about the management and organizational revolution that's already underway:

> ". . . . if you go back in history and think about the fall of the Roman Empire, I think this set of years that we've experienced in the last 10 or 15 may actually be characterized as the fall of the traditional business empire and the rise or the emergence of collaborative and virtual empires around the world.
>
> You know, [it's] kind of a sound bite that maybe not everybody gets yet, but as I look at the industrial powers as we knew . . . know them, or, knew

them, it really should be, I don't think they exist as powerfully as they would have thought they would have been 10 years ago."

(Source: "IBM and the Future of Work," a podcast; a transcription is also available, at: http://www.ibm.com/investor/viewpoint/podcast/pdf/27-03-06-1.pdf).

Maybe the most fundamental question that every CEO needs to ask is, how can I ensure that all those people in "my" organization who are making hundreds of thousands of decisions every day, in far-flung places and often without direct supervision, are making the "right" decisions?

The way industrial corporations dealt with that challenge of control was through strict, tight procedures, policy manuals ("Thou Shalt" and "Thou Shalt Not"), and close-in supervision by front-line supervisors. In today's world, where semi-independent knowledge professionals are making those decisions on their own all day long, we believe the only way to get "control" is to ensure that your employees *understand* what you need, and why; and—more importantly—to *want* what you want.

That's why the notion of employee engagement has become so important. It's no longer a matter of telling employees what to do. The only way to succeed today is to let them know what you need, give them reasons to "buy in," and then get the hell out of their way.

So we think it's way past time for a genuine revolution in management practice and organizational design. We remember that President John F Kennedy once observed that, "Those who make peaceful revolution impossible make violent revolution inevitable." Enough said.

(Charlie Grantham, Executive Producer, The Work Design Collaborative, LLC, Prescott, Arizona.

Jim Ware, Executive Producer, The Work Design Collaborative, LLC, Berkeley, California.)

4

The Changing Face of Leadership – Defining Competencies for the 21st Century

This article shows the transition of leadership perspective for traditional leadership to the leadership perspective of future or 21st century. The traditionalists say that the key elements of leadership remain the same, whilst others argue against the command and control style in favour of persuasive leadership and modernist approaches that are now more appropriate to today's complex environment. The article explains the nature of the transactional leader (BC - 1960) and the transition from transactional to transformational leader from 1960s to 1980s. The period 1980-1990 saw the change leader as the transformational leadership was gaining ground and it coincided with a period of intense change across all business sectors. The leaders of future, leadership competencies and related issues are dealt with in this article, which throws light on global leaders, leaders in technology and leaders in the New Economy. Finally, the article highlights the essential building blocks for the future as a 'core cluster' and how it is being developed by an organization, according to its requirement, is explained.

1. Introduction

The leadership 'industry' is burgeoning. Two thousand books on the subject published in the last year and web searches that provide a myriad of academic papers, training programmes and conferences are proof of the continuing quest for leadership understanding.

The traditionalists will say that the key elements of leadership remain the same whilst the others argue against the 'command and control' style in favour of 'persuasive leadership' and modernist approaches that are now more appropriate to today's complex environment. Even today at conferences, debates still reign over the 'nature or nurture' 'born or bred' approach to leadership development. This all adds to the confusion and perhaps explains why so many people are trying to gain a greater understanding of what leadership means today and how it will look in the 21st Century.

As with all such debates, there is something that can be taken from the different viewpoints to improve understanding. Initially, this paper takes an historical perspective, providing a backdrop to the way in which leadership competences have developed. In doing so, it demonstrates that, where the description of a good leader and leadership competences may have been relatively static for many centuries, the 20th Century, and in particular the latter part, has seen a dramatic change in pace and the beliefs in what makes a good leader. The 21st Century is now requiring leaders to develop new competences at a rapidly increasing rate to match that of their changing operating environment. The paper goes on to define five core leadership competences that draw together the best from the past and yet focus clearly on the needs of the future.

2. The Historical Perspective

2.1. The Transactional Leader – (BC – 1960)

From the traditionalist's perspective, it is certainly true that, throughout the 20th Century business world, there remained an adherence to organisational leadership styles and structures that had their genesis in Greek and Roman times. These were formalised and reinforced by Taylor and other management 'scientists' after the industrial revolution and in the early part of the 20th Century as business processes were focused on manufacturing and production. Leadership at that time was synonymous with positions of authority in the organisation and rarely questioned. It bred the 'command and control' elements of transactional leadership with an emphasis on conditional reward, management-by-exception and 'leading from the front'—often this meant leading in isolation. This attitude to leadership in the first part of the 20th Century was further influenced in the United Kingdom by three other factors:

- There remained a clearly defined social strata which meant that leadership roles, whether in politics, the military, the clergy, or the professions, were, in most cases, the preserve of the privileged, educated and well-connected. This reinforced the paternal style of leadership and unquestioning 'followership' that had prevailed in earlier times.
- The industrialists who built their business empires and who did not come from the privileged classes still aspired to 'gentrification' and modelled themselves on existing leadership styles to perpetuate the way in which a leader should behave. They became the 'new squires'.
- Throughout most of the 20th Century until the early 1960s most men experienced military leadership through active service or conscription and that became the accepted style that was often easily understood and translated into civilian working environments.

The leadership competencies during this period were focused around the task and direction and, whilst they might also be categorised under 'management' competences, a number remain as relevant today in a leadership role:

- Focus on Delivery – achieving results, organising resources.
- Providing Direction – setting goals, establishing priorities and objectives.
- Strategic Thinking – focus on external environment, analytical.

2.2 Transactional to Transformational (1960-1980)

By the 1970s the transactional model of leadership had become largely outdated along with the blurring of social boundaries and more opportunities for a wider variety of people to take leadership roles. The increase in service industries and professional knowledge workers also changed the focus of the leadership role away from the needs of the more controlled environments of the manufacturing and production industries. The authoritarian leadership and highly structured organizational hierarchies of the past became too restrictive to elicit motivation, high levels of performance and customer expectations.

The transformational leadership approach gained favour in the 1980s with its aim of bringing both leaders and followers to high levels of motivation and morality. Characteristics often associated with transformational leaders include: determining and building a common vision, inspiring followers, encouraging new approaches to problem solving, continuously developing the skills of subordinates, and establishing superior performance. In many ways these characteristics were the antithesis of the transactional leader with their emphasis on inclusion and yet the very best leaders were able to combine and flex styles to suit the situation and the operating environment. This resulted in a broader set of leadership competences that embraced the 'people' aspects of leadership alongside the more traditional ones. Transformational leader competences began to emerge that considered the personal and interpersonal aspects of leadership and the need to 'sell' and motivate rather than 'tell' and dominate. Typically these involved:

- Getting the best from people – coaching, motivating, inspiring, challenging
- Learning and improving – sharing knowledge, seeking learning opportunities
- Making a personal impact – building relationships, role modelling
- Communicating effectively – active listening, openly communicating.

Whilst these are provided as generic examples, any set of leadership competences needs to be congruent with the organisational culture and operating environment. To be truly effective, they also need to be aligned with other systems and processes to reward the appropriate behaviours.

2.3 The Change Leader (1980-1990)

As transformational leadership was gaining ground it coincided with a period of intense change across all business sectors in the 1980s. It has continued ever since, has now become the accepted norm and continues to escalate – to gauge the escalation it is only 15 years ago that most business communication was paper based and mobile phones were as large as car batteries. Driven by technology, consumer demands and globalisation, the pace of change began to increase exponentially and this added to the competences expected of the 'new leader'. Whilst they may be linked to other areas, many leadership competences began to emerge in organisation specifically to measure and develop skills and abilities in:

- Leading change – communicating, involving others, setting the vision
- Building commitment for change
- Catalysing Change.

This period also coincided with the emergence of situational leadership that advocated the need to flex leadership styles according to the situation. It encouraged leaders to consider the appropriate style across the spectrum of directive leadership to participative leadership. Thus flexibility and adaptability became important aspects of the leadership role and started to feature in competence frameworks.

2.4 Leading from Within (1990-2003)

Where there had been little change in the requirements of a leader in the decades and centuries before 1960, by the end of the 1980s there had been a significant shift with a variety of views. The opinions were building on each other and merely reflecting the changes in the business environment and socio-cultural expectations, but they often only served to fuel the debate about what leaders really do and add to the confusion.

By the early 1990s the focus was placed firmly on individual attributes, with David McLelland's research linking emotional intelligence to business results making it a powerful message. The four core capabilities of self-awareness, self-management, social awareness and social skills encompass many of the previous competencies under their headings. For example, social skill also includes change catalyst and setting a compelling vision. This made EI an attractive way of bringing together many of the previous competences under one model—although many organisations used it as a base and linked it with existing competencies to tailor it to their own needs.

Since the mid-1990s this focus on the individual has been taken to another level that considers the impact of an individual's beliefs and spirituality on their leadership behaviours. It links most easily with EI's self-awareness capability. There are a number of theories but in simplistic terms it can be illustrated as an hierarchy:

Environment	:	Where a person operates – physical context.
Behaviour	:	What someone is seen to do.
Capability	:	What someone is capable of – skills, knowledge.
Beliefs	:	Fundamental principles and perceptions that somebody has about life and how to live it.
Identity	:	What someone believes themselves to be – self-perception, self-value.
Spirituality	:	Connection with mankind and the universe.

In both cases, they add to the competences that could be used to define leadership. The progression from the 1960s therefore sees a gradual change from the task and process competences through the people aspects of interpersonal skills to the deeper level of individual understanding.

3. Leaders of the Future

3.1 From 2003 – 2010

In view of the way in which attitudes to leadership have changed in recent decades, it would be foolhardy to predict much further than 10 years into the future. Yet, just as in the 1990s when EI was making an impact and has retained its relevance, there are still trends emerging today which signpost the new competences by which leaders will be measured. There is little doubt that the impact of technology and globalisation will continue to accelerate its impact on the leadership role at the highest levels. Also at that level, the demands of increased corporate social responsibility, changes to corporate governance and regulation will all require a leadership style that will need to meet the expectations of a wider range of stakeholders. Beyond the senior levels of the organisation, there will be a greater recognition that leadership roles and responsibilities need to be cascaded throughout the organisation if they are to be adaptive in a complex operating environment. This then links in with the need for organisations to 'grow their own' leaders as the war for talent will inevitably gather pace over the next decade. The next section considers some of the issues above and the impact this may have on leadership competences of the future in the areas of:

- Global Leaders
- Leaders in technology
- Leaders in the 'new economy'.

3.1.1 Global leaders

A snapshot of the future is provided in recent research involving four international financial and development institutions; the International Monetary Fund (IMF); the World Bank; the Inter-American Development Bank, and the Inter-American Investment Corporation.

The international leaders interviewed identified the following future challenges and opportunities for global leaders, including the following:

- coping with the speed of interrelated international events and crises, including the speed of technology;
- managing and leading in the growing complexity of a global society;
- the role of the corporation and its responsibilities in a 'caring' society
- becoming more adaptable and flexible in creating, accepting, and adapting to change;
- maintaining a vision that incorporates people from different cultures; and
- recognizing the decline of nation states/boundaries and the convergence of cultures as education and technology break down barriers.

A comparison of what the current leaders indicate as key qualities for future leaders shows that, as expected, there is agreement and support for the development of the competencies of strategic vision, communication, and building relationships.

However, a "leadership development gap" exists regarding the two competencies of adaptability and fostering teamwork. There was also a view that it would also seem important to expand the definition of the leadership competency to include such factors as honesty/integrity, continuous learning, humility and generosity, multidiscipline or breadth of experience, and commitment to the success of the organization.

3.1.2 Leaders in technology

The digital revolution has meant that it is no longer possible to innovate and deliver at the old incremental rates and expect to keep pace. Digital has already been a major driving force in accelerating the pace of change to an entirely new level and this has set new challenges for leaders. Retaining the best staff, dealing with diversity and managing increased stakeholders in the complex environment that increased connectivity brings places emphasis on a different set of leadership competences.

Leaders in the era of new technology will need to be 'intellectually agile' to embrace new developments and manage their impact from a leadership perspective. Those researching the 'technological leader' also emphasise the importance of paying careful attention to the congruence of personal and organisational values when the pace of change is so intense. A reinforcement of emotional intelligence and self-awareness is also seen in the research as key competencies for leaders in the digital age.

3.1.3 The 'new economy' leader

The 1980s and 1990s saw leaders focused on short-term performance where shareholders were the key. In the years ahead, society will be looking at organisations, both big and small, to expand their range of focus to a wider stakeholder group that is interested in the organisation's contribution to the 'greater good'. Leaders of the future will be expected to develop more sophisticated relationship and influencing skills to accommodate the demands of an increasingly diverse stakeholder group beyond the financial world and their own business sector. This will be compounded by the expectations of employees who will be influenced by the organisation's ability to present themselves as socially responsible.

Changes to corporate governance going into the 21st century, have also placed new challenges on business leaders. Where reckless behaviour and risk taking was eulogised in the recent past, there is an increasing trend towards the opposite with business leaders wanting to play it safe. A key competence for successful leaders in the next decade will be the resolve to take risks but the intellect to make them as 'calculated' as possible and to mitigate any adverse fall-out.

3.2 Leadership Competences for the 21st Century

In developing leaders for the future, the difficulty for an organisation today is to determine the 'core' leadership competences that it feels will meet the demands of their anticipated operating environment. The emphasis on specific competences and the behavioural indicators that provide the descriptors will be determined by the culture of the organisation and its strategy. However, an organisation has to start somewhere. In an effort to gain some clarity from the confused picture presented by the historical perspective and the competences highlighted as essential to the future, OPP has used its experience to highlight those competencies that should be considered as the essential 'building blocks' for the future as a 'core cluster'.

3.2.1 Core Cluster 1

Creating a vision and giving purpose

Leaders who can spark the imagination with a compelling vision are the ones we have followed in the past and will continue to do so in the future. Successful leaders translate their vision into clear objectives and their commitment is made obvious by their repeated communication of what needs to be achieved. Among the sub-set of this core competence would be:

- Thinking strategically – sensitive to wider and external organisational context.
- Communicates a compelling view of the future clearly and persuasively.
- Agrees clear responsibilities and objectives for getting results.
- Instils faith, respect, trust and a strong sense of values among followers.

3.2.2 Core Cluster 2

Managing complexity and change

This is a key factor that distinguishes those with the capacity to hold high level roles from managers unlikely to progress further in the organisation. The most senior roles deal with complex market or industry dynamics, possibly a global scope and extended timeframes. They place heavy demands on managers' ability to handle strategic, complex and ambiguous issues – in other words their ability to think 'outside the box'. This is not just about 'intellectual horsepower' or 'IQ'. Some managers can score highly on standard reasoning tests yet still have difficulty in handling complex or strategic issues. This becomes further complicated when mapped against a backdrop of accelerating change in terms of technology and the competitive environment.

Leaders of the future will be able to flourish in a work environment that has fewer boundaries and a wider variety of challenges and stakeholders. The emphasis in this core competence area is placed on influencing, building relationships and networks and managing the politics of business life both inside and outside of the organisation. Among the sub-set of this core competence would be:

- Creates structure out of chaos and calm in times of crisis.
- Creates and shapes change rather than passively accepting it.
- Assimilates and makes sense of complex and conflicting data and different perspectives.
- Uses flexible influencing skills to build productive relationships with people across and outside of the organisation.
- Accepts and encourages a level of considered risk to exploit business opportunities.
- Recognises and acts on the currents of organisational life, builds decision networks and navigates organisation poilitics.

3.2.3 Core Cluster 3

Developing self and others

Research by Morgan McCall and his colleagues in the US has found that leaders with advanced learning skills progress more rapidly than others. People with 'learning agility' are highly proactive in seeking out opportunities to learn and stretch themselves; they actively seek feedback from others and act on what they have learned. In turn, they encourage others to develop and are often the catalyst in promoting development in others. Leaders of the future will need 'learning agility' to continually update their knowledge in a fast-changing and complex environment. They will also need to focus on the development of others as a means of winning the 'war for talent'. A sub-set of this core cluster would be:

- Aware of own strengths, weaknesses and motivation.
- Applies learning from own experiences and actively seeks new or different opportunities to learn.
- Readily shares knowledge with others and encourages their development.
- Identifies and brings on talent and gets to know individuals and their aspirations.
- Gives and expects frequent feedback and coaches individuals so that they give their best.

3.2.4 Core Cluster 4

Emotional alignment

There is now very strong evidence to support the importance of so-called 'soft' skills in distinguishing those leaders who will move furthest fastest. The ability to lead and influence others and to have high levels of self-awareness, resilience and motivation are consistently found to distinguish high flyers from others. The EI work that emerged in the 1990s still holds a high degree of relevance for the future, according to the majority of observers. We are now seeing this being taken to new levels towards spirituality and, whilst there may be a continuing trend in this direction, it remains a subject of debate. However, there is a now a broad acceptance that 'persuasive leadership' underpinned by EI is here to stay. The real key for leaders of the future is to seek 'alignment' between their own emotional awareness, those of their 'followers' and how this links with attitudes in the organisation. A key sub-set of this core cluster is the need for leaders to become increasingly self-aware in terms of their own beliefs and values.

- Demonstrates an ability to read and understand their own emotions and recognise the impact they may have on others and in the workplace.
- Has a strong and positive sense of self-worth and a realistic view of strengths and limitations.
- Empathises with others, senses their emotions, understands their perspectives and takes an active interest in their concerns.
- Demonstrates an inner drive to meet high personal standards of excellence.

3.2.5 Core Cluster 5

Focus on delivery

The leaders of the future will need to draw upon the competences of those in the past in terms of achieving results. With this cluster comes a sub-set of competences that reflect the behaviours and skills that will mean that the task will be achieved, although in the future they become more important. In the past the task may have been achieved through 'command and control' with less reliance on the behaviours below as authority and a style of transactional leadership assured success. The 'followers' of today and in the future expect a transformational and 'persuasive' style of leadership, where the qualities of the leader become an increasingly important aspect of getting the right result. The sub-set of this core cluster would include:

- Demonstrates a resilience and determination to overcome obstacles.
- Challenges and is prepared to be challenged.
- Seizes opportunities through initiative and manages the risks.
- Motivates and makes best use of resources, technology and talent to achieve results.
- Demonstrates confidence, honesty and integrity.

5

The Seven Deadly Sins of Leadership Theory

Mitch McCrimmon

The article focuses on the development of a new leadership framework. We have been carrying on about the leadership with the old industries in focus, thereby committing a sin in not understanding the true meaning of leadership. This article describes in detail the seven deadly sins of leadership: The organizational sin, The sin of consideration versus structure, The sin of killing off management, The transformational sin, The sin of learnable process, The sin of character and emotional intelligence, The sin of parental dependency. There is a shift in focus of the industries, individuals and the working groups, and the perceptions need to be changed to manage people in the organization. The author emphasizes that leadership is nothing other than promotion of new directions and not only that it is also associated with senior organizational roles.

We are today assailed by so many diverse accounts of leadership that its essence is now murkier than ever. If we can agree on anything about leadership, it is surely its growing elusiveness. The problem is that our foundations are rotten.

We are trying to build an understanding of leadership on a faulty image, erroneous assumptions and a biased starting point. Contemporary leadership theory might not be guilty of all of the traditional seven deadly sins, but accusing it of gluttony and greed would not be unfair, given its currently bloated nature and its elimination of any constructive role for management. The strident call to replace all managers with leaders is responsible for leadership's current obesity.

The seven deadly sins of leadership theory refer to erroneous preconceptions about the nature of leadership. We can only hope to achieve agreement on what leadership means if we can rid ourselves of these faulty assumptions. After listing them I will explain what I mean in more detail, then offer a very different but sounder conception of leadership, one based on a clearer distinction between leadership and management where the latter is restored to its rightful place in organizations.

The Bottom Line

Leadership needs to be recast as focusing only on challenging the *status quo* to provide new directions, while everything to do with getting things done through people is assigned to management. Some surprising and unconventional conclusions follow from this realignment of the two functions. Most critically, leadership has nothing to do with implementation or managing people to get things done. Everything to do with empowering, coaching and developing people falls within the sphere of management recast along the lines of the sports coach as opposed to the controlling bureaucrat. Limiting leadership to promoting new directions is the only way to make sense of the fact that leadership can be shown upward as well as down or how it can be shown by organizational outsiders. Further, a purely functional distinction between leadership and management means that they can both use the same influencing tactics, hence leaders can be inspiring or quiet and so can managers. The essential difference between this view and transformational leadership theory is that both leaders and managers can be transformational, only their focus separates them. Hence, it is a mistake to align leadership with being transformational while limiting management to being transactional. Other equally unconventional implications follow, but let's look at the preconceptions currently blocking us from moving away from our dysfunctional view of leadership.

The Seven Deadly Sins

One broader sin underlies all the others and that is our focus on what it means to be the head of a group to understand leadership. As we shall see, the group as a model for leadership breaks down in a world driven by innovation where any group's direction can be as easily moved by outside or bottom-up influences as the CEO's vision. I discuss the shifting fortune of the group after we look at the 7 deadly sins.

1. **The organizational sin** – By modelling leadership on what it takes to run a group, with the CEO as our primary image of the leader, we distort leadership to the aim of getting things done through an organization. This view fails to capture the leadership of non-organizational leaders such as Martin Luther King and other lone voices in the wilderness who challenge the *status quo* without the CEO's power to execute. Further, thinking in positional terms, formal or informal, makes leadership a downward only force, ruling out upward leadership which has nothing to do with managing a group of people to execute a task.
2. **The sin of consideration versus structure** – Popular views of leadership and management are still rooted in the old distinction between showing consideration for people and initiating structure. These are the classic twin levers for managing organizational performance. This way of viewing the world stems directly from the first sin, associating leadership with occupying an executive role. But when we assign both processes to management and recast leadership as promoting new directions, we free leadership from everything to do with managing people by any means, a totally different slant on things.
3. **The sin of killing off management** – By defining management as mechanistically controlling, leadership claims all the "good guy" territory, relegating management to the "tough guy" tasks, the dirty work. The crusade to replace managers with leaders was an over reaction to the 1970's business success of the Japanese.
4. **The transformational sin** – By limiting leadership to being transformational (visionary, inspiring, morally uplifting), all forms of quiet, factual or

evidence-based leadership are ruled out. Transformational leadership is merely "showing consideration for people" on steroids, not the revolution it is cracked up to be.

5. **The sin of learnable process** – By viewing both management and leadership as processes we fail to see that leadership is not as transferable across contexts as management, that leadership is more closely aligned to unique *content*—it makes a statement about a particular subject unlike management which facilitates results across situations. Portraying leadership as a set of transferable skills, makes it seem learnable. But, if we break leadership into two elements—content (saying something new about a subject matter) and influencing skills, we get a different picture. Influencing skills can be learned, but the inclination and the courage to challenge the *status quo* in relation to entrenched content depends on youthful rebelliousness, not a skill set, learned or otherwise.
6. **The sin of character and emotional intelligence** – Our preferred image of the leader is an executive with admirable character traits, including emotional intelligence. Managers need to be trustworthy and capable of showing appropriate sensitivity toward people, but leadership does not require such traits, simply because it is possible for technical experts with poor interpersonal skills to show leadership viewed as challenging the *status quo*.
7. **The sin of parental dependency** – Our motivation to regard leaders as heroes is deeply entrenched, but worse, we have a specific heroic model in mind, not the high achieving sports person, scientist or artist but rather the parental hero, the omnipotent parent figure who we wanted from an early age to take care of everything for us and soothe all our anxieties. Unless we rid ourselves of this model of leadership we will never get any closer to agreeing what it means to lead in a contemporary organizational context.

1. The Organizational Sin

The basic question CEOs ask is: "How can I execute my goals through this group of people as effectively as possible?" CEOs achieve results through the vehicle of an organization and they have the authority to do so. The comparable question a non-organizational leader, such as Martin Luther King, Nelson Mandela or

Gandhi, would ask is: "How can I influence those in power to change their ways, beliefs, attitudes and values?" CEOs look *downward* to organize and motivate a group of subordinates to achieve a task while non-organizational leaders focus *upward* to influence those in charge to change their minds. CEOs achieve their goals *through* their followers, while the followers of Martin Luther King, for example, actually join him on the leadership stage to challenge the prevailing views of government and the population at large. Martin Luther King could not work through his followers to achieve his aims. Quite the opposite, they helped him to show leadership to the real target audience: those in power who make policy.

What is the core difference between these two types of leadership? Because non-organizational leaders lack the power to implement their visions, their leadership has nothing to do with implementation. Their leadership comes to an end, it achieves its objectives, when those in power decide to change their policies. Government officials, in turn, must take responsibility for implementation. By challenging the *status quo*, such leaders are offering new directions. CEOs who promote a new vision are also offering a new direction but we tend to understand their leadership, at least partly, in terms of implementation, not limiting it to merely selling their vision.

In addition, positional leadership, conceptualized as inducing a team to perform at a high level, rules out upward leadership where the target audience does not report to those attempting to show such leadership. Consider thought leadership, the promotion of new ideas. This is a form of leadership that can be shown upward and sideways as well as down. Anyone who argues for doing something different is showing thought leadership. But, like the leadership of Martin Luther King, Nelson Mandela and Gandhi, thought leadership has nothing to do with implementation. It comes to an end once the target audience, those in power, accept the new ideas. For example, thought leaders promoting new products to their superiors must leave it to them to implement the new products. Showing such leadership is simply a matter of doing a convincing job of selling good ideas. It has nothing to do with managing a team to achieve a goal. Again, implementation is a separate phase.

The bottom line here is that, if we want a single theory of leadership, one that covers both in-group and out-group situations, then we must say that leadership is about challenging the *status quo* and offering a new direction, end of story. Implementation is a separate sphere of action or phase that, even in organizations, may not be managed by the Chief Executive. The implications of this shift for our conventional understanding of leadership are massive. So much of traditional leadership theory and talk of leadership style revolve around how best to manage a team to achieve a task within a working group or team. But focusing leadership on selling new directions means that leadership has nothing to do with the actual management of a team of people. This is a managerial job. Leaders sell the tickets for the journey but managers drive the bus to the destination.

To avoid the first sin, therefore, we need a conception of leadership that unites positional and non-positional, organizational and non-organizational, in-group and out-group leadership. Such an account portrays leadership as challenging the *status quo* to provide new directions. This form of leadership can be shown by CEOs as well as knowledge workers leading upward and outsiders calling for change from the sidelines.

2. The Sin of Consideration versus Structure

This sin stems directly from the first, specifically from the basic question CEOs ask about how to obtain maximum productivity from the group of people reporting to them. The old and still popular answer is to strike the right balance between initiating structure and showing consideration for people. We didn't worry about whether management differed from leadership when this solution first saw the light of day. It was only later that leadership became associated with the people side while management was consigned to initiating structure. This move lent itself neatly to early attempts to offer a functional differentiation between leadership and management. It was easy to say that leadership dealt with change and worked through inspirational consideration for people, while management dealt with the task side through planning, organizing and controlling.

But this is surely to confuse ends and means. A purely functional distinction between leadership and management points only to their differing ends, implying nothing about means. So, leadership is well conceived as championing change, while management can be seen as executing the new directions that leadership promotes. But, and this is the key point, both leaders and managers can use the same means of moving people. Leaders can be inspiring when necessary or quiet and factual. Similarly managers can either routinely reward performance or they can be inspiring when their team is up against a difficult challenge such as achieving a nearly impossible deadline. On this view, the basic question a CEO asks about how to maximize productivity is a managerial one, nothing to do with leadership. Managers can both initiate structure *and* show consideration for people. Leaders are interested in championing new directions. When they move into implementation mode, they put on a managerial hat, throwing in only occasional injections of leadership when (or if) new resistance develops. Leadership, as a function, does not govern implementation.

We need to rid ourselves, therefore, of old-fashioned attempts to differentiate leadership and management functionally that carry the added obsolete baggage of allowing only leaders to be inspiring (transformational) while managers are limited to being controlling drones (transactional). While managers may not champion change, they surely can be inspiring in the way they motivate exceptional performance. But so long as their focus is execution, not the promotion of new directions, they are operating as managers not leaders. This means that managers can be as transformational, empowering and emotionally engaging as the situation demands.

3. The Sin of Killing off Management

Management is not as admired as it deserves to be. It is still too often seen as bureaucratic and controlling rather than value adding or facilitating. There are two main sources of this disrepute. One is Fredrick Taylor's identification of management with the efficiency of the assembly line and the other is the way American commentators reacted to the Japanese commercial invasion in the 1970s. A scapegoat was needed to blame for US industry's lack of competitiveness when the Japanese struck. Management was fingered for this role. But the real problem was the way management was practiced at the time. Because there was little incentive to innovate or radically reinvent processes, US and other Western managers could focus on making minor upgrades in efficiency or products. The truth is that US industry was uncompetitive because it had not had to face serious competition prior to the arrival of Japanese businesses. It was this lack of pressure to change that was the cause of *both* its poor performance against the Japanese *and* the way management was practiced. Management was not the source of the problem but one of the outcomes of a lack of competitive pressure.

This sin is clearly related to the sin of structure versus consideration. Management was vilified for placing too much emphasis on control, hence stifling innovation, but it was the *style* of management that was the problem, not the actual function of management. (Recall the point about confusing ends and means.) All we needed to do was adopt a more empowering, facilitative, coaching and developmental style of management, not throw it out altogether and put all the burden of achieving excellence on the shoulders of leadership. Our image of management should be something like that of the sports coach, not that of the controlling disciplinarian or bureaucrat.

What follows from our story so far? Well, by resurrecting management and assigning it the function of getting things done in a manner that makes the best use of all resources available, we can reserve leadership for inspiring change. This means that everything to do with getting the best out of people in relation to achieving a set of organizational goals calls for good management. Not convinced? Why would we not want to allow leadership a hand in implementation? Because, as we saw in discussing our earlier sins, upward leadership must stop once the boss is convinced. Such leaders do not manage implementation through their bosses—the target of their leadership efforts. This means that, if we want a general conception of leadership, one that encompasses both in-group and out-group leadership, we must say that leadership has nothing to do with implementation except where a change needs periodic reselling. But everything to do with motivating people and achieving high performance calls for excellent managerial motivation, coaching and empowerment, not leadership.

It is critical to note that leadership as characterized here is not about *change management* and management is not restricted to keeping static operations ticking over as many have claimed who differentiate between leadership and management along functional lines. Leaders promote new directions and managers implement all major change in addition to running current operations efficiently. This is not to say that leadership is no longer required once major change initiatives are launched. Periodic injections of leadership may still be necessary to resell the benefits of change. But if we apply the 80/20 rule, the bulk of getting to the destination requires a combination of good project management skills and managerial motivation. The latter includes coaching, empowerment, inspiration, emotional engagement and all necessary people development activities. These are all managerial actions so long as the focus is on implementation, not the promotion of new directions.

4. The Transformational Sin

The remarkable fact about transformational leadership is that anyone could ever have taken it as a model for all leadership. It is so obviously possible to show leadership quietly or by example without even being aware of it, let alone explicitly making a stirring, visionary speech that it is puzzling why transformational leadership has had such a long run. The reason it has been at all credible is because we admire heroic, larger-than-life people. But we now must recognize that being transformational is no more than a situational requirement, useful in situations of major change or conflict. It is not a template for a general understanding of leadership, precisely because it rules out all forms of quieter leadership. For example, the health sector is big on evidence-based practice. Showing leadership in this context depends on an ability to cite hard evidence for new proposals, regardless of whether the pitch is made in an emotionally inspiring manner or not.

The transformational sin is really just a corollary of the sin of structure versus consideration because it is merely an extension of the earlier view of how best to maximize performance—to show consideration for people. What we need is a conception of leadership which says that it helps if you can be transformational when you have to tackle massive resistance to your ideas or when you are trying to get people to change their fundamental, dearly held values. But if you are championing a new product and your prospective followers are out and out opportunists, they might jump on the bandwagon with little persuasion at all from you, let alone requiring a visionary, inspiring appeal. The truth is that all particular influencing styles, whether transformational or quiet and factual, are situational facilitators rather than essential definitional elements of leadership.

5. The Sin of Learnable Process

Again, this sin stems from the first one, conceptualizing leadership in organizational terms with a focus on what it takes to operate effectively in a senior position within a working group. It also ties in with the sin of consideration versus structure where being effective in an executive position meant being able to shift between the use of the two core processes of initiating structure and showing consideration for people. Certainly, these two factors are processes, but they are both managerial processes, not a basis for differentiating leadership from management.

Let's take a closer look at the nature of leadership conceived as challenging the *status quo* and offering a new direction. There are two components comprising such leadership: having something new to say and having the ability to say or demonstrate it in a manner that wins the support of the target audience (within or outside your immediate team). So, there is content and influencing skills. The latter has a process feel to it, but the former refers to a concrete subject matter, not a process at all. It is not impossibly difficult to shift from being a business leader to taking a leadership stance in politics, but it is not so easy to be a leader in molecular genetics one day and a leader in software development or financial services the next. To the extent that leadership says something new about a subject area, the harder it is to show leadership across widely divergent subjects. Conversely, the management skills of utilizing people and other resources in a manner that yields the highest return on the investment of those resources is much more readily transferable across widely diverse industries. Content is less important to manage well. Hence, we can more readily view management as a set of process skills.

Why does this point matter? Well, it is easier to associate a process with a role such as CEO, but the fact is that CEOs don't have all the answers when it comes to content, which is why, to be fully effective, organizations today need to foster leadership in all of their content experts or knowledge workers as well as looking for it outside the organization. (Outsourced leadership?) A related point is that younger or new employees with good ideas are the real leaders in organizations and that promoting them to positions of responsibility does not amount to making leaders out of them. Rather, we are turning employees who are already leaders into managers, some of whom might still be good leaders and poor managers. Others may become good managers but lose their leadership edge. A few excel at both.

Talk of processes suggests a learnable set of steps, most clearly true for management and influencing skills. Showing leadership no doubt requires influencing skills but these can range from unwitting example through explicit but logical, factual arguments to inspirational vision statements. There are two other essential ingredients: having something novel to say about a particular subject and having the courage to stand up and say it, to challenge the *status quo*, to risk group rejection and ridicule. Content knowledge and insight into how a field might progress are acquired through close study and hard thinking about the domain in question, but the other essential ingredients are associated with youthful rebelliousness. Creativity is not required because leaders can be early adopters of new ideas developed by others, but the essential traits for leadership overlap with those that underpin creativity – a drive to differentiate yourself by doing something new or different and a curiosity about how things work. Such traits emerge in people naturally. They are not learned skills or a formulaic process. While they are not the exclusive province of youth, creativity flourishes more readily in the young, just as does youthful rebelliousness. And, naturally, some are more rebellious than others. Some rebels become deviants, dropouts or criminals. Not all channel their spirit of adventure in productive directions, thereby becoming leaders.

It is nothing new to say that leadership involves content and influence. All great leaders are said to have a vision—a new idea for a better future or direction, supplemented by great influencing skills. But, because we so strongly admire powerful influencing skills, we have over emphasized them as the key to being a leader. But this is a dead end because leadership is ultimately in the eyes of the beholder and, the fact is, some people are more swayed by hard facts than an emotional appeal, so particular styles of influencing can only be situational, not definitional. Also, as we move inexorably into a knowledge-driven world, the emphasis needs to shift to the power of ideas and away from the force of personality to move us. As we now say: "Content is king." What is less understandable is why we have overlooked the similarity of leadership to creativity such that both are underpinned by youthful rebelliousness, an unlearned spirit of adventure.

The implications of moving away from the sin of learnable process is that we can develop managers and rounded executives, but only foster leadership just as we can only foster creativity. It is important to add, however, that everyone can show a degree of leadership because much of it is very small scale and local—such as suggesting a small improvement in an operating process. Leadership only needs to be seen as heroic when we associate it with the ability to ascend to the top of a vast organization or move hordes of people in the domain of human values. Much of business leadership occurs in very technical domains where basic human values do not play a key part.

6. The Sin of Character and Emotional Intelligence

Leadership conceived as challenging the *status quo* can range from an interpersonally sensitive, emotionally uplifting appeal to an aggressive frontal attack. Consider, for example, a software developer who is very unreliable, who regularly fails to show up for work and who relates to others in a rude, aggressive and insensitive manner but who develops a revolutionary new piece of software. He attacks management for weeks, promoting his product and verbally abusing management for sticking with their pet products. Because he can demonstrate the superiority of his product and begins to gain serious interest from customers, management finally gives in. The new product requires a fundamental reorganization of the business as the new product takes them into a totally new market. No one likes this developer and many resent his success in moving the organization in a new direction. He cannot even manage himself so is not given any responsibility for managing the new product or the organizational change process. This is an example of leadership, however, despite the total absence of admirable character traits or emotional intelligence. Such traits are necessary, however, for anyone in a role with responsibility for people—a manager or executive. We have to place our trust in managers because they hold the fate of our careers in their hands. To earn our trust, they must have a reputable character and display a modicum of emotional intelligence. Not so for leadership. Having such traits is situationally valuable for leadership to influence people who only respond to such approaches but they are not universally necessary so cannot form any part of our definition of leadership. Hence, the meaning of leadership is totally independent of all style considerations.

7. The Sin of Parental Dependency

Why have we over-emphasized powerful influencing skills in our efforts to understand leadership? Why do we so admire such people? It is not just that we tend to admire heroes. Conventional leaders are a specific sort of heroes—they take the place in our minds of powerful parental figures, usually fathers. Traditional leadership theory is, therefore, inescapably paternalistic. It is also biologically primitive because all higher primates tend to align themselves into hierarchies. Our intuitive or unconscious distinction between leadership and management parallels our image of the good and bad father. The former protects, guides and supports us while the latter controls and punishes us for stepping out of line. As children we needed to trust our fathers. Not surprisingly, we fly into a rage when "leaders" disappoint us or betray our trust. One of the main reasons why many will be dissatisfied with a conception of leadership that allows every obscure knowledge worker in the lower reaches of organizations to show leadership merely by flogging a new product is that it clashes head on with our paternal image of the leader. Such knowledge workers may be capable of successfully promoting new directions but many are neither able nor interested in being managers or having parental authority over people. Hence, they just do not fit the image of the conventional leader.

This is the crunch. I think we need to rid ourselves of our paternal, biologically primitive, image of leadership if we are ever to succeed in fully understanding and capitalizing on leadership properly recast for a digital age. We may not get rid of our hard wired tendencies to form ourselves into hierarchies or to look up to father figures but we can stop calling such people leaders. Senior executives are executives. They may be successful simply by being effective managers. They may also show some leadership, where leadership is seen as an occasional activity, not a role or position. CEOs and political leaders such as Churchill or Roosevelt or any other admired head of state display a mixture of management, genuine directional leadership and paternal leadership. The latter is what they are mostly admired for but it is not what propels businesses that compete through rampant innovation.

In Summary, what is Leadership?

Leadership is the promotion of new directions through challenging the *status quo*. It is complemented by management which focuses on all aspects of getting things done efficiently through people. Style is another matter altogether. Leadership champions a new perspective on some content or subject matter. It is successful when people are willingly influenced to accept the leadership attempt. How they are moved is a completely situational or contextual matter, not definitional.

Benefits of a more Sharply Focused Concept of Leadership

- Executives are better able to focus their energies where they can best add value by not having to be all things to all people.
- Greater engagement, motivation and retention of key knowledge workers by encouraging them to be leaders now.
- More employees thinking about how to improve the business due to more widely dispersed ownership over future directions.
- Greater receptivity to new ideas and upward challenges as executives better understand their roles as managers, coaches and facilitators and as they learn to relinquish their monopoly on leadership.

The Fading Fortune of Ingroup Dynamics as a Foundation for Leadership

Our model of leadership is distorted by our focus on working groups because it leads us to study the person who emerges as the most influential within the group. But Martin Luther King, Nelson Mandela and Gandhi attempted to show leadership to people who were outside their working group—governmental authorities and the general public. Similarly, lowly but innovative knowledge workers who promote new products to their superiors are striving to lead people who are not, strictly speaking, members of their working groups or teams. Thirdly, leadership can be shown to whole organizations by industry gurus or market leading competitors—again a source of leadership that emerges from outside the groups that experience the leadership impact. A working group or team can both decide what to do and then proceed to do it. But there are separate actors involved when outsiders influence a group to change direction. The outsider leader has no part in enabling or overseeing the group's movement toward its goals. Hence, such leadership must come to an end once the group decides to move. Another example of what might be called out-group leadership was Churchill trying to persuade the US government to get involved in World War II. Churchill was not an American leader. He was the head of a different group. His leadership intent was to win US commitment to take a more direct part in the war effort. It was not about managing or inspiring his organization to reach a goal.

Consider the following three themes:

1. How the basic goals of groups have shifted from (a) stability through (b) efficient production of a product to (c) being able to change quickly.
2. How the forces that move groups have shifted away from the personal power of the group leader to all manner of forces external to that individual's control.
3. How the boundaries between groups are breaking down.

The Shifting of Group Goals

The objective of a primitive tribe or group of higher primates is subsistence – to eat and reproduce free from external threats. Leadership in such groups is clearly a position and a relatively stable one at that. Being a leader means having the power to attain and hold the top slot. Such groups do not have a product, they do not make or even do anything other than whatever it takes to survive. Stability, not effective change, is the measure of success.

By contrast, the goal of early business groups was to produce a product efficiently. It was not enough simply to exist as a group and do nothing. Successful forward movement is also required for the person in charge to be seen as an effective leader. Now leaders needed to accomplish two things: they had to display enough personal power to gain the top position in the first place. Then they had to get the group producing its product effectively. In this context leadership researchers had two questions to answer:

- What does it take to make it to the top?
- What do you have to do to get a group producing effectively?

Since the early 1970s, business groups have developed a third goal beyond efficient production of a product and that is to continually evolve to keep up with a rapidly changing environment of aggressive competitors and rapidly shifting customer demands. Now, efficient productivity is the new stability and effective leadership must be aligned with engendering successful change. Unfortunately, for positional leaders, this shift in group goals destabilizes their power base for the simple reason that the world is now too complex for any one person to figure out what to do next. Brute strength was once enough to hold onto a leadership position, followed later by the force of larger-than-life personality, but now there is the added pressure to divine new directions fast, while wearing a blindfold. A wide range of other voices are now crying out to be heard.

The Shifting Forces that Move Groups

In primitive groups it was not safe to challenge authority. Death or excommunication surely followed. As recently as the time of Galileo and Martin Luther, questioning received wisdom was done at great personal risk—you could be burnt at the stake. Leadership in this world was a win-lose monopoly. Either you had the power to topple the leader or you pay the ultimate price. You could take the safe option and say nothing, of course. Even in our time, Nelson Mandela was imprisoned for his challenge to the *status quo,* while Martin Luther King was assassinated.

Within the political realm, deeply held values cause seemingly irresolvable conflict making change nearly impossible in many cases. Not so in business where rapid change driven by innovation is unstoppable. The key point here is that, for groups that operate in an innovation-driven world, new ideas are the motor that propels change and, most critically, such ideas can come from any source other than (but not excluding) the person in charge of the group. This rise to prominence of external group forces complements the group's new goal of continually reinventing itself discussed above where no single person has a monopoly on good ideas.

Breakdown of Group Boundaries

In primitive times, when two groups clashed, one was defeated and the leader replaced by the winner. Much the same still happens today when a business is acquired. But in modern business, it is possible for several groups to compete in the same markets without any of them getting acquired or killed off. Winning has become less absolute, more relative. This makes business a bit like a multi-team sports league where one team is temporarily in the lead and others must sit for a while in second or a lower place. In this context, lower ranked groups often look to their betters for leadership which means that their sole or main source of leadership need no longer be the person in charge of their own group. Rapid change and growing complexity have also led to strategic alliances and complex outsourcing arrangements where it is unclear who is leading whom. Further, employees are unsure who is their leader in such complex marriages. Who is an outsourced employee's formal leader? With what group do such employees identify or belong?

Implications for leadership

The fundamental implication of the shifting fortunes of groups is that we can no longer restrict our efforts to understand leadership to the dynamics *within* groups. We now need a concept of leadership based on a much wider set of dynamics. The traditional small group, such as the street corner gang are *closed* in the sense that direction and power revolve around the one person acknowledged as the group's leader. By contrast, innovation-driven organizations are considerably much more *open* to outside influences.

Here are just a few key implications of the shifting fortunes of the group:

- Leadership must be reframed strictly as a call to change direction because it can come as easily from outside an organization or from its frontlines as from the top.
- If leadership can be bottom-up, where the successful leadership attempt ends when those in power accept the proposal, then leadership cannot be formulated in terms of overseeing a group's journey toward a new goal. This means that everything to do with people management and implementation must be recast as a management function, having nothing to do with leadership.
- If leadership entails nothing more than challenging the *status quo* to offer a new direction, rather than facilitating the achievement of a group goal, then leadership is not a process. It is, rather, an impact based on someone's insight into how the world could be better, combined with the nerve to

speak up. This is youthful rebelliousness, not a relationship, process, or learned skill set.

- If leadership, viewed as a successful challenge to the *status quo*, can be done in an aggressive manner, then leadership does not require emotional intelligence.

Conclusion

What does it mean to be a CEO in this revised leadership framework? CEOs do not need to display genuine leadership if there is no need to champion new directions. Industries that, relatively speaking, major on service, cost and quality, rather than rampant innovation, need effective management and not so much leadership. On the other hand, all CEOs admired by their organization members display primitive or paternal leadership. There is nothing wrong with acknowledging a legitimate place for someone to help employees allay their anxieties, but it is confusing and old fashioned to call this leadership.

There are some interesting postmodern themes running through the shift in our understanding of leadership that I am advocating. Although postmodernism is not as popular as it was a few years ago, some of its tenets are likely here to stay. One of these is the view that there are no authorities, that we are all our own authorities. In organizations, the power to generate novel directions is inexorably slipping through the hands of those in positions of authority to everyone else. Knowledge (content) is increasingly more powerful than position and the force of personality. Accordingly, we need a conception of leadership that captures the central role of innovation, the promotion of new ideas. Boundarylessness is another postmodern theme. Thought leadership is not only shown by positionless knowledge workers at the bottom of the pile, it can also come from outside the organization. In simpler times we could get away with limiting our attempts to understand leadership by studying what happens within groups. But boundaries are breaking down and the impact of the world outside immediate groups is now such that we need a theory of leadership that can account for cross-group, out-group or lone operator influences on group action.

If we can agree that leadership is nothing other than the promotion of new directions rather than associated with senior organizational roles, then we can now effectively capture the fact that some whole organizations are better followers than leaders. Microsoft would be an example. But even those organizations that are leading edge might occasionally follow the lead of external gurus or innovators.

In conclusion, for this view of leadership to be accepted, we need to rebuild our conception of management and stop calling executives leaders no matter how much they meet our emotional needs for guidance, support and anxiety reduction.

(Mitch McCrimmon, Ph.D is a business psychologist with over 30 years experience of management assessment and executive coaching. His latest book is Burn! 7 Leadership Myths in Ashes, 2006. He is based in Canada and the UK.)

6

A Case Study: Changing Human Resource Management Education to Fit the Field

Michael Bedell and Gary H Kritz

The field of Human Resource Management has embarked upon a process of significant change. To keep up with changes in the field, Barksdale (1998) exhorted to update HR education. This article describes the effort that changed the HR educational model from a functional, silos-focused model to an integrated, outcome-based model. The logic for the change, what changes were made, and comments about the outcomes are also presented.

Introduction

"The competitive landscape is changing, and new models of competitiveness are needed to deal with the challenges ahead. These responses reveal a new competitive reality demanding organizational capabilities that will enable firms to better serve their customers and to differentiate themselves from their competitors." (Ulrich, 1997, p.1).

The maintenance and development of human capital is necessary to sustain an organization's competitive position. Quite simply, the organization needs to

Source: www.coastal.edu, The Coastal Business Journal, Volume 5, Number 1, Spring 2006.

have a human capital mix (e.g., knowledge, skills, and abilities) that will facilitate goal achievement year after year. Organizations that fail to take a proactive approach to developing and maintaining human capital will be less competitive. As Pfeffer (1998) notes, "Companies that manage people right will outperform companies that don't by 30% to 40%." There are a variety of other authors that seem to concur with Pfeffer's comments (e.g., Pfau & Kay, 2002).

The management and development of human capital is one challenge presented by an increasingly complex marketplace. Other challenges to the organization may include global, capability awareness and development, change management, technology, and the employee life-cycle (Ulrich, 1997, p. 2-14). Ulrich (1997, p. 23) suggests that the Human Resource (HR) function is ideally positioned to help the organization manage these challenges. Becker & Huselid (1999) suggest that the HR function must reinvent itself as both a strategic partner and service provider within the organization. As a strategic partner, the HR function is responsible for ensuring that adequate number of employees exist, with the right skills, in the right positions, so that the organization can achieve the goals that are set by the senior management team (profitability, expansion into new markets). As a service provider the HR function's role is to provide managers with information about people-related issues, provide employees with timely paychecks, benefit information, provide training and many other tasks. Fitz-enz (2001) suggests that HR has clearly evolved and to remain relevant, it must change with the times and learn to use data to make intelligent decisions. In other words, HR needs to measure and make sure that it is using its resources as well as possible.

The push to become a strategic partner and service provider of the organization has changed the skills-mix that organizations seek when hiring HR graduates. The role of the HR faculty member is to make sure that the Knowledge, Skills, and Abilities (KSA) mix provided by the HR curriculum "generally" matches the needs of HR—present and future—so that when students complete their degrees they are employable. This discussion does not intend to suggest that Business Schools are vocational schools. Instead, Business Schools should perceive themselves and be perceived as a development organization. And as a development organization the goal is to develop individuals that (1) have an appropriate/current mix of KSA's to meet future human capital needs, and (2) sufficient foundation to continue developing themselves.

Consistent with the arguments that the HR function in organizations needs to update itself, Barksdale (1998) in the *Journal of Management Education* argues that we also must update HR education. He identifies four reasons why we should update HR education: the HR image problem; an overemphasis on compliance; ignorance of the financial side of business; and that HR has forgotten what it does well. A discussion with most HR professionals demonstrates that these reasons are valid, and there are probably several others that could also be included (e.g., strategic HR and changing technology). When these reasons are coupled with the growing chorus of industry and academic leaders who are increasingly talking about the link between treating people well and enhanced profitability, the argument to update HR education is even more compelling.

The evidence presented by both academic thought leaders and HR professionals is consistent. New HR professionals require skills—beyond the traditional HR tools (i.e., recruiting, compensation, etc.)—such as technology skills (Gartner Group, 1999; Miller, 2000; Shrivastava & Shaw, 2003; Thompson, 2000), the ability to think strategically (Becker, Huselid, Pickus, & Spratt, 1997), and the ability to understand how to measure and benchmark HR processes (Fitz-enz, 2001). Becker, Huselid, & Ulrich (2001, p. 12) note that most HR managers are very competent with regard to HR tasks but less competent at meeting strategic HR needs.

The Society for Human Resource Management (SHRM) presents a knowledge model as a recommendation for every HR professional (SHRM, 2005). The SHRM model recommends that every HR professional should have: (a) knowledge of his/her business; (b) an understanding of HR technology; (c) ethical behavior and the demonstration of personal credibility; and (d) knowledge of traditional HR needs and delivery. The linkage between these components and the strategic contribution of HR also needs to be understood.

Purpose of this Paper

The purpose of this article is to go beyond the call for discussion presented by Barksdale (1998) to update HR education and provide a case example as to how one management department updated its HR concentration. Ideally, this article will start discussion and perhaps fan the flames of change.

The curriculum changes presented within were developed with input from a variety of stakeholders. The list of stakeholders includes HR professionals, current students, and students who graduated and started working in HR or management positions within the last several years. In addition, the authors relied upon: (1) one author's work experience as an Organizational Development specialist with a global retailer; (2) routine contacts with HR and management professionals in the business communities; (3) service with the local Society for Human Resource Management (SHRM) Board of Directors; and (4) service with a global provider of Human Resource Information Systems, (HRIS), and Supply Chain information systems—both of which are subsets of Enterprise Resource Planning (ERP) and software systems which are used to run entire organizations.

The Starting Point

An examination of various Human Resource curricula finds a heavy emphasis on the traditional HR tools with some focus on strategic HR and HRIS—and ours was no different. When we began this process, our curriculum was composed of the traditional list of courses with each one focusing on a subset of the traditional HR toolbox: (a) Introduction to Human Resources; (b) Compensation & Benefits; (c) Staffing, Recruiting, & Selection; (d) Training & Development; and (e) a Special Topics course. Students took four of the courses (see Figure 1) of which one was a required prerequisite. Although our curriculum did not, some curricula also include an HR Information Systems component to demonstrate how data can be used to make hiring decisions, to track training courses taken, and to help manage placement of people based on their skills. Feedback from our constituents strongly suggested that our HR students were well-versed in the traditional HR tools.

Courses were heavily focused on the "how to" of the traditional HR tools, and they provided great detail on these tools. There was little discussion that focused on the linkages that could be developed between traditional HR tools or as to how they could be implemented to facilitate the achievement of desired outcomes. Any discussion of linkages between the functional HR areas (compensation, recruiting) and strategic organizational goals (such as profitability or physical capacity growth) existed in a hypothetical and sometimes case study fashion, but these discussions would have been much more powerful if they had occurred consistently in every class and if the focus had been at the level of the HR department and not on the functional silo (recruiting). For the purpose of this paper, functional silos are defined as a focused subset of activities within the HR function. For example, compensation and all the activities related to compensation decisions would occur within the functional silo responsible for compensation.

Figure 1: Pre 2001 Model – Functional Silo Curriculum

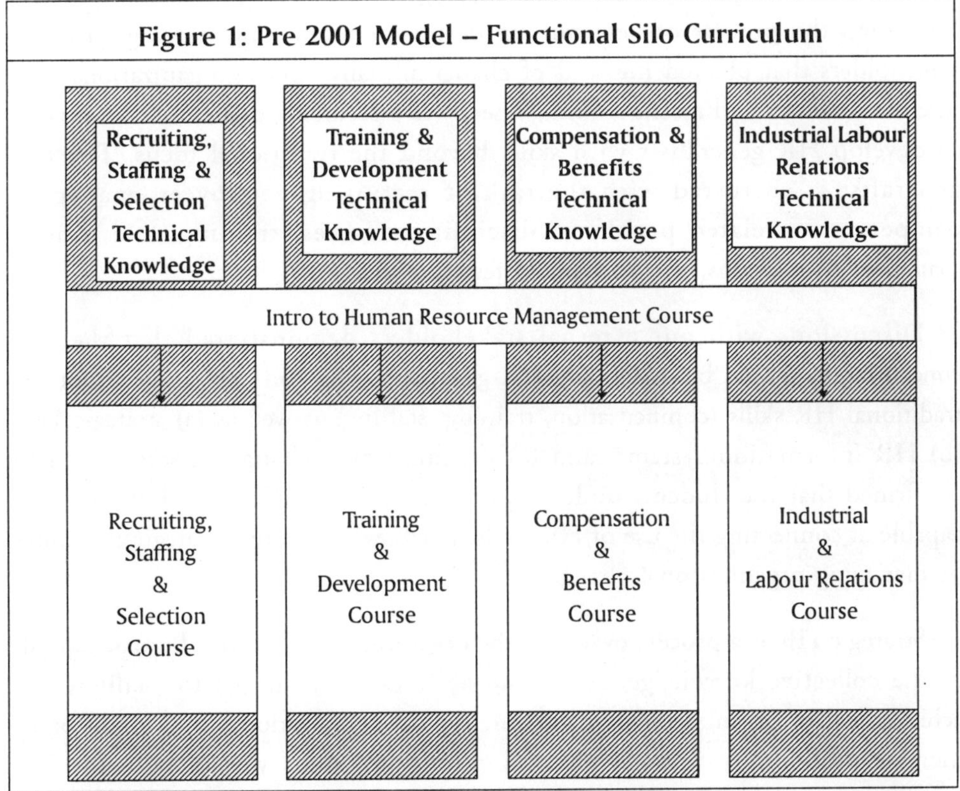

Barksdale (1998) notes that the traditional focus has three weaknesses. First, this approach reflects the historical development of HR and is heavily compliance-oriented. Second, this approach tends to teach the traditional HR tools in a vacuum. That is, it teaches HR tools without accounting for the necessity of being able to: (a) connect HR practices to the achievement of strategic organizational goals; (b) benchmark HR processes; (c) measure HR financial effectiveness; (d) manage change; and (e) completely understand modern HR information systems. Third, the traditional HR tools were developed by examining the desired capabilities of personnel professionals of an earlier time.

Re-Engineering

Based on these arguments and other trends in the field, we began re-engineering our HR concentration during the 2001/2002 academic year. The change process started with a simple re-engineering question—"What outcomes are desired?" We began the process of determining desired outcomes by starting with the stakeholders that planted the seed of change initially—those organizations who hire our students and recent alumni. There was a recurring theme that we needed to develop HR generalists with skills beyond the traditional focus. The HR generalist is entrusted with the task of recruiting employees, managing compensation-related problems, disciplinary issues, training, and union-management relations, just to name a few activities.

Discussions with our external stakeholders demonstrated that the HR concentration should be developing HR generalists who had knowledge about the traditional HR skills (compensation, training, staffing) as well as (a) strategic HR, (b) HR information systems, and (c) organizational change. Assessment data confirmed that the students understood the traditional HR tools, but were less capable at connecting the use of HR tools to achieving desired strategic outcomes or managing organizational change.

Strategic HR is a process by which the organization's collective human capital, or the collective knowledge, skills, and abilities are managed to facilitate the achievement of organizational goals. One typical organizational goal might be to increase profitability through physical expansion, which would mean the HR function should identify, train, decide on compensation, and physically move the individuals that would be likely to be successful in a new location. Another organizational goal might be to reduce reliance on outside contractors in the information technology sector, which means the HR function needs to manage an aggressive hiring campaign and then make sure that the compensation plan is in place so that adequate numbers of employees with the right skills can be hired to replace the outside contractors. Strategic HR is the process of identifying the organization's goals, translating those goals into strategic HR goals, and then coordinating the various areas within HR in their movement towards goal achievement. The new HR professional needs to understand the linkages present in order to be part of these processes.

Human Resource Information Systems are database software products that manage all of the data that organizations maintain about their employees. Much like the introduction of spreadsheets and accounting information systems to accounting students, new HR graduates are expected to understand how an HRIS works and ideally have some familiarity. For example, when making a recommendation about which employee to interview for an open position, the HRIS can be used to match the specific tasks required of the job with all applicants and their skills. This results in a much faster decision about who is qualified so that valuable interview time and resources are not wasted on an unqualified applicant. The HRIS can also help by automating some processes, such as payroll, so that the HR professional can be left to work on strategic decisions.

Many of the traditional HR tools can be easily adapted to help manage change. For example, training is often used to manage change. The difference between training for jobs and training for change is the focus of the training. Recruiting might also be used to facilitate change by changing the kind of individual knowledge, skills, or abilities that are desired in the next hire.

When we began this process the goal was simple—determine the best way to add or augment courses to meet the identified knowledge goals. As the re-engineering process began, it was discovered that simply adding material would not necessarily develop the additional knowledge in a way that was useful to the student and more importantly transferable by the student into the workplace. The number of hours available in the HR concentration also served as a constraint. Six months and many conversations with stakeholders later—a new HR concentration was developed.

A New Curriculum

The 2002/2003 academic year began with a streamlined and focused HR concentration with fewer course choices. The new concentration was designed by first deciding how to put the goals listed previously into practice in the classroom. Once the desired outcomes were defined, courses could be developed that would teach the desired HR skills with the linkages to those desired outcomes. The new concentration continued to be four courses—now consisting of three required courses and one elective (see Figure 2). The new course list is:

- Introduction to Human Resource Management (required prerequisite)
- Human Resource Information Systems (required)
- Strategic Human Resource Management (required)
- Change Management or Negotiation Skills or Organizational Theory.

Figure 2: 2002/2003 Model – Outcome Based Curriculum

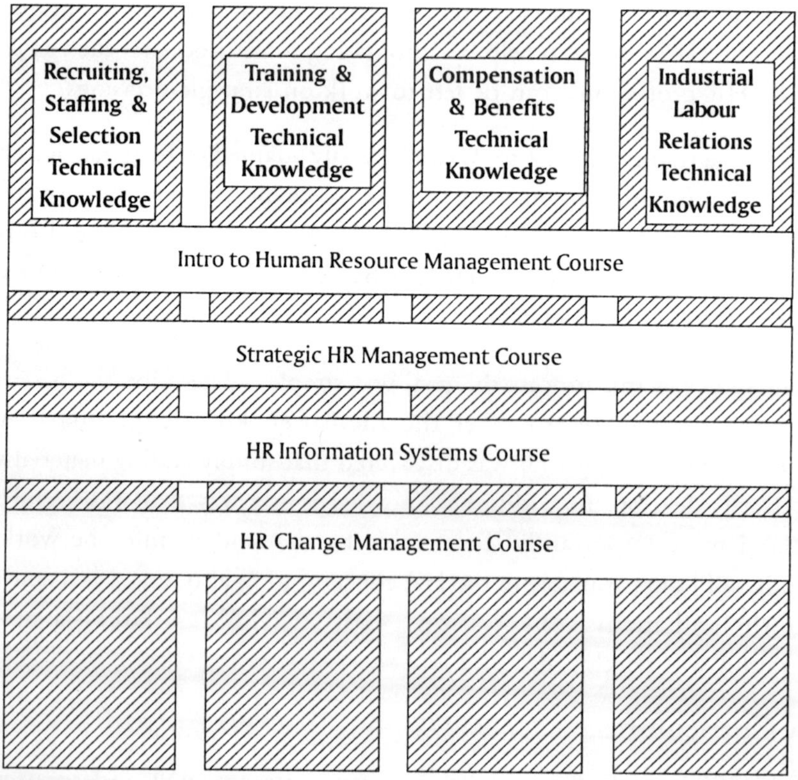

Recruiting, Staffing & Selection Technical Knowledge

Training & Development Technical Knowledge

Compensation & Benefits Technical Knowledge

Industrial Labour Relations Technical Knowledge

Intro to Human Resource Management Course

Strategic HR Management Course

HR Information Systems Course

HR Change Management Course

The logic behind this was that the traditional HR tools could continue to be taught, but now they would be taught as part of the process towards achieving specific outcomes. In other words, the focus would start with outcomes and work "backwards" to the traditional HR tools instead of simply teaching the tools. This would develop linkages, an understanding of the HR system and processes, and knowledge of how each HR capability could contribute to a specific desired outcome. For example, instead of a specific focus on an HR tool or practice in an entire class (e.g., staffing and selection), each student would receive some aspect of staffing and selection in any course where it was relevant to the desired outcomes. This approach requires the student to use all of the traditional tools in the HR toolbox while the old approach focused on one HR process at a time.

As an alternative, the simple addition of a capstone course to the original course sequence was considered. There are two reasons that we elected this other option. First, there were not enough free credit hours to require an HR capstone. The students would have developed depth in only two areas; and for a capstone course to work well, the students should be competent in all of the HR functional areas. Second, the integrated model would provide multiple opportunities to work with the traditional HR tools and the relationship that each HR tool has to the defined outcomes. As most training methodologies have demonstrated, when more opportunities are provided to develop new skills, greater learning is more likely.

Conclusion: What Have We Learned?

As with any new curriculum, it is vital that assessment be completed to determine if the modifications have been successful. Much to the delight of the people that hire our students, the new curriculum seems be helping us to develop new HR employees with desired competencies. The most often mentioned positive feedback indicates that our students understand the big picture and also how to strategically partner with top management to develop, implement, and interpret HR metrics.

The most significant opportunity for improvement—as mentioned by our HR advisory board—is that the traditional HR skills (e.g., compensation, training, recruiting) are not as strong as they used to be in some of the students. In hindsight, perhaps we went too far. When we combine this feedback with the feedback we receive from our recent alumni, we find another opportunity for fine-tuning. Several recent alumni (and new entrants into the workforce) suggested that the HRIS course could be tailored to better fit the role of the HR generalist instead of the HRIS specialist. HR generalists work throughout the entire field of HR making daily decisions about hiring, compensation, training, and terminations, and they use an HR information system to support these activities. HRIS specialists focus on the decision support role of the HRIS as a delivered product, while their daily activities focus on system implementation. A solid suggestion is to replace the time spent developing HRIS specialist knowledge with additional time on working with the HR tools such as compensation, training, or recruiting (see Figure 3).

Figure 3: The Next Model?

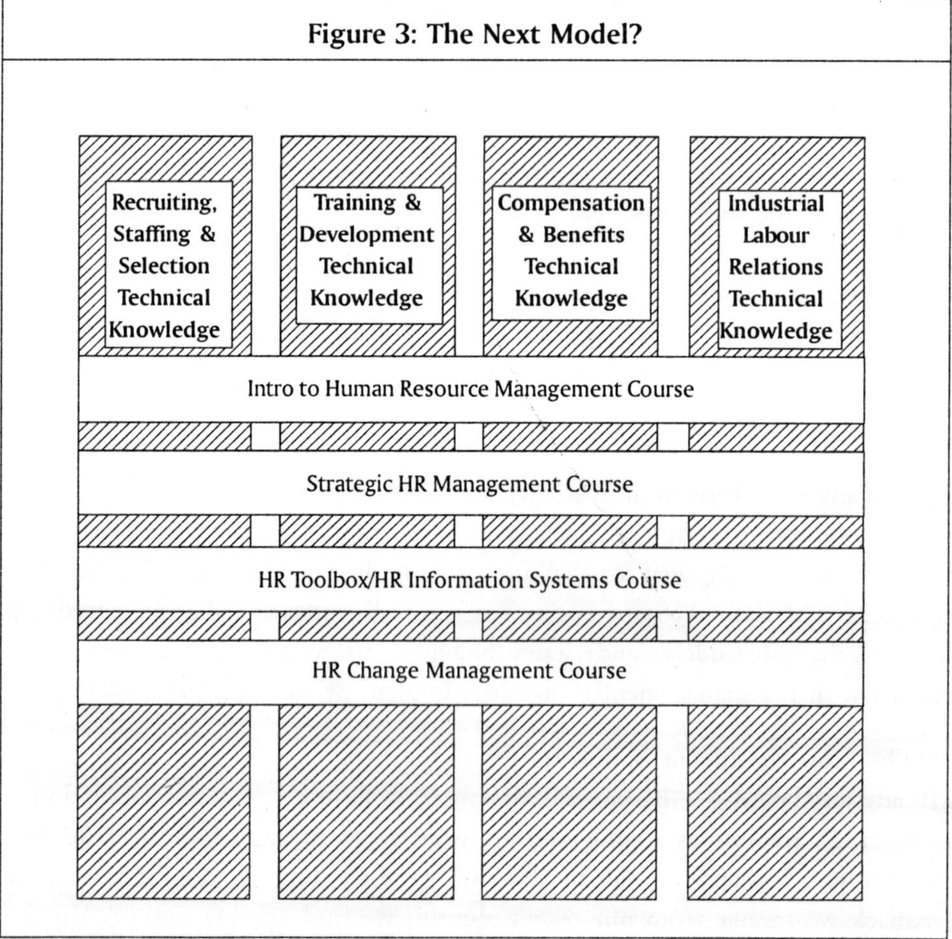

While it is possible to focus too closely on the traditional HR tools, it is also possible to go too far the other direction and develop strategic thinkers that are not as familiar as they should be with the HR functional tools. Most of the thought leaders in HR strongly suggest that HR professionals need to add the strategic capability, metrics, and technology to their toolkits (Barksdale, 1998; Fitz-enz, 2001; Pfeffer, 1998; Ulrich, 1997). However, these same thought leaders say nothing about abandoning the traditional HR tools.

Another approach might be to examine HR from the perspective of the supply chain. In the supply chain model the focus is on processes that are used to deliver products or services to the final customer. The supply chain is broadly conceptualized in that it examines the entire manufacturing/service process from final customer back to initial suppliers of raw materials. However, to the sides of this supply chain there must be financial capital and human capital. This suggests that the role of HR is to ensure that adequate levels of human capital, as defined by desired knowledge, skills, and abilities, are provided such that the supply chain can continue functioning. This is not such a stretch as the role of accounting/finance is to ensure that adequate financial capital exists such that the supply chain can continue functioning. This approach would certainly focus on meeting the human capital needs of the supply chain, although there is a potential for a short-term human capital focus to develop.

As many have suggested, the HR function must change to embrace the business that they are within; so also most of those who develop the HR professional. We must go beyond the simple addition of new topics by continuously monitoring our key constituent groups—the employing organization and the soon-to-graduate student who will want to be employable. In the spirit of continuous improvement we should also consider improving our assessments of what the students are learning. We must also go beyond simple assessment to systematically request feedback from our HR professional graduates. We might also consider working more closely with the professional organizations as their content more rapidly reflects workplace realities and changes.

Another way that the effectiveness of this change may be assessed is in actions taken by the outside stakeholder group. The general level of interest in our students has increased, and placement rates have increased for interns and new full-time positions. Several members of the local Society for Human Resource Management chapter—including the Vice-President of HR of a large local hospital; the Director of HR for the County Courts; and the College Recruiters for two global oil companies with a presence—have commented that the new curriculum has had a noticeable effect in that the interns and new HR professionals have a better understanding of how HR activities fit into the big picture of the organization. This is not a task to be taken lightly. Much like designing a new product, the right stakeholders need to be involved, and the right questions must be asked. The end result, though, appears to be promising and worth the time and effort spent.

(Michael Bedell, PhD., is an Associate Professor of Management, MBA Program Director with the School of Business & Public Administration at California State University, Bakersfield.

Gary H Kritz, PhD., is Assistant Professor of Marketing and Faculty Fellow of the Institute for International Business, Stillman School of Business, Seton Hall University.)

References

Barksdale, K. (1998). "Why We Should Update HR Education." *Journal of Management Education, 22*, 4, 526-530.

Becker, B. & Huselid, M. (1999). "Strategic Human Resource Management in Five Leading Firms." *Human Resource Management, 38*, 2, 287-301.

Becker, B., Huselid, M., & Ulrich, D. (2001). *The HR Scorecard: Linking People, Strategy, and Performance*. Cambridge, MA: Harvard Business Publishing, 4 & 12.

Becker, B., Huselid, M., Pickus, P., & Spratt, M. (1997). "HR as a Source of Shareholder Value: Research and Recommendations." *Human Resource Management, 36*, 1, 39-47.

Fitz-enz, J. (2001). *How to Measure Human Resources Management*. 3rd ed., NY, NY: McGraw-Hill, 14.

Gartner Group, (1999). *Special Report: The CIO Top Ten 1999-2003*. Stanford, CT: Gartner Group Inc.

Miller, H. (2000). White Paper on IT Skills. Arlington, VA: Information Technology Association of America.

Personal communication. CSUB HR Advisory Board. Various dates between 2000 and now.

Pfau, B.N., & Kay, I.T. (2002). *The Human Capital Edge: 21 People Management Practices Your Company Must Implement (or Avoid) to Maximize Shareholder Value*. NY, NY: McGraw-Hill.

Pfeffer, J. (1998). The Human Equation: Building Profits by Putting People First. Cambridge, MA: Harvard Business School Press.

Shrivastava, S. & Shaw, J.B. (2003). "Liberating HR Through Technology." *Human Resource Management. 42*, 3, 201-222.

Society for Human Resource Management (SHRM) (2005). "HRCI Knowledge Model" on the website. *www.hrci.org*. Alexandria, VA.

Thompson, R. (2000). "Tech Skills, While Daunting, Are Essential for Today's HR Professional." *HR News, 19*, 9, 1-2.

Ulrich, D. (1997). *Human Resource Champions: The Next Agenda for Adding Value and Delivering Results*. Cambridge, MA: Harvard Business School Press. 25-27, 53-81.

Section II

Studies

7

The Validity and Usefulness of Management Theories: A Review

J P Cornelissen and R Thorpe

In this paper, an attempt is made at widening the scope of the current debate about the relationship between management theory and managerial practice. This is done by subjecting the widely held claim within the management literature—that management theory can be validated through successful applications in organizational settings—to critical appraisal. The analysis of this claim, its warrant and grounds has interesting and far-reaching implications for the relationship between management theory and practice, and for the working relationship between academic researchers and practicing managers.

Introduction

One of the most perennial issues in the field of management involves the status and role of management theorizing in the light of the practice that it aims to illuminate. Bearing upon different images of the role and use of academic research within professional fields—as a 'pure' enterprise without any accounting towards management practice or as a more 'applied', action-oriented enterprise concerned with producing usable knowledge for practicing managers—the issue seems hardly resolved (e.g., Beyer, 1997), yet it has become more salient than ever before. In particular, fuelled by a number of societal forces, including industry and federal support for academic research (Leydesdorff and Etzkowitz, 1998), the emergence of 'techno-sciences' in many disciplinary fields (Gibbons, Limoges, Nowotny, Scott, and Trow, 1994), and the assumed importance of science-based knowledge to the management technology and innovation process (Rynes, McNatt, and Bretz, 1999), the call for a greater relevance and applicability of management theory to organizational problems and situations have gained momentum and has become more prominent than ever before (Hambrick, 1994; Tranfield and Starkey, 1997; Mohrman, 2001; *Organization,* 2001; *Human Relations,* 2001; *British Journal of Management,* 2001; *Management Science,* 2002). Yet, despite these admissions, little research and commentary has focused on whether management theory indeed can or should have a clear application-basis to grant or validate its claims. Rather, as Miner (1984) already suggested, statements emphasizing the applicability of management theory as a test of its validity such as Lewin's epigram that "nothing is as practical as a good theory" (Lewin, 1945, 129) have in much of the management literature been treated as "something of a dictum, almost as self-evident" (Miner, 1984, 296). The present paper therefore sheds light upon the solidity of the claim that academic management theories are or can be validated by successful practical applications. In the next sections, we subject this claim and the line of argument underlying it to critical appraisal. Our objective involves drawing attention to the fact that this particular claim concerning the validation of theory through application has important implications for one's view of the relationship between management theory and practice, and that this claim is, at least, open to question. Our intention, then, is to generate discussion of the issues, rather than to forestall further argument by means of a final, conclusive analysis. We start with introducing the different perspectives of the relationship between management theory and practice before subjecting the claim that management theory can be validated through practical application to further analysis.

Management Theory and Practice

The relationship between academia, the conduct of scientific research, and professional fields of practice has been a subject of continuing debate in most disciplines within the physical and social sciences, fuelled by the significant increase in industry's share of academic research over the past two decades, from 3.1 percent in 1975 to 6.9 percent in 1995 (National Science Board, 1996). In the larger scientific community, reactions to the latter development in particular have been mixed. Most observers have emphasized the benefits, which can be attributed to these partnerships between industry and academia including improved transfer of knowledge and technology, increased relevance of education, and, in the case of practically useful science-derived technology and knowledge, improved competitiveness and economic development. However, others have been less enthusiastic, emphasizing the potential costs of a closer alignment of the domains in which industry and universities have traditionally operated. Already in the early 1980s, for example, hearings in the US House of Representatives examined two issues within the biomedical sciences (US House of Representatives, 1981): (1) whether university-industry research relationships violated scientific and academic freedom and responsibilities, and (2) whether these relationships best served the interests of the American public.

Similar issues regarding the relationship among theory, academic research, and practice, have been at the center of a series of debates within the field of management as shown in a number of recent special journal issues devoted to the topic (*Journal of Management Inquiry,* 1997; *Academy of Management Journal,* 2001; *Organization,* 2001; *Human Relations,* 2001; *British Journal of Management,* 2001; *Management Science,* 2002). Conflicting images and prescriptions of the relationship between scientific theory and research, and management practice prevail in these debates. On the one hand, subscribing to the belief that scientific development is tied in with an enterprise directed at fundamental understanding *per se* rather than understanding for use by managers, a number of academic observers (Kover, 1979; Shrivastava and Mitroff, 1984; Blackler and Shimmin, 1984; Brinberg and Hirschman, 1986; Astley and Zammuto, 1992) have argued that academic and practitioner orientations to management problems are intrinsically distinct. From this perspective, knowledge is constituted differently in the academic and practitioner realms according to varying interests, purposes, conventions, and criteria of adequacy. As such, theory (as the outcome of academic deliberations and research) and practice are seen as disparate, with the two domains being too far removed and insulated to have any direct and sustained impact on one another. Judgments of efficacy and validity of what 'counts' as knowledge therefore principally differ between academic and practitioner contexts, and hence practitioner judgments of practical efficacy cannot serve un-problematically to validate academic knowledge-claims which have been proposed in connection with a different interpretative context and in relation to different objectives. Mauws and Phillips (1995), following Astley and Zammuto (1992), illustrate the latter presumption well in their further exploration of the distinct language games in which academics and practitioners in the field of management partake: "the distance between the language game that characterizes organization science and the language game that characterizes management practice is simply too great to allow organizational researchers to produce tools and techniques that are actually useful to managers" (Mauws and Phillips, 1995, 324). And, hence, it follows from this perspective that from the successful use of tools and techniques in practice one cannot possibly infer the validity of a management theory (e.g., Beyer, 1997; Grey, 2001).

On the other hand, a growing group of academic researchers and commentators have started to emphasize the need for the integration of academic research and practice (Koontz, 1980; Dunbar, 1983; Lawler, 1985; Pettigrew, 1985; Shrivastava, 1987; Donaldson, 1992; Argyris, 1996; Wind and Nueno, 1998; Mohrman, 2001; Mohrman, Gibson, and Mohrman, 2001), arguing that although there may be some general differences in orientations of academics and practitioners (evident in a quest for basic understanding versus usable knowledge relevant to a particular case), both orientations should be seen as complementary and as closely related, rather than competitive or mutually exclusive. Seemingly sticking to Merlon's adage that "just as inquiries aimed at fundamental knowledge have repeatedly turned up unsuspected applications, so inquiries aimed at application have, though perhaps less often, turned up unsuspected understandings of uniformities in nature and society" (Merton, 1963, 87-88), the stock of management knowledge is seen to increase with the alignment of academic and practitioner orientations to management research (see also Brinberg and Hirschman, 1986). From such a perspective, benefits are also seen to accrue from directly relating research inquiries to practice such as, for instance, providing anchorage for abstractions, and data and tests for hypotheses, and new understandings that arise from putting knowledge into practice. The academic discipline of management is thus seen as, at least in part, applied and action-oriented towards management practice (Tranfield and Starkey, 1997; Starkey and Madan, 2001). It is because of this applied, action-oriented nature that academics are expected to utilize collaborative links with practitioners to ensure validity in the collection and codification of data and to develop theorizing and conduct research that is relevant and usable for practicing managers in professional settings (Mohrman, 2001).

One further argument for the linking of academic management research and managerial practice is the relatively widespread claim that the validity of management theory hinges upon an objective criterion which is used to certify the validity of scientific knowledge claims, namely, the criterion of practical utility (e.g., Koontz, 1980; Jacoby, 1985; Montgomery, Wernerfelt, and Balakrishan, 1989; Seth and Zinkhan, 1991; Donaldson, 1992; Hitt, 1998; Gabriel, 2002).

> "A number of theories in this [organizational] field claim to be of practical use to managers, who claim to make use of some of them and for those theories which are meant to be effectively put into practice, practical successes are claimed. Thus, the impression is sometimes created that the different theories of organization amount to a toolkit for practicing managers" (Gabriel, 2002,134).

In this sense, knowledge produced through academic research and as captured in management theories is considered to be valid because it 'works', in a way that both academics and practicing managers must accept: it seems to be objectively valid in the sense that it gives efficient control over many aspects of the managerial world. Crucial to ascribing such a role to management theory as working through practical applications is, as Gabriel (2002) outlines, the view that management theory aims to "understand events in order to anticipate them, and to anticipate them in order to control them. Thus, in practice, control has undoubtedly been a central reason for the perceived value of organizational theory" (Gabriel, 2002, 134). A fervent proponent of such a perspective of management theory is Donaldson (1992; 1995; 1999), who throughout his writings has argued that based upon positivist and rigorous analytical research (as in the case of structural contingency theory), management and organization theories embrace both situational specificity and operational precision leading to theories that consists of concepts that are thus "specific enough to be capable of giving, deductively, practical guidance to those who are seeking to manage in the real world" (Donaldson, 1992, 465). And, as such, Donaldson (1992) adds, "practical action is to be served by the construction and validation of theoretical models that state in language that has operational implications whose approach is optimal in any specific situation given the policy and value objectives" (Donaldson, 1992, 461).

From such a viewpoint, theory thus acquires what Jacoby (1985) calls "a decidedly real-world orientation" where "the principal criterion for evaluating theory is not elegance, nor parsimony, but utility, i.e., does it work, and, if so, how widely?" (Jacoby, 1985, 157). In other words, validity of a theory thus hinges, at least in part, on successful use through application in management practice. This particular claim, and the implications for the relationship between management theory and practice, and for the working relationship between academic researchers and practicing managers that follow from it, are subjected to analysis in the remainder of the paper. To do this, we explore, firstly, whether there is a connection between management scientific endeavor, on the one hand, and management technologies and practice, on the other, followed by an analysis of the claim that management theory can be logically and methodically validated through practical application.

How Far is Management Technology and Practice Dependent on Management Science?

When we indeed argue that the special epistemological position of management science[1] is established, at least in part, by the technological productivity and management practices of modern corporations, we appear to be assuming that most effective practical techniques created today are a fairly direct product or outcome of scientific knowledge, and also that most scientific knowledge generates such techniques. The very terminology which management academics, and also practitioners, have used to describe the relationship between management science and technology clearly expresses these assumptions. Thus, the processes whereby knowledge is produced and put into operation have typically been depicted as taking place along a continuum from 'basic' or 'pure' research, to 'technological

[1] Management science is defined here as all academic research within the management discipline, including the whole plethora of quantitative, qualitative and critical research methodologies, and aimed at producing general, context-free knowledge or idiographic knowledge about a managerial situation or problem (through dramatizing the coincidence of events purposive).

development', to 'application' or 'practice' (e.g., Gruber and Miles, 1975; Cohen, Nelson, and Walsh, 2002). As outlined in the preceding section, many academics and observers have been inclined to take it for granted that the conclusions reached at the 'basic' end of the continuum are in general validated by practical activities occurring at the 'application' or 'practice' end. Yet, when looking more closely at the empirical evidence relevant to the issue, we find little indication of any clear or close links between basic academic research, technological development and management practice.

When considering the spillover from science or theory to management practice, we find, firstly, that within the management field, or any other scientific field for that matter, most knowledge-claims do not appear to 'work' in a practical sense at all. Certain areas of management theory (for example, validity generalization theory, meta-analysis, and utility analysis) are never seen by practicing managers or other observers as having any relevance to practical application, and are even read as a paean to inutility (Beyer, 1997; Hodgkinson, Herriot, and Anderson, 2001; Rynes, Bartunek, and Daft, 2001). Consequently, when we talk of scientific management knowledge demonstrating its objectivity through successful application, we are at most referring to a minority of scientific knowledge claims within a limited number of research areas. We cannot, therefore, use this argument to show that the intellectual products of management science *in general* enjoy a special epistemological status through practical application. This negative conclusion is strengthened by the fact that the literature of 'public' or university research and science tend to remain fairly separate from technology and professional practice literatures, with little cross-referencing and with significantly different patterns of internal citation (Spencer, 2001; cf. Leydesdorff and Etzkowitz, 1998).

The view that the relationship between academic management research and practical application is often weak and indirect receives further support from the Carnegie Mellon Survey on industrial R&D (Cohen, Nelson, and Walsh 2000; Cohen, Nelson, and Walsh, 2002). Surveying the application of public (university and government) research within a broad range of industries, Cohen, Nelson, and Walsh (2002) found that the 'linear' model in which upstream 'basic' research is seen to play an initiating role leading to industrial innovation as outlined above is not granted as industrial innovation "emerges from a complicated process where fundamental research need not play an initiating role, nor, at times, any role" (Cohen, Nelson, and Walsh, 2002, 1). In effect, although 'public' research was found to have a substantial impact upon industrial R&D, notably in the pharmaceutical industry and across broad segments of the manufacturing sector, this impact is slight compared to sources in the industrial chain (see also Klevorick, Levin, Nelson, and Winter, 1995). That is, results of the Carnegie Mellon survey on industrial R&D suggest that a preponderance of industrial R&D projects are initiated in response to information from buyers or from the firm's own manufacturing operations, which is perhaps unsurprising given the centrality of the latter "to process innovation and the importance of 'manufacturability' for product innovation" (Cohen, Nelson, and Walsh, 2002, 7). Furthermore, apart from playing a more peripheral role alongside sources of knowledge in the firm's own value chain, public research's impact upon industrial R&D was also found to be more indirect and less immediate with its principal contribution lying in providing managers and R&D departments with general and conceptual research findings—the less tangible and more intermediate input of disembodied knowledge —rather than 'prototypes' or new instruments and techniques (Cohen, Nelson, and Walsh, 2002). In a sense, the latter finding suggests that practical application and what has traditionally been called 'basic' research can be seen to take place in different social contexts, whereby the social separation and divergent internal dynamics of these contexts operate to prevent any immediate and direct cognitive interaction (see Cohen, Florida, Randazzese, and Walsh, 1998). This observation is further strengthened by analyses of the genealogy of particular management concepts that have emerged and become entrenched in academic and practitioner languages and frames of reference. Abrahamson and Fairchild (1999), for instance, emphasized that although the concepts of quality circles and total quality management had in the early 1990s found resonance in both the academic and practitioner realms, this was primarily rhetorical or linguistic (cf. Astley and Zammuto, 1992; Mauws and Phillips, 1995) as academics and practitioners had adopted the basic terminology surrounding these concepts, while their accounts significantly differed in the coverage and extensions ascribed to these concepts.

The line of argument developed here should, however, not be taken too far, as there have been some notable and documented cases where academic research undertaken in pursuit of fundamental scientific knowledge has indeed led directly to successful management applications (for example, contingency theory, see Donaldson, 1999). There is also the phenomenon of 'embodiment', which occurs when scientific knowledge becomes embodied in a specific management technique or procedure, such as conjoint analysis (Green, Krieger, and Wind, 2001), which is then used and may give rise to further techniques and management applications. There may be a subsequent tendency in such cases to treat the second generation of management techniques and applications as growing out of prior technology alone and to ignore the original scientific contribution. There is also the difficulty of estimating the extent to which basic science contributes to technological advance and management practice by means of public and personal interactions (through, for example, publications, consultancy and conferences) between academic researchers and practitioners (Rynes, McNatt, and Bretz, 1999; Cohen, Nelson, and Walsh, 2002). Nevertheless, the evidence summarized above makes problematic—the simple view that in general the technologies and management practices of modern corporations are a direct by-product of a growing body of scientific knowledge. So far, we have concentrated on the connection, or lack of connection, between management technology and basic management science; and have only commented in passing on the question of whether, even when there is a direct link, the practical application of knowledge can actually serve to validate that knowledge. The next section takes up this latter issue in more detail.

Can Successful Application Validate a Scientific Management Theory?

As indicated in the preceding sections, it has customarily been taken as self-evident that when a theory is actually used as the basis for successful practical action, this necessarily validates the theory (e.g., Miner, 1984; Jacoby, 1985; Donaldson, 1992). There are, however, as already suggested by the weak and indirect links between industry innovation and management science identified above, strong grounds for maintaining that effective practical application is insufficient to provide such validation. In the first place, it needs to be recognized that any theory, whether of a more or less formal kind, is composed of a number of propositions (specifying relationships among constructs that are potentially testable and falsifiable), and that it is therefore always possible that only some of these propositions contribute significantly to its successful practical application. It thus appears that the most we can conclude from using a theory to good practical effect is that some *part* of that theory is valid, or approximately so. Moreover, much management theory consists of conceptual devices, which do not (yet) count as formal theories and can instead be referred to as precursors to formal theory, such as analytical categorisations and generalisations, classification schemes and typologies, and metaphors (e.g., Doty and Glick, 1994). Such a conceptual device, while serving a clear heuristic purpose in theorizing and research, lacks a clearly specified and tested framework of causal dynamics between specific management phenomena (in contrast to formal management theory) that would allow a direct instrumental application, on the basis of which inferences as to its practical use and validity could then be made. This observation of the nature of many management theories and the particular difficulties in inferring their validity through application also leads us to another consideration; that the complexity of everyday practical situations and the impossibility of controlling all relevant variables (Schon, 1983; Latour, 1987) would also make it difficult, if not impossible, to establish clear theoretical inferences on the basis of practical success, compared with the relative clarity of inference attainable in the laboratory or its equivalent, where some close approximation can often be made to the idealized relationships between phenomena with which scientific theory deals. Taking this point a bit further, given the complexity and the particularities of problems and situations with which managers are faced in organizational settings, it would also make it very unlikely that a formal management theory that suggests "linear causal relationships between predefined sets of variables" would in itself suffice or be successful as such theory fails to take account of "the host of other organizational variables that may be internally connected to them in practice" (Shrivastava and Mitroff, 1984, 24).

It follows from these deliberations that it is usually impossible to identify by means of successful practical action alone, which elements of theory have been responsible for, and hence validated, by the successful achievement. It is therefore misleading to talk of scientific knowledge being validated by the actions and practices of managers in organizational settings. Another important consideration which strengthens these conclusions is, as mentioned, that the idealized formulations of scientific theory have always to be not only re-formulated, but also combined with other cognitive elements when they are brought to bear upon the complexity of day-to-day problems with which managers deal. As Wagner and Sternberg (1985) have documented, practicing managers translate and integrate the knowledge contained in scientific theories with alternative sources of knowledge such as industry market intelligence, managerial expertise, and experience for solving management problems. It thus follows that any type of scientific theory is never used in an unaltered form as managers actively translate and modify it to fit the specifics of the management problem or situation for which it is sourced. As such, rather than using management theory instrumentally —which, as mentioned, is inhibited because of the dearth of formal theories that are operational enough and that also fully account for the situational contingencies of the everyday world of practicing managers—managers have been found to use management theory conceptually, i.e., for general enlightenment (Pelz, 1978; Weiss and Bucuvalas, 1980; Beyer and Trice, 1982; Beyer, 1997; Rynes, McNatt, and Bretz, 1999; Cohen, Nelson, and Walsh, 2002). Conceptual devices, as precursors of formal substantive theory, in particular, have offered considerable scope for conceptual use within practitioner settings (Astley and Zammuto, 1992), because they give great latitude to practitioners in selecting, redefining, altering, combining and generally reinterpreting scientific theory and the declarative knowledge that it contains to fit a wide variety of circumstances and purposes. As Schon (1983) amongst others has documented, managers pick up parts of new ideas from management theories, they interpret and adjust the retrieved concepts against their own background and interests, and adhere or inscribe this jumble of new ideas together with existing practices into the organizational culture and structure of the organization.

It is also important here to realize that accuracy requirements of practice are very different from, and usually far less stringent than, those applied in research undertaken with no immediate practical objective (Nelson and Winter, 1982; Blackler and Shimmin, 1984; Shrivastava and Mitroff, 1984). An approximate, descriptive and local theory, a theory-in-use, will often be sufficient for practical purposes, even when from an academic perspective such a theory might, as mentioned, be considered inadequate. Taken together, these considerations—that is, reformulation of theories in practical contexts, conceptual use of a theory, low accuracy requirements, and the complexity of practical situations—show that infinitely many possible rival theories can yield results which are identical in practical terms and that it is therefore clearly not possible to consider application as an exclusive test for any theory's validity. In other words, we have established that successful practical application has no conclusive validating force. However, we might still wish to object to this conclusion on the claim that, although the validity of substantive management theory is principally independent of its possible use or application in practice, the validity of methodological theories and models generated through modelling and researching within the context of management application effectively hinges upon such practical use.

It is indeed true that within the management discipline, a distinct 'technological management science', which is explicitly organized around problems arising in the pursuit of practical objectives, emerged in the early 1960s and has developed into a substantial body of work (e.g. Little, 1960; Charnes and Cooper, 1966; Charnes, Cooper, Learner, and Philips, 1985; Clark, 1992; Rosenzweig, 1994; Interfaces, 2001). This 'technological management science' sub-discipline is located mainly within the academic community, whilst retaining close links with industry and management practitioners. However, such a technological science sub-discipline is, as Gibbons, Limoges, Nowotny, Scott, and Trow (1994) have emphasized, intellectually as well as socially distinct from the autonomous generalizing science which sociologists of science have considered to be the main repositories of certified scientific knowledge. Gibbons, Limoges, Nowotny, Scott, and Trow (1994; see also Nowotny, Scott, and Gibbons, 2001) distinguish here between what they term as Mode 1 science production where research is carried out following the codes of practice relevant to a particular academic discipline and with the aim of developing generalisable, fundamental and disciplinary-based theories and knowledge, and Mode 2 science production, where research and problem solving are primarily organized around a particular application. While both these modes of research and the theorizing and knowledge involved comprise empirical and theoretical components and are therefore undeniably contributions to knowledge, insofar as the mode 2 type of technological science approaches practice, so its cognitive content appears to diverge from the universal formulations of the basic scientific disciplines (Gibbons, Limoges, Nowotny, Scott, and Trow, 1994; Zuzovsky, 1994/1995). Therefore, whenever basic science is used as the foundation for technological science (and hence for the production of technology), it requires a considerable amount of reformulation. In effect, in order to make basic management science 'work', it has to be radically re-interpreted by technologists and managers in accordance with the requirements of the organizational context of practical application (Gruber and Miles, 1975; Beyer and Trice, 1982; Schon, 1983; Latour, 1987; Astley and Zammuto, 1992).

> "Putting management knowledge into a form which causes change, the management technologist makes possible 'mutual understanding' between the manager and the scientist by reducing the abstractness of scientific knowledge to a level that managers can understand. Technologists in management translate a scientific understanding of industrial and organizational phenomena into a means of carrying out managerial functions. Management scientists are concerned with pushing the frontier of knowledge outwards, while technologists work within this frontier" (Gruber and Miles, 1975:957).

This seems to illustrate that, not that practical utility furnishes an objective criterion of the universal validity of scientific propositions, but rather that judgments of adequacy vary with academic and practitioner contexts (see Shrivastava and Mitroff, 1984; Blackler and Shimmin, 1984; Brinberg and Hirschman, 1986; Astley and Zammuto, 1992). It certainly makes it far from obvious that we can treat the practical success of technology or applications (through technological science applications) as validating the formulations of basic science, for the latter actually undergo major transformations of meaning as they come nearer to the realm of application and management practice. Nonetheless, as the following section outlines, technological science applications and tools *per se*, for which we reserve the term 'methodological theories', have a more direct and instrumental impact upon practice, and hence their application does indicate their validity *and* use.

The Validity and Usefulness of Management Theory Reconsidered

What thus emerges is a distinction between the relationship of substantive theories (following the tenets of Mode 1 science production) and practice, which at least in part works through mediation from technologists (academic translators and consultants), and methodological theories (following the tenets of Mode 2) produced by academics for direct application within management practice. In the first perspective, as mentioned, knowledge is constituted differently in the academic and practitioner realms according to varying interests, purposes, conventions and criteria of adequacy. And, hence, as substantive theory (including both formal theories and conceptual devices) is principally separated from action and application in practice; the impact of theorizing upon practice consist, at most, of indirectly providing some general conceptual insights and ideas that get transformed and altered by practitioners for dealing with problems in their organizational settings. As such, the validity of substantive theory is exclusively established within the academic community (independent from industry and practicing managers) through conventional criteria of science (Shrivastava and Mitroff, 1984), although it may have some derived practical use in drawing attention to actions or tendencies that would otherwise have gone unnoticed by the practicing manager thus challenging and complementing the assumptions guiding what managers think and do (Astley and Zammuto, 1992; Abrahamson and Eisenman, 2001).

While substantive, explanatory theory and practical understanding and actions indeed differ in "essential and unsurmountable ways" (Sandelands, 1990, 253), methodological theories do not stand apart from practice in such a way. When considering methodological theories—including (1) models and methods of assembling and treating management data that are mathematically based and often decision and/or optimization oriented (e.g., forecasting, simulation, decision support systems) (Charnes, Cooper, Learner, and Philips, 1985; Clark, 1992), and (2) research methods and techniques of statistical sampling and inference of data sets (e.g. motivation research and projective techniques, experimental and panel designs (ANOVA) and conjoint analysis) (Green, Krieger, and Wind, 2001) —their development, dissemination and use require a close working relationship between academics and practitioners in the context of application. More specific, the largely procedural knowledge of these methodological theories is first and foremost displayed in action through instrumental application, and its validity is thus indeed directly tied in with its particular application or use.

> "Tools [including methodological theories] are of practice and are invented and evolve according to its necessities (their form follows function). [Substantive] theories are no better than about practice and are invented and evolve according to conceptual necessities, rather than practical ones" (Sandelands, 1990, 254).

In the case of methodological theories, the orientation and role of practitioners allies therefore with the orientation and objectives of academics, as both groups are geared towards developing solutions in the form of procedural knowledge that get implemented to solve actual management problems (see Wittink, 2001), and their relationship could therefore best be described by metaphors or models like 'collaboration' or 'propinquity' (see Pringle, 2001).

One crucial difference between substantive and methodological theories as for their relationship with management practice is thus that substantive theories typically contain declarative knowledge: general factual or conceptual knowledge about management phenomena, objects and events, and their relationships, while methodological theories are premised on procedural knowledge: knowledge representations in the form of procedure-based models and techniques that encode how to achieve a particular management result (cf. Anderson, 1993). In other words, substantive theory is focused on 'knowing that' (i.e., knowledge for prepositional argument and explanation), while methodological theory is concerned with 'knowing how' (i.e., knowledge that is inscribed in action) (Sandelands, 1990; Greenwood and Levin, 2001; Pettigrew, 2001). As such, methodological theories aim to be directly relevant and useful in the knowledge that they provide to practising managers supplying them with "knowledge that get things done" (Sandelands, 1990, 235). It follows that in contrast to substantive theory, the validity of methodological theories indeed can and need be directly inferred from applications in practice.

Substantive and methodological management theories, and the declarative and procedural knowledge that they contain, should, however, be seen as complementary rather than competitive or mutually exclusive (cf. Susman and Evered, 1978; Anderson, 1993; Sandelands, 1990) as both serve the purposes of science and contribute to the general body of knowledge in the management field. Moreover, theorizing and research which is carried out following the codes of practice relevant to substantive theorizing within the academic management discipline, and theorizing and research which is primarily organized around a particular application are mutually influential, where procedural knowledge—generated and sustained through the use of a methodological theory in the context of application—for instance "may enter into and fertilize any number of disciplinary sciences" (Gibbons, Limoges, Nowotny, Scott, and Trow, 1994, 9).

Concluding Comments

Through our analysis we have arrived at seemingly radical, but well-founded assessments of the application of theory in managerial practice, and of whether such application can validate a theory's prepositional apparatus. In doing so, we have clarified the ways in which management theory and practice are related, providing a base from which further deliberations and debate upon the topic may depart. Like others before us who have started to decipher and qualify the nature of the relationship(s) between theory, academic research and practice (Sandelands, 1990; Starkey and Madan, 2001), we hope that this paper will help in the never-ending process of sorting the wheat from the chaff, in further research and discussions on the subject. On a particular note, the paper has established that the validity of substantive management theory cannot be inferred from technological applications and management practices, but did provide the case for such inferences in the case of methodological theories in the context of application. While further deliberations are obviously needed to research and evaluate the solidity of this claim, one central message of guidance for further research already emerged. Rather than talking of theory and practice in general, unidimensional terms, and considering their relationship as primarily 'linear', theory development, dissemination and application processes are far more complex, dynamic and multi-faceted. Further work would indeed benefit from adopting an expanded perspective that accounts for this dynamism and variety, but, importantly, such further theoretical deliberations ultimately need to be added to by empirical research and observations upon the relationship between theory and practice within the management field.

(J P Cornelissen, Lecturer in Marketing (Corporate and Marketing Communications), Marketing Division, University of Leeds Business School, Leeds, United Kingdom. He can be reached at jpc@lubs.leeds.ac.uk

R Thorpe, Professor of Management Development, Management Division, University of Leeds Business School, Leeds, United Kingdom.)

Acknowledgement

Thanks are given to Loet Leydesdorff (University of Amsterdam) and staff and PhD students of the Graduate School of Business at the Manchester Metropolitan University for input concerning the details of the argument presented.

References

Abrahamson, E., and Eisenman, M. (2001) 'Why management scholars must intervene strategically in the management knowledge market', *Human Relations,* 54:67-75.

Abrahamson E, and Fairchild G. (1999), 'Management fashion: Lifecycles, triggers, and collective learning processes', *Administrative Science Quarterly,* 44:708-740.

Academy of Management Journal (2001) [special topic forum on knowledge creation and diffusion between academics and practitioners] 44.

Anderson, J. R. (1993) *Rules of the mind.* Hillsdale, NJ: Lawrence Erlbaum.

Argyris, C. (1996) 'Actionable knowledge: Design causality in the service of consequential theory', *Journal of Applied Behavioral Science,* 32:309-406.

Astley, W.G., and Zammuto, R.F. (1992) 'Organization science, managers, and language games', *Organization Science,* 3:443-460.

Beyer, J. M. (1997) 'Research Utilization: Bridging a Cultural Gap Between Communities', *Journal of Management Inquiry,* 7:17-23.

Beyer, J.M., and Trice, H.M. (1982) 'The utilization process: A conceptual framework and synthesis of empirical findings', *Administrative Science Quarterly,* 27:591-622.

Blackler, F., and Shimmin, S. (1984) *Applying psychology in organizations.* London: Methuen.

Brinberg, D., and Hirschman, E.G. (1986) 'Multiple orientations for the conduct of marketing research: An analysis of the academic/practitioner distinction', *Journal of Marketing,* 50: 161-173.

British Journal of Management (2001) [special issue on the relevance of management research] 12.

Charnes, A., and Cooper, W.W. (1966) 'Management sciences and management – Some requirements for further development', *Management Science,* 13: C3-C9.

Charnes, A., Cooper, W.W., Learner, D.B., and Philips, F.Y. (1985) 'Management science and marketing management', *Journal of Marketing,* 49:93-105.

Clark, D. (1992) 'A literature analysis of the use of management science tools in strategic planning', *The Journal of the Operational Research Society,* 43:859-870.

Cohen, W.M., Florida, R, Randazzese, L, and Walsh, J.P. (1998) 'Industry and the academy: Uneasy partners in the cause of technological advance', in R.G. Noll (ed.), *Challenges to research universities,* chapter 7. Washington DC: Brookings Institute Press.

Cohen, W.M., Nelson, R.R., and Walsh, J.P. (2000) *Links and impacts: Survey results on the influence of public research on industrial R&D.* Carnegie Mellon University: Mimeo.

Cohen, W.M., Nelson, R.R., and Walsh, J.P. (2002) 'Links and impacts: The influence of public research on industrial R&D', *Management Science,* 48:1-23.

Donaldson, L. (1985) *In defence of organisation theory: A reply to the critics.* Cambridge: Cambridge University Press.

Donaldson, L. (1992) 'The Weick stuff: Managing beyond games', *Organization Science,* 4: 461-466.

Donaldson, L. (1999) 'The normal science of structural contingency theory', in S. Clegg, and C. Hardy (Eds.), *Studying Organization: Theory and Method:* 51-70. London: Sage.

Doty, D.H., and Glick, W.H. (1994) 'Typologies as a unique form of theory building: Toward Improved understanding and modeling', *Academy of Management Review,* 19:230-251.

Dunbar, R. (1983) 'Toward an applied administrative science'. *Administrative Science Quarterly,* 28:129-144.

Gabriel, Y. (2002) 'On paragrammatic uses of organizational theory – A provocation', *Organization Studies,* 23:133-151.

Gibbons, M., Limoges, C., Nowotny, H., Scott, P., and Trow, M. (1994) *The new production of knowledge: The dynamics of science and research in contemporary societies.* London: Sage.

Green, P.E., Krieger, A.M., and Wind, Y. (2001) 'Thirty years of conjoint analysis: Reflections and prospects', *Interfaces,* 31: S56-S73.

Greenwood, D., and Levin, M. (2001) 'Re-organizing universities and 'knowing how': University restructuring and knowledge creation for the 21st century', *Organization,* 8:433-440.

Grey, C. (2001) 'Re-imagining relevance: A response to Starkey and Madan', *British Journal of Management,* 12: S27-S32.

Gruber, W.H., and Miles, J.S. (1975) 'The science-technology-utilization relationship in management', *Management Science* 21:956-963.

Hambrick, D. (1994) 'What if the academy actually mattered?', *Academy of Management Review,* 19:11-16.

Hitt, M.A. (1998) 'Twenty-first century organizations: Business firms, business schools and the academy', *Academy of Management Review,* 23:218-224.

Hodgkinson, G., Herriot, P. and Anderson, N. (2001) 'Re-aligning the stakeholders in management research: Lessons from industrial, work and organizational psychology', *British Journal of Management,* 12: S41-S48.

Human Relations (2001) [special issue on re-viewing organization] 54. Interfaces (2001) [special issue on marketing engineering] 31.

Jacoby, J. (1985) 'Serving two masters: Perspectives on consulting', in E.G. Hirschman, and M.B. Holbrook (Eds.), *Advances in Consumer Research* (volume 13): 157-163. Ann Arbor, MI: Association for Consumer Research.

Journal of Management Inquiry (1997) [special issue on rigor, relevance and research utilization] 6.

Klevorick, A.K., Levin, R., Nelson, R.R., and Winter, S. (1995) 'On the sources and significance of inter-industry differences in technological opportunities', *Research Policy,* 24:195-205.

Koontz, H. (1980) The management theory jungle revisited', *Academy of Management Review,* 5:175-187.

Kover, A.J. (1976) 'Careers and noncommunication: The case of academic and applied marketing research', *Journal of Marketing Research,* 13:339-344.

Latour, B. (1987) *Science in action: How to follow scientists and engineers through society.* Cambridge, Mass.: Harvard University Press.

Lawler, E.E. (1985) 'Challenging traditional research assumptions', in E.E. Lawler, A.M. Mohrman, S.A. Mohrman, G.E. Ledford, and T.G. Cummings (Eds.), *Doing research that is useful to practice:* 1-17. San Francisco: Jossey-Bass.

Lewin, K. (1945) 'The research center for group dynamics at Massachusetts Institute of Technology', *Sociometry,* 8:126-136.

Leydesdorff, L, and Etzkowitz, H. (1998) 'The triple helix as a model for innovation studies', *Science and Public Policy,* 25:195-203.

Little, J. (1970) 'Models and managers: The concept of a decision calculus', *Management Science,* 16: B466-485.

Management Science (2002) [special issue on university entrepreneurship and technology transfer] 48.

Mauws, M.K., and Phillips, N. (1995) 'Understanding language games', *Organization Science,* 6:322-335.

Merton, Robert (1963) 'Basic research and potentials of relevance', *American Behavioral Scientist,* 6:86-90.

Miner, J.B. (1984) The validity and usefulness of theories in an emerging organizational science', *Academy of Management Review,* 9:296-306.

Mohrman, S. (2001) 'Seize the day: Organizational studies can and should make a difference', *Human Relations,* 54:57-65.

Mohrman, S.A., Gibson, C.B., and Mohrman, A.M. (2001) 'Doing research that is useful to practice: A model and empirical exploration', *Academy of Management Journal,* 44:357-376.

Montgomery, C., Wernerfelt, B., and Balakrishan, S. (1989) 'Strategy content and the research process: A critique and commentary', *Strategic Management Journal,* 10:189-197.

National Science Board (1993) *Science and engineering indicators.* Washington, DC: National Science Board.

Nelson, R.R., and Winter, S.G. (1982) *An evolutionary theory of economic change.* Boston, MA: Harvard University Press.

Nowotny, H., Scott, P., and Gibbons, M. (2001) *Re-thinking science: Knowledge and the public in an age of uncertainty.* Polity Press.

Organization (2001) [special issue on re-organizing knowledge and transforming institutions] 8.

Pelz, D.C. (1978) 'Some expanded perspectives on use of social science in public policy', in M. Yinger, and S.J. Cutler (Eds.), *Major social issues: A multidisciplinary view:* 346-357. New York: Free Press.

Pettigrew, A. (1985) 'Contextualist research and relevance', in Lawler, E.E., A.M. Mohrman, S.A. Mohrman, G.E. Ledford, and T.G. Cummings (Eds.), *Doing research that is useful to practice.* 222-248. San Francisco: Jossey-Bass.

Pettigrew, A. (2001) The co-production and co-dissemination of knowledge across practitioner and international boundaries. Paper presented to the All Academy Symposium on Practitioner and Practice Grounded Research (Academy of Management Annual Conference, Washington DC, August 6-8).

Pringle, L. (2001) 'The academy and the practice: In principle, theory and practice are different. But, in practice, they never are', *Marketing Science,* 20:373-381.

Rosenzweig, P. (1994) 'When can management science research be generalized internationally?', *Management Science,* 40:28-39.

Rynes, S.L., Bartunek, J.M., and Daft, R.L. (2001) 'Across the great divide: Knowledge creation and transfer between practitioners and academics', *Academy of Management Journal,* 44:340-355.

Rynes, S.L., McNatt, B., and Bretz, R.D. (1999) 'Academic research inside organizations: Inputs, processes and outcomes', *Personnel Psychology,* 52:869-898.

Sandelands, L. (1990) 'What is so practical about theory? Lewin revisited', *Journal for the Theory of Social Behavior,* 20:235-262.

Schon, D. (1983) *The reflective practitioner: How professionals think in action.* New York: Basic Books.

Seth, A., and Zinkhan, G. (1991) 'Strategy and the research process: A comment', *Strategic Management Journal,* 12:75-82.

Shrivastava, P. (1987) 'Rigor and practical usefulness of research in strategic management', *Strategic Management Journal,* 8:77-92.

Shrivastava, P., and Mitroff, I.I. (1984) 'Enhancing organizational research utilization: The role of decision makers' assumptions', *Academy of Management Review,* 9:18-26.

Spencer, J.W. (2001) 'How relevant is university-based research to private high-technology firms? A United States-Japan comparison', *Academy of Management Journal*, 44:432-441.

Starkey, K., and Madan, P. (2001) 'Bridging the relevance gap: Aligning the stakeholders in the future of management research', *British Journal of Management*, 12: S3-S26.

Susman, G.I., and Evered, R.D. (1978) 'An assessment of the scientific merits of action research', *Administrative Science Quarterly*, 23:582-603.

Tranfield, D., and Starkey, K. (1998) 'The nature, social organization and promotion of management research: Towards policy', *British Journal of Management*, 9:341-353.

U.S. House of Representatives (1981) 'Commercialization of academic biomedical research', *Committee on Science and Technology; Subcommittee on Investigations and Oversight.* Hearings held June 8-9,1981.

Wagner, R.K., and Sternberg, R.J. (1985) 'Practical intelligence in real-world pursuits: The role of tacit knowledge', *Journal of Personality and Social Psychology*, 49:436-458.

Weiss, C.H., and Bucuvalas, M.J. (1980) *Social science research and decision making.* New York: Columbia University Press.

Wind, J., and Neuno, P. (1998) *The impact imperative: Closing the gap of academic management research.* The International Academy of Management – a proposed manifesto for the IAM, presented and discussed during the IAM's North America Meeting on May 28.

Wittink, D. (2001) 'Market measurement and analysis: The first 'marketing science' conference', *Marketing Science* 20:349-356.

Zuzovsky, R. (1994/1995) 'Utilization of research findings: A matter of research tradition', *Knowledge and Policy*, 7:78-94.

December 2004 Issue 1

1. 'The Validity and Usefulness of Management Theories: A Review' by J. Cornelissen and R. Thorpe.
2. 'Measurements of Probability Sensitivity and Attractiveness in Decision under Risk' by P. Wickham.
3. "Me Time': Life Temporality and Customised Working Patterns of Employees without Childcare Responsibilities' by E. Roberts.
4. 'Ambiguity Seeking as a Result of the Status Quo Bias' by M. Roca.

8

Designing a New Organisation: A Complexity Approach

Eve Mitleton-Kelly

Organisations often assume that it is possible to 'design' an organisation in the same way that engineers can design a new product, but this is an erroneous assumption and the repeated failure of organisational restructuring provides significant evidence that a different approach is required. The paper will describe an alternative approach based on the logic of complexity, with reference to a specific case. It will also describe the different qualitative and quantitative tools and methods used that helped to identify the social, cultural, technical and political conditions that together led to the co-creation of an enabling framework as the basis for the 'design' of a new organisation.

Introduction

Human systems are complex in the sense that they are able to self-organise, to influence each other and be influenced, in turn, and this reciprocal influence can change ideas, behaviour, ways of thinking, working and relating—that is, humans are able to co-evolve, to self-organise and to create something new that is emergent in the sense that it could not have been predicted at the outset. They create intricate networks of relationships sustained through communication and other forms of feedback, with varying degrees of interdependence. Although heavily influenced by their history and culture they can transcend both when necessary. When they meet a constraint they are able to explore the space of possibilities and find a different way of doing things, i.e., they are creative and innovative. However, they can also develop patterns of behaviour that when repeated over and again, become very difficult to change; yet when that pattern finally collapses they are able to start something totally new—but not always!

Organisational restructuring often attempts to create a new organisational form or way of organising by merely changing the structure, while repeating old dysfunctional patterns of behaviour. An alternative approach might be to identify the conditions that both enabled and constrained the attainment of objectives in the 'old' organisation, and to co-create a new environment that may help to avoid the repetition of dysfunctional patterns of behaviour, while building on the enablers. The paper will describe a process, as part of an integrated methodology, which helped an organisation in the public sector in the UK, to design a new organisation that would facilitate creativity and innovation and become agile and robust.

The old organisation (OldOrg) was part of a very large public sector service provider. It had been set up to help the parent become more innovative by identifying and sharing new ideas, procedures and processes throughout the parent organisation. OldOrg had grown from 50 to 850 employees in two years; it did so by taking over the activities of several disparate projects that already existed within the parent organisation. One of the consequences of this growth by acquisition was a lack of clarity of identity. Individuals felt greater allegiance to their project than to OldOrg as an entity. This was characterised by a lack of coherence in its policies and lack of communication between the projects; it was also evident in the interaction of its 70 senior managers when meeting as a management team.

The research project with the LSE Complexity Research Group started in September 2003. At that time the LSE team was asked to work with the senior management group and to reflect back to them the characteristics that enabled and constrained the aims of OldOrg, using the principles of complexity. However, at the same time that the work was taking place the Government decided to restructure OldOrg. The LSE team then worked with a small core group from OldOrg to help them identify the *social, cultural, technical, economic and political conditions of an enabling framework, that would help them achieve the aims and objectives of NewOrg.* An enabling framework provides a different approach to 'designing' organisations, based on the theory of complexity. It is a dual bottom-up and top-down approach, based on the co-creation of an enabling environment with significant involvement from employees. It provides clarity of direction but allows the organisational form to co-evolve with its changing environment.

The logic is that if organisations can grow organically, then they can explore possible alternatives and find the most appropriate ways of working suitable to the task; this is not an argument for total lack of structure or accountability or leadership. All those are necessary, but this approach suggests that structure needs to be sufficiently flexible to allow for self-organisation, emergence and co-evolution. Organisations, both in the private and public sectors that have adopted this approach found that individual responsibility increased to a significant degree and accountability became clearer and stronger. They also found that they developed true distributed leadership, as everyone acted as a responsible agent working towards a shared vision, exploring possibilities and taking initiatives that nevertheless fitted well into the overall strategic direction. They achieved this through a strong network of relationships and peer support (rather than pressure).

The official 'leader' then became a person who held that space for them, negotiated with other stakeholders and was free to scan the horizon for new patterns and to influence the overall direction, as well as to facilitate new partnerships with others in the same and related industries.

The paper is in four parts. The first describes the various tools and methods used in the OldOrg case, the second describes the contribution of complexity, the third outlines the benefits and the fourth describes some of the findings in terms of the Enabling Framework.

1. Methodology

The tools and methods used in the OldOrg case were the following (for a fuller discussion on the methodology and a description of all the tools and methods used in the Integrated Methodology, please see two papers by Mitleton-Kelly E.[1]):

a. **In-depth semi-structured interviews** with 22 members of the senior management group. The transcripts were analysed by four researchers to identify common themes, key questions, dilemmas (equally desirable objectives that cannot apparently be achieved at the same time) and underlying assumptions. Individual respondents are seen as fractal representatives of the whole, not as a statistical sample. This approach, as well as the power of the interviewing method and the analysis mean that relatively small numbers are needed.

b. Diagnosis of preference profiles based on an email questionnaire (60 questionnaires were returned, giving a response rate of 70%)—the tool used is known as the *Landscape of the Mind (LoM)*[2]. This provided a group profile as well as individual profiles.

c. **Individual feedback sessions on LoM profiles.** This provided individuals with a fuller understanding of the tool as well as discussing individual profiles. These sessions are confidential.

d. **Reflect Back Workshop** with the interviewees and others to validate the findings both from the interviews and LoM.

e. **Mapping of email connectivity** to show formal and informal networks within and across teams and projects – the tool is known as *NetMap*[3]. It had access to a server that covered at least half of the 850 employees within the organisation.

---

1 Mitleton-Kelly E. 2003 *"Complexity Research – Approaches and Methods: The LSE Complexity Group Integrated Methodology"* in Keskinen A, Aaltonen M, Mitleton-Kelly E *"Organisational Complexity"*. Foreword by Stuart Kauffinan. Scientific Papers 1/2003, TUTU Publications, Finland Futures Research Centre, Helsinki Mitleton-Kelly E., Puszczynski L.R. 2005 (in print) *'An Integrated Methodology to Facilitate The Emergence of New Ways of Organising'* in Unifying Themes in Complex Systems, Vol. V, NECSI Knowledge Press Both papers are available on *http://www.lse.ac.uk/complexity*

2 LoM has been developed by Kate Hopkinson [hopkinson@innerskills.co.uk].

3 NetMap was developed by Prof. John Galloway [JGalloway@netmap.com.au].

f. Four LSE researchers were involved in the project and the analysis; they also *attended meetings* of the senior management group and one conference. This provided significant understanding of the issues in different working settings.

g. Three meetings of a *Core Group* to identify the conditions for an enabling framework that will contribute to the design of the new organisation. Based on the report from the interview findings and their own experience, the Core Group identified patterns of behaviour that proved generative and could be further developed in the new organisation and those patterns that should be avoided. They also identified the social, cultural, technical and political conditions for an enabling environment for the new organisation, as well as those conditions that might facilitate or inhibit the enabling environment.

h. A professional *facilitator*[4] facilitated the Reflect Back Workshop and Core Group meetings.

i. **Complexity Thinking** Workshops to introduce the theory (Mitleton-Kelly E. 2003[5]) to OldOrg members and to discuss its application in day-to-day operations. The application of the theory has been tested with several organisations including Rolls-Royce, Shell, BT, Humberside Training & Enterprise Council, the World Bank (Washington DC), Citibank (New York), and many others. It provides a rigorous and robust theoretical underpinning to strategy, the re-design of organisations, leadership, innovation, etc.

The methodology provided significant *weight of evidence* using different methods and tools that complemented each other; and *validated* the findings through the Reflect-Back Workshop, the 3 Core Group meetings and discussions with individuals.

2. Contribution of Complexity

Complex behaviour of systems arises from the *inter-relationship, interaction,* and *inter-connectivity* of elements within a system and between a system and its environment.

[4] The facilitator was Nazreen A Subhan [nazreen_phoenix@hotmail.com] who is also a change agent.

[5] Mitleton-Kelly, E Chapter 2 *'Ten Principles of Complexity & Enabling Infrastructures'* in 'Complex Systems and Evolutionary Perspectives on Organisations: The Application of Complexity Theory to Organisations' Elsevier 2003, ISBN: 0-08-043957-8.

These relationships also create intricate *interdependencies* throughout a system. In a human system, connectivity and interdependence mean that a decision or action by any individual (group, organisation, institution, or human system) may affect related individuals and systems. When this influence is in one direction we may see *adaptation* of one entity as a response to the influence of other entities (or collectively, the influence of the environment or ecosystem). When the influence and response are reciprocal we may see *co-evolution* or change in all interacting entities. Both Netmap and Agent Based Modelling (ABM was not used with OldOrg) show the interaction of individuals and the *emergent* properties (e.g., patterns of connectivity, informal groups, etc.) that arise as a result of that interaction. The connections are also good indicators of feedback; Netmap in particular acts as an indicator of feedback as it depends on an exchange of emails (or other media) and information (we are aware however that no such tool can provide an exhaustive picture on all feedback processes). Both tools also show *self-organisation* and when repeated they can show the *evolution of relationships* over time. Landscape of the Mind (LoM) also looks at individuals and the way they relate within a group, in other words LoM can show *epistatic interations*— i.e., the extent to which the fitness contribution made by one individual depends on related individuals. Complexity principles are scale invariant and apply to all scales from the individual, to the group and the whole organisation. All three tools can show characteristics at different scales. Working with these tools an organisation is also able to look at alternatives and thus *explore its spaces of possibilities.*

Connectivity and interdependence is one aspect of how complex behaviour arises. Another important and closely related aspect is that complex systems are *multidimensional,* and all the dimensions interact and influence each other. In a human context the social, cultural, technical, economic, political and global dimensions may impinge upon and influence each other. The narrative analysis based on the interviews can identify these multiple dimensions as well as the connectivities, interdependencies, self-organisation, co-evolution, far-from-equilibrium conditions, historicity and time, feedback, emergence, path-dependence and the creation of new order. In the later stages of the methodology, when the research team works closely with a core group from the organisation to identify the conditions for the enabling framework and finally when the organisation co-creates an enabling environment, all the principles come into play. This process is supported by the Complexity Thinking Workshops when members of the organisation are introduced to complexity thinking and its language. It continues throughout a project as the theory is constantly exemplified through practical examples from the organisation, thus making the theory tangible and accessible.

Complexity, however, is not a methodology or a set of tools. Complexity theory provides a conceptual framework, *a way of thinking, and a way of seeing the world.* The way it has been articulated and used by the LSE Complexity Group is that any complex evolving system has a set of characteristics or principles. When all of these characteristics are evident and the system is able to create new order, then it may be called 'complex' otherwise it is 'complicated'. Any methodology that purports to be based on complexity must therefore be based on those principles.

Why So Many Tools?

We use so many tools because they triangulate the data and provide robust and rigorous findings. But that is not the only reason. They each provide different but complementary information about the organisation. So when several tools and methods are used the organisation ends up with a very rich and deep understanding of itself. The findings can then be used as an informed basis for building the enabling infrastructure. This last part is a *co-creation* activity. We work with a core team of 'volunteers who can make a difference' to identify the social, cultural and technical conditions (within a political and economic context) that together will help the organisation co-create the kind of environment conducive to change and the emergence of new ways of organising (ways of working and relating). But this is not a one-off process, the new ways of thinking based on complexity, the new relationships, procedures, processes, structures, etc., need to become embedded in the business culture if they are to be sustainable. Ideally, the organisation will build the capacity to continue the process of *co-evolutionary sustainability.*

When the tools are used a second or third time in a longitudinal study, they show organisational evolution over time. However, the emphasis on co-creation and collaboration keeps the research team in close touch with the business partner and helps to monitor these changes. To facilitate reflection on organisational evolution, we also hold regular reflecting meetings within the team as well as with our business partners.

It is not necessary to use all the tools and we may choose the most appropriate 2-3 to use in each case. In addition, there are regular *inter-organisational workshops* and meetings with the *business and academic Advisors.* These will help in learning between partners.

We use these specific tools and methods because at present we find them relevant and appropriate to a methodology using the logic of complexity. Individual tools and methods may be familiar to our business partners (some are well established) and their familiarity is an advantage as it provides a useful transition from the known and familiar towards the new and unfamiliar concepts of complexity. There could also be other tools that could be used and we are constantly exploring new ideas. The methodology is not, and cannot be, static. It has to evolve and to co-evolve with the needs of our business partners and the requirements of sound research. *In addition the methodology is NOT just a set of tools—it is about connectivity, collaboration and co-creation – but also about enabling individuals and teams to self-organise, and about being open to a significant degree of emergence and innovation.*

3. The Benefits

Organisations want to perform efficiently and effectively. But if organisations are complex, evolving systems with a specific purpose, we need new ways such as those based on complexity theory to review and understand areas in which organisational performance can be improved. In the case under discussion, the project was influential in evaluating the change process in the OldOrg and in designing the NewOrg. Our business partners describe the contribution of the research project thus:

> "**An enabling framework for the new organisation:** This work has assisted in ensuring that a wide variety of lessons were learned from the setting up and operation of the 'OldOrg' to ensure that they were not replicated in the 'NewOrg'. This has been of substantial benefit, and much of the research has been built into, for example, new business processes as part of the enabling framework.
>
> **Co-creation and Co-development:** Our learning about complex, adaptive systems has been extensive. A feature of complexity has been the notion of

co-evolution and co-creation with our systems partners. This has influenced our strategy to develop the new organisation and its products. A key design feature of the systems and processes of the new organisation has been the explicit design-in of the voice of our customers and stakeholders.

Evaluation: The outcomes from this work are being used as part of the evaluation of the overall Change Process within the MA over the past 18 months."

4. The Enabling Framework

The following conditions for an enabling framework are based on all the findings and on work done with the core group. The social, cultural, technical and political conditions have to be seen as a whole and cannot be separated. A complex organisation exists within a complex social ecosystem where all the conditions interact and influence each other. When conditions are isolated then they become unrealistic as they are taken out of their rich co-evolving context. Some 23 recommendations were made to help facilitate this.

The following section is an edited extract (to protect the identity of the organisation) from the Findings Report and outlines both the conditions and the relevant recommendations for designing the enabling framework of the NewOrg. Most of the conditions given, however, would also be relevant to other organisations.

a) **Cultural Conditions**

Clear vision and clear scope: the new organisation needed to be clear about its purpose and function, about what the organisation was tasked to do and what did not come within its remit. This was unclear for the OldOrg and created a great deal of uncertainty.

When the scope is clear then demonstrating the impact and the implications of actions and initiatives will also become easier.

Corporate identity and brand: OldOrg felt fragmented and did not have an overall *corporate identity.* This was one of the main themes repeated by most interviewees. It felt like a conglomerate of disparate parts. Having a strong corporate identity does not, however, mean uniformity. On the contrary, a clear overarching identity provides the space for diversity and for the variety of skills, competences, ways of working and thinking that will be necessary for the new organisation.

Brand is different. This is the product that the organisation delivers. It can be one brand identified with the new organisation, giving it visibility and building its credibility.

Need to do things differently: *"everything we do will need to be focussed on impact, adoption and sustainability".* There were many issues packed in these three themes, summarised by a core group member. Demonstrating impact was a weakness; but impact does not mean just measuring the *quantifiable* outcomes, it also means evaluating the *qualitative* impact on employees and others. *The new organisation will need to learn how to evaluate both quantitative and qualitative impact and to demonstrate that value.*

Adoption and sustainability are implicated with sharing the learning. The OldOrg placed a great deal of emphasis on the building and development of relationships, which should have facilitated the identification, capture and dissemination of learning, but this was patchy, excellent in some contexts, but poor in others. Successful sharing of learning involved a *sharing of values, trust, knowledge and experience.* The new organisation will need to *develop the skills to capture and disseminate learning.* Part of that skill development will involve *transferring the learning from successful experiments or initiatives.* It is impossible to precisely copy or to replicate a set of activities in a complex human system. Actions and decisions as well as initial conditions are always different when the context and the individuals involved change. But what can be done is to identify generaliseable principles, gather insights, and learn from the process that was undertaken, the mistakes and successes. *Identify the enabling and inhibiting conditions and offer them as a framework that others can adopt and adapt to their specific context.*

When the transfer of learning was successful in OldOrg, *three Cs* were always present: *communication, collaboration* and *co-creation.* It was not enough just to write about the case or to put it on a website, it needed a great deal more and

OldOrg's strength in developing good relationships was used to its maximum and produced the desired benefit.

Sustainability, however, means the continuing development of such an approach and makes learning an active process that feeds into making an organisation flexible and responsive to a changing environment. This does not mean blind adaptation to external changes, but active reciprocal influence or co-evolution with that environment. A clear vision is essential—but no vision is immutable. The argument here is for a balance between adaptation and influence. The two processes working to reciprocal advantage. This is called *co-evolutionary sustainability* and allows an organisation to change with a changing environment without constant restructuring, which has a high cost in terms of effort, resources and morale. Co-evolutionary sustainability does not always mean gradual change, but includes significant step changes, when necessary. Nor does it mean a loss of identity but an evolution of that identity over time. Co-evolutionary sustainability could be seen as a primary objective for the new organisation.

Needing to do things differently may also mean looking afresh at how the job is done by *exploring* alternatives or the *space-of-possibilities.* However, exploring alternative solutions often means that not every experiment will work and those that do not succeed cannot be seen as failures, they are part of the exploration process. This process cannot happen within a blame-culture, it can only be effective in a culture that welcomes responsible experimentation.

A lack of readiness to improve or even active resistance to improvement within the parent organisation, created a great deal of tension in OldOrg, called the 'burden of help'. OldOrg was expected to hold two incompatible roles: being invited in to help versus imposing improvement. This, in turn, led to a further tension or *dilemma,* which was *using a creative versus a directive style.* One way to resolve the tension or dilemma would be to demonstrate success through a supporting approach—by facilitating an enabling environment for those in the field to make the changes, rather than imposing change. Then creating the right climate for those that are weak and need to improve to *want* to change. Resistance is not always bloody mindedness—it often has an underlying rationale that needs to be understood and worked with. One example identified by OldOrg members was using incentives rather than performance management. Performance-based management, using inappropriate measurement, which was, in turn, based on what could easily be measured, exacerbated the tension. Seen from another perspective, OldOrg was asked to performance-manage the wrong things, which created the dilemma of pleasing one set of stakeholder versus meeting targets. The latter were quantitative measures that took priority and ignored both the positive and negative qualitative effects on employees and others.

One of the inhibitors to effective working within OldOrg was *fragmentation* of the teams and projects. Staff talked about *"working in silos"* and longed for greater integration. Fragmentation, by not treating all the stakeholders as a whole, gave different messages, which was confusing and often led to disenfranchised staff. Greater integration, on the other hand, facilitates cross-linkages and learning and increases the benefits exponentially. The new organisation will have to be very aware of this pattern of working and focus on greater integration, by involving all stakeholders and by improving the links between teams.

Another possibility to explore would be *distributed leadership and distributed power.* Large global corporates are learning that distributed local power and leadership is the only way to manage large and diverse organisations. *Centralised control no longer works.* The parent organisation is a large employer; at its best it exemplifies the move to distributed leadership and power, but the pull towards centralised control is a constant counter-force negating some of the benefits.

Finally, the new organisation could provide a *reflective space for sense making,* for re-evaluating what needs to be done and how; for the *exploration of new possibilities,* facilitating *self-organisation,* identifying *new patterns as they emerge* and pro-actively preparing the parent organisation to address new changes.

b) **Social or Organisational Conditions**

Many of the conditions discussed under culture above would also apply to this section. In addition, the new organisation will need appropriate *business and management systems* (i.e. ways of organizing time, money, people, bureaucratic dimension, project management), which are *continuously evaluated for appropriateness and relevance and are fit for purpose.* One of the weaknesses of

OldOrg was lack of effective management systems and an effective cost model that could be used to justify its activities. In addition the strategic fit of the business systems was not questioned, since the strategic direction was not clear.

This was often confused with structure and much time and effort was expended in discussing the structure of the organisation, which became more cumbersome as OldOrg grew.

Both management systems and structure were identified with bureaucracy—but a small agile organisation should not need a bureaucratic structure. Once the new organisation knows what it needs to do it—will need relevant systems to support it, to facilitate its work and to provide the necessary checks and balances required in a public body, but without a heavy bureaucratic overload.

"Valuing staff, acknowledging their contribution and honouring their time was a weakness in OldOrg that will need to be addressed by the new organisation. Other examples were a need to improve *diary and time management* and to respect other peoples' time.

Co-ordination of objectives would also be necessary. The OldOrg suffered from objectives agreed at different levels, by different people with little overall co-ordination. The new organisation will need to develop a *good governance model* that will be appropriate to its scope, function and size within a clear strategic direction. It will be a question of getting the balance right—and this cannot be a once for all time action. *In a constantly changing complex social ecosystem there is no single universal optimum, but many changing local optima.*

c) Technical Conditions

An integrated IT system to support staff would be essential for the new organisation, perhaps based on the current proposal for integration and the provision of a single IT system. The OldOrg had incompatible legacy IT systems and email that made life on the road extremely difficult, as the different systems did not 'talk to each other'; files could often not be attached and access to certain information was awkward. In addition the system would often crash and much time was wasted trying to restart it. Technical problems absorbed too much valuable time from the job at hand.

A better understanding of the use of technology and how it can contribute to improvement would also be essential. Technological innovation would need to co-evolve with organisational improvement innovation. The lack of alignment of understanding of (a) what the technology can offer and (b) what the organisation needs currently and in the future, is a problem faced by many organisations. Some have resolved it through greater interaction between the IT technologists and the users and the new organisation will need to build in this type of continuing interaction. Technology could also be utilised to demonstrate success, impact and ROI in a robust way.

The different systems also meant different standards were used and OldOrg members asked for agreement on best practice. Furthermore, ensuring that the back-end (infrastructure) was correct and stayed constant would allow the front-end (applications) to remain flexible and to respond to changes in the organisation. Furthermore, an appropriate and effective technology infrastructure would help with information management, to connect and capture both internal and external knowledge.

Another issue was retaining the experience and knowledge when people leave. One way to retain it would be to migrate the information to a good IT system and this would certainly help. However, it is worth noting that this would not capture the experiential learning of each individual. So other ways will need to be found to share the experience and knowledge.

d) **Political Conditions**

The political environment of the new organisation is changing and the following issues will therefore need to be addressed.

Clarity of vision with clear agreement from the parent organisation, to ensure adherence to the vision, purpose and function of the new organisation.

Strong leadership with political awareness to help position the new organisation effectively in the changing political environment. Identifying those who set the agenda would be part of the job, ensuring that the new organisation will be agile within the political system. The new organisation should be able to both influence and be influenced in the appropriate way—i.e., *to co-evolve effectively within the political environment.*

Clarity on who will be the new organisation's sponsorers, paymasters and customers is required. These roles were not always clear for the OldOrg and adversely influenced the way the work and its impact were evaluated.

Conclusion

If organisations are seen as complex evolving systems that need to co-evolve with a constantly changing environment, then the 'design' of a new organisation needs to be considered from a new perspective. Organisational restructuring, when it focuses primarily on the structure of the organisation, is not enough. All the key conditions need to be seen as a whole, with dimensions that interact and influence each other. Therefore the social, cultural, technical, political, economic (and other relevant) conditions need to be considered. This includes ways of thinking and relating, as the old mental models also need to change. It is therefore a process of constant learning and reciprocal influence creating new structures, procedures, processes, relationships and ways of thinking.

Working collaboratively with organisations in both the private and public sectors in the UK and USA over a period of ten years to apply the principles of complexity has led to some insights. One is that true collaborative working, with genuine involvement of staff at all levels, helps to co-create a flexible and responsive culture and an organisational form that becomes very responsive to needed changes. Another is that distributed leadership, distributed intelligence and distributed power throughout the organisation contributes significantly to its survival through engagement and constant innovation. Innovation is also enhanced by facilitating self-organisation and the exploration of alternative solutions. But such exploration needs to be done within a 'no-blame' culture. That does not mean that individuals have free rein; when they are trusted to look after the interests of the organisation they develop a strong sense of accountability and responsibility and they do work within self-imposed boundaries. Furthermore, any 'mistakes' or 'misjudgements' tend to be corrected through peer support.

As in the case of OldOrg, clarity of vision and direction are essential. This allows for local exploration of alternative solutions to achieve the vision and thus provides the organisation with multiple micro-strategies for attaining its goals. So when external conditions change it is prepared and is not hampered by a single and no longer appropriate strategy. But exploration by itself is not enough, as with OldOrg, it worked best when the 3Cs were present: communication, collaboration and co-creation. This ensured that good ideas were shared and one part learned from the other. It also meant that when working collaboratively across silos (whether functions or different projects), they were able to co-create something new and innovative and finally to co-create a new organisational form for NewOrg.

(Eve Mitleton-Kelly, Director, Complexity Research Programme, London School of Economics and Visiting Professor at Open University, UK. He can be reached at E.Mitleton-Kelly@lse.ac.uk).

Acknowledgments

The LSE Complexity Group's research and the development of the methodology have been enabled by the support of our business partners and by four **EPSRC** (Engineering and Physical Science Research Council) awards, including the 3-year collaborative action research project ICoSS under the Systems Integration Initiative entitled *'Enabling the Integration of Diverse Socio-cultural and Technical Systems within a Turbulent Social Ecosystem'* (GR/R37753). Details of the LSE Complexity Research Programme at *http://www.lse.ac.uk/comp.lexitv.*

9

Corporate Rejuvenation: A Study of Indian Firms' Post-Economic Reforms

Amita Mital

This is a research paper where the author studies the process of corporate rejuvenation in line with Indian deregulation and liberalization process. An in-depth analysis has been made of the external and internal factors contributing to the decline and strategies for turnaround/rejuvenation process. In the internal causes of decline, the author has submitted literature survey contribution and categorized five heads—top management and planning skills, financial management, operation management, human relations management and marketing management. The most important contributors for decline are the labor-related problems and uneconomic wage levels. The author has described at length and in tabulated forms the strategies adopted by the corporate to turnaround. Chief amongst these are the cost reduction issues and the culture-building exercises.

Introduction

India undertook a cascading set of economic reforms beginning in June 1991. Industrial controls over most investments and also controls over diversification and expansion were removed. Import controls, except for most consumer goods, were dismantled. Foreign investment restrictions came to an end in an effort to attract investment. Financial sector reforms were initiated with the objective of increasing management efficiency by providing greater autonomy to financial institutions in terms of interest rate structures and operational matters. The Government also sought better management by introducing competition to areas of public sector monopoly by allowing the entry of new private sector firms (Bhagwati, 1994). Structural reforms aimed at deregulating the economy and shifting from a path of relatively protected by inward-looking industrialization as a new phase based on greater competition in the domestic markets, openness to trade and investment, and fuller integration with the global economy was also implemented (Ahluwalia, 1994).

These reforms were mainly aimed at ending the era of central planning through persistent measures towards deregulating the domestic markets, increasing their integration with the global economy, reducing the role of Government and promoting market mechanisms to regulate the economy (Ray, 2003). A borderless economy meant allowing free access to global players in various economic activities such as reduction in tariff and other protectionist measures including modification of various Government policies (Kumar, 2001). The policy changes were in two broad categories, stabilization policy intended towards short-term correction of the grim financial situation being faced by the economy; and structural reforms policy intended to accelerate economic growth over the medium term (Rangarajan, 1993).

As a result of these reforms, the veil of protectionism thrown around the Indian industry in terms of high import tariffs, licensing of industries, etc., was gradually dismantled by bringing in competition both within India and from outside. While this was a healthy sign indicating a trend towards near-perfect competition, it proved to be a source of much anxiety for firms in India which had always lived under the protectionist umbrella, as they were not geared up in terms of financial muscle and orientation to compete globally. Competitiveness, technology upgradation, modernization, economies of scale and rationalization of operations became the key for survival (Podar, 1993). Though there was a positive response from industry to gear itself to meet the new challenges, the industry had to contend with adverse factors like severe import concessions, reduced domestic demand because of slow GDP growth and decline in public sector investment outlays and reduced overseas demand (Dhuldhoya, 1993).

An analysis of the financial performance of the listed companies for the period 1990-2002 based on CMIE[1] database indicated that the industrial sector was witnessing a decline. While during 1990, 79% of the listed firms were making profits, by the close of 2001, only 40% were making profits, 60% were not in good condition including 32% that were not reporting (Kumar, 2003). Further analysis also reveals that only 278 companies out of the total 7,532 listed companies, never went into losses during 1990 to 2001 and another 290 companies went into losses for 1-2 years but could rejuvenate and emerge from the downtrend and sustain positive profits for at least three consecutive years thereafter. The Gross Fixed Assets of companies making losses were INR 760,510 millions and of companies not reporting INR 623,990 million (Kumar, 2003), which was more than 12% of the GDP of India. In this situation rather than looking for unique context-turnaround fits, scholars may look for effective turnaround modes for each contextual condition so that they can be compared to provide a choice to practitioners (Khandwalla, 2001).

The present Indian context suggests deregulation and liberalization have impacted the external causes, which, in turn, have impacted the internal processes and functioning of companies that has led to their decline. Given this economy-wide situation, there was need for Corporate Rejuvenation, which can be defined as building of effective systems and skills needed to create sustainable growth (Stopford & Baden-Fuller, 1990). The study was undertaken with the objective of building knowledge about the post-economic reforms environment by addressing three issues—identification of factors that would determine success or decline of firms; identification of rejuvenation strategies adopted by firms; and establishing processes for rejuvenation adopted by successful firm. The study

[1] CMIE- Centre for Monitoring Indian Economy is a leading provider of financial data of Indian Companies.

incorporates a review of literature to identify factors causing decline and strategies for turnaround brought out by earlier researchers and studying their relevance in the post-economic reform context of India. A study of turnaround of declining companies needs to necessarily incorporate causes of decline to identify the symptoms that indicate decline. There is a need to know what is the likely cause of failure, what is the prognosis for the severity… what treatment there is… what preventive medicines there are and what healthy companies should do and not do to stay healthy (Argenti, 1976). Therefore, explicitly recognizing the cause of a firm's (Barker & Ardekani, 1995).

Corporate decline may be the outcome of natural processes of the organizational life cycle (Greiner, 1972; Tushman, Newman & Romanelli, 1986) or of the changes in external environment and/or changes in management (Cameron & Zammuto, 1983). Under such conditions, frame-breaking changes cannot be avoided and will have to be made either proactively or under crisis/turnaround condition (Tushman, Newman & Romanelli, 1986). However, research has brought out that when business conditions change, the most successful companies are often the slowest to adapt, due to the effect of active inertia (Sull, 1999). Success leads to specialization and exaggeration, to confidence and complacency, to dogma and ritual (Miller, 1992). Though Altman (1983) developed a scale, the Z-Score, for predicting bankruptcy, when decline is on account of discontinuous environmental changes, as happened in case of India, the prediction may not leave adequate time for firms to adapt to the changing environment.

Research indicates that in only about 9% of the cases, external factors are the sole cause of decline (Bibeault, 1982). In 20% of the cases, decline is caused by both internal and external factors and in about 70% decline is internally caused though it may be triggered by external forces. However, in case of India, only 278 (4%) companies continued to remain profitable post-economic reforms. This led to the objective of analyzing on the basis of literature, what has caused decline—external factors, internal factors or both.

Research Design

Two aspects were integrated in the research—one was a literature review to identify causes of decline and strategies for turnaround and/or rejuvenation brought out by earlier research and the second was studying the relevance of all these factors through intensive case analysis of 8 companies selected from the identified 290 Indian companies, that felt the impact of economic reforms, went into decline for 1-2 years, but rejuvenated and had sustained profits for at least three consecutive years.

Sample Selection

All the publicly listed companies as per the CMIE Prowess database as on March 31, 2001 were taken as the population. The net profit after tax was taken as the criterion for short-listing. Five parameters were considered, i.e., profitability, sustainability, present health of the company, cyclic factors impacting firms and stage in the life cycle of the firm. Starting with profitability, firms at the two ends of the continuum, firms that were never in loss (278) and firms that were never in profit (743) during FY 1990 to 2002 were removed. Next, firms that did not sustain profits, firms that had profits for only one year (564) or two years (876) during the same period were removed. The firms that did were not in good health as on the close of FY 2002, i.e., did not have profits in one or all of the years 2000 to 2002 (3038) and were removed. Firms which had profits (184) only on account of some cyclic upswing but had not reported profits in the preceding 3 years were removed. Lastly, firms that had losses (1412) on account of their being in the early 1-2 years of existence were removed and firms with overall losses in more than 2 years (147) were also removed. Thus we were left with 290 firms (Table 1).

These short-listed firms were analyzed for ascertaining whether there was any relation with type of industry, ownership, size and/or age. The analysis revealed that these firms were not specific to any industry, rather they were a blend of 215 (74%) manufacturing and 75 (26%) service firms, pursuing 110 types of different activities. In terms of ownership, they comprised 15 firms with Government ownership, 32 firms with private (foreign ownership), 113 small ownership, and the remaining 130 firms owned by Indian business houses. In terms of size, these comprised 199 firms having GFA of less that INR 1000, 66 firms in the range of INR 1000-4000 million and 25 firms with GFA of more than INR 4000 million. In terms of turnover, there were 162 firms with turnover of less than INR 1000 million, 79 firms in the range of INR 1000-4000 million and

Table 1: Process of Short-Listing Firms for Study

Criteria	Firms Removed	Balance Firms
Total No. of Listed Firms as per CMIE Prowess		7532
Profitability		
– Firms that never had losses	278	
– Firms that never had profits	743	6511
Sustainability		
– Firms that had profits for only 1 or 2 years	1440	5071
Present Health		
– Firms that did not have profits for some or all of the years 2000-2002	3038	2033
Cyclic Factors		
– Firms that had profits in last 3 years but did not report in preceding years	184	1849
Stage in lifecycle		
– Firms that had loss or did not report in early years of existence	1412	437
– Firms with more than 2 years of losses	147	290

49 firms with turnover of more than INR 4000 million. In terms of age these ranged from firms incorporated 4 year ago to 90 year ago.

This indicated that decline in firms is irrespective of industry, ownership, size and age. Hence 8 firms were picked up for study, 6 (75%) from manufacturing and 2 (25%) from service industry. In terms of age, they ranged from firms incorporated in 1945 to 1990. In terms of assets they ranged from INR 350 million to INR 23210 million and in terms of turnover from INR 490 million to INR 51000 million. A summary is depicted in Table 2.

Data Collection and Analysis

Primarily qualitative data was collected interspersed with quantitative data. Qualitative data consisted of two kinds of data collection—in-depth, open-ended interviews; and written documents including annual reports, house journals and reports prepared for reviews. The topic and purpose of research were described to

Table 2: Characteristics of Sample Firms Selected for Study

Industry	Automobile 2 wheelers		Iron & Steel		Paper		Hotels & Restaurants	
Name of Company	**HHML**	**TVSM**	**TML**	**TSIL**	**BILT**	**SBPM**	**JHL**	**AGHL**
Yr. of Incorporation	1984	1982	1990	1982	1945	1979	1980	1970
Business Group	Hero Munjal	TVS Iyengar	Tata Group	Tata Group	Thapar	Private	Jai Prakash Group	ITC
Turnover (INR Million)	51000	19300	1320	1430	15790	490	1120	560
Assets (INR Million)	11560	8300	750	1100	23210	350	2210	1510
Share of Industry	48	19	3	3	8	1	5	3

Legend:

HHML – Hero Honda Motors Ltd.
TVSM – TVS Motor Company Ltd.
TML – Tata Metaliks Ltd.
TSIL – Tata Sponge Iron Ltd.
BILT – Ballarpur Industries Ltd.
SBPM – Shree Bhawani Paper Mills
JHL – Jaypee Hotels Ltd.
AGHL – Adayar Gate Hotel Limited

the participants prior to the interview (Graebner, 2004). To bring in relevance and to get richer inputs, data from secondary sources was reviewed prior to the interview. Document analysis yielded excerpts, quotations and correspondence; official publications and reports and open ended response to questions (Quinn, 1990). Data collected were transcribed after collection and emerging patterns were analyzed. The analysis was aimed at validating the factors of decline and strategies for turnaround/rejuvenation brought out by earlier research and also identifying a framework for the rejuvenation process.

Literature Survey

External Causes of Decline

External causes of decline have been attributed to economic changes (Argenti, 1976; Dutt, 1980; Bibeault, 1982; Frost & Joson, 1998; Grinyer, Mayes & McKiernan, 1988; Pandit, 1998; Kaveri, 1983; Balgobin & Pandit, 2001); competitive changes (Argenti, 1976; Schendel, Patton & Riggs, 1976; Chakraborty, 1980; Porter, 1980; Harrigan, 1980; Bibeault, 1982; Slatter, 1984-

a; Grinyer, Mayes & McKiernan, 1988, 1990; Pandit, 1998, Goldstein, 1988; Balgobin & Pandit, 2001); sociological changes (Argenti, 1976; Dutt, 1980; Grinyer, Mayes & McKiernan, 1988; Goldstein, 1988; Harrigan, 1980; Porter, 1980; Bibeault, 1982; Frost & Joson, 1998); technological change (Argenti, 1976; Harrigan, 1980; Bibeault, 1982; Goldstein, 1988; Grinyer, Mayes & McKiernan, 1988; Manimala, 1991); Government constraints (Dutt, 1980, Bibeault, 1982; Goldstein, 1988; Gopal, 1991; Frost & Joson, 1998; Khandwalla, 2001); general calamities (Dutt, 1980; Gopal, 1991) and other factors like non-availability of inputs including power, transport (Dutt, 1980; Kaveri, 1983; Gopal, 1991; Manimala, 1991; Mathur, 199; Khandwalla, 2001), delayed release of funds by financial institutions (Dutt, 1980, Manimala, 1991; Mathur, 1999) and adverse industrial relations environment (Kaveri, 1983; Mathur, 1999; Khandwalla, 2001).

Internal Causes of Decline

The internal causes of decline may be due to strategic factors or operating factors and accordingly firms have to adopt strategic or operating cures (Schendel, Patton & Riggs 1976). Internal causes may be categorized under five heads—top management and planning skills; financial management and control skills; operations management; human resource management; and marketing management.

Top Management and Planning Skills

Some of the most frequent top management related factors are one man-rule (Argenti, 1976; Bibeault, 1982; Balgobin, 2001; Kaveri, 1983; Manimala, 1991; Mathur, 1999; Schendel, Patton & Riggs, 1976; Grinyer, 1988, 1990; Slatter, 1984-a; Gopal, 1991; Mckiernan, 1982; Frost & Joson, 1998; Pandit, 2000); weak/non-participative board (Argenti, 1976; Bibeault, 1982; Slatter, 1984-a; Gopal, 1991; Khandwalla, 1992, 2001; Frost, 1998); lack of management depth (Slatter, 1984-a); bureaucratic management (Frost & Joson, 1998); poorly conceived schemes (Dutt, 1980; Grinyer, 1988,1990); faulty planning/ implementation of projects (Argenti, 1976; Kaveri, 1983; Manimala, 1991; Goldstein, 1988; Slatter, 1984-a; Khandwalla, 1992, 2001); tardy debtor collections (Chakraborty, 1980; Mathur, 1999); inappropriate collaborations (Dutt, 1980; Slatter, 1984-a); bad location (Dutt, 1980; Goldstein, 1988; Kaveri,

1983); dishonesty of entrepreneurs (Manimala, 1991; Khandwalla, 1992, 2001); internal conflicts (Dutt, 1980; Chakraborty, 1980); dissension among partners (Manimala, 1991; Khandwalla, 1992, 2001); and non-responsiveness to change (Argenti, 1976).

Financial Management and Control Skills

Financial management and control includes inadequate control (Argenti, 1976; Bibeault, 1982; Chakraborty, 1980; Mathur, 1999; Goldstein, 1988; Slatter, 1984-a; Khandwalla, 1992, 2001; Balgobin & Pandit, 2001); lack of inventory and cost control (Argenti, 1976; Kaveri, 1983; Grinyer, 1988, 1990; Slatter, 1984-a; Gopal, 1991; Khandwalla, 1992, 2001; Frost, 1998); faulty accounting (Argenti, 1976; Kaveri, 1983; Chakraborty, 1980; Slatter, 1984-a; Khandwalla, 1992, 2001); low capital base/high leverage (Argenti, 1976; Dutt, 1980; Goldstein, 1988); inadequate working capital (Frost & Joson 1998); over-expansion/diversification (Goldstein, 1988; Grinyer, 1988, 1990; Slatter, 1984-a; Gopal, 1991; Khandwalla, 1992, 2001); diversion of funds (Dutt, 1980); cost over-runs (Dutt, 1980; Slatter, 1984-a); delayed distribution of profits (Dutt, 1980); and overtrading (Argenti, 1976; Slatter, 1984-a).

Marketing Management

The most widely acknowledged marketing management errors are lack of marketing efforts (Mathur, 1999; Goldstein, 1988; Grinyer, Mayes & McKiernan, 1988, 1990; Slatter, 1984-a; Khandwalla, 1992, 2001; Pandit, 1998); dependence on few buyers (Mathur, 1999; Goldstein, 1988; Grinyer, Mayes & McKiernan, 1988,1990; Slatter, 1984-a; Khandwalla, 1992, 2001; Pandit, 1998); lack of market research (Slatter, 1984-a); ineffective advertising (Slatter, 1984-a); and poor after-sales service (Slatter, 1984-a).

Operations Management

Operating inefficiencies include high-cost structure (Schendel, Patton & Riggs, 1976; Chakraborty, 1980; Slatter, 1984-a; Porter, 1980; Balgobin & Pandit, 2001); inefficient machines (Dutt, 1980; Chakraborty, 1980; Mathur, 1999); raw material scarcity (Manimala, 1991; Chakraborty, 1980); shortage of infrastructure (Manimala, 1991; Mathur, 1999); capacity underutilization (Manimala, 1991; Chakraborty, 1980; Mathur, 1999); faulty production programs (Manimala, 1991); dependence on few suppliers (Mathur, 1999; Goldstein, 1988; Grinyer, Mayes & McKiernan, 1988,1990; Slatter, 1984-a; Khandwalla, 1992, 2001; Pandit, 2000); poor quality (Grinyer, Mayes & McKiernan, 1988, 1990); technological obsolescence (Harrigan, 1980; Dutt, 1980; Manimala, 1991; Chakraborty, 1980; Mathur, 1999); and lack of R&D (Mathur, 1999; Khandwalla, 1992, 2001).

Human Resource Management

The most widely acknowledged human resource management errors are labor-related problems (Schendel, Patton & Riggs, 1976; Dutt, 1980; Manimala, 1991; Frost & Joson, 1998); and uneconomic wage levels (Manimala, 1991).

A mere list of causes and symptoms, no matter how coherent and comprehensive it may be, is not enough as it does not give adequate importance to the dynamics of failure (Argenti, 1976). Decline may occur over several years although there are situations when extraordinary events occurring over a shorter period of time can place a firm in peril (Tranfield, 1998). The rejuvenation strategy of firms would normally depend on the stage of decline, early comprising firms that are anticipatory and make incremental or strategic changes to reverse decline; intermediate when response to changes is reactive and actions by firms are in response to symptoms of the problem rather than the problem itself; or late when organizations face relatively sharp decline, but high exit barriers force them to remain in business (McKiernan, 1982). Slatter (1984-b) identified hidden crisis, crisis denial, organizational disintegration and organizational collapses as the four stages of crisis development.

A successful recovery may range from a subdued form, involving mere survival to its most positive form, leading to the firm achieving sustainable, superior competitive positions in its chosen areas of activity (Bibeault, 1982). A review of literature was also undertaken for identifying the rejuvenation/turnaround strategies identified by earlier research.

Rejuvenation/Turnaround Strategies

Studies on rejuvenation have been few and diverse with some authors focusing on the financial aspects, some on HR aspect and few on an integrated approach. In terms of approach of study, some have conducted studies using econometric models, while some have gone in for case study-based analysis. However, it has not been possible to make generalizations for successful turnaround. This is understandable, as there can be no turnaround formulae as there are many types of turnarounds and differing circumstances within each type (Bibeàult, 1982). The successful strategy will almost always depend on causes of decline and suitable customized solution for each case. Accurate attribution of causes, timely action and adequate resources are always required to effect a turnaround (Chowdhury & Lang, 1993).

Rejuvenation strategies should be attempted only when the business itself is worth saving. Rejuvenation strategies may be strategic or operating. The strategic ones include two types—product market refocus (O'Neill, & McKiernan, 1988, 1990; Slatter, 1984-a; McKiernan, 1982; Manimala, 1991; Khandwalla, 1992, 2001; Pandit, 2000; Harrigan, 1980; Hambrick & Schecter, 1983; Gopal, 1991; Schendel, Patton & Riggs, 1976); and large-scale expansion (Schendel, Patton & Riggs, 1976, Grinyer, Mayes & McKiernan, 1988 &1990; Slatter, 1984-a; Manimala, 1991). There are four operation strategies that are observed to be pursued. They are revenue-increasing strategies (Harrigan, 1980; Slatter, 1984-a; Pandit, 2000; Bibeault, 1982; Hambrick & Schecter, 1983; O'Neill, 1986), cost-decreasing strategies (Goldstein, 1988; Gopal, 1991; Grinyer, Mayes & McKiernan, 1988 & 1990; Hofer, 1980; Manimala, 1991; Khandwalla, 1999 & 2001; Slatter, 1984-a; Frost & Joson, 1998; Pandit, 1998 & 2000; Schendel, Patton & Riggs, 1976; Arogyaswamy, Barker & Ardekani, 1995; Eitel, 1995; Hambrick & Schecter, 1983); asset reduction strategies (Goldstein, 1988; Gopal, 1991; Hofer, 1980; Slatter, 1984-a; Manimala, 1991; Frost & Joson, 1998; Harrigan, 1980; McKiernan, 1982; O'Neill, 1986; Pandit, 1998); and combination strategies (Hofer 1980).

Depending on the nature and extent of the decline, chances of revival and financial muscle, firms may make a choice among expansion (Schendel, Patton & Riggs, 1976, Manimala, 1991), growth (O'Neill), acquisition (Grinyer, Mayes & McKiernan, 1988, 1990; Slatter, 1984-1986-a), investment (Harrigan, 1980; Slatter, 1984-a, Pandit, 2000), 1986, Manimala, 1991), diversification (Schendel Patton & Riggs, 1976; Grinyer, Mayes & McKiernan, 1988, 1990; Gopal 1991), strengthening core business (Harrigan, 1980, Bibeault, 1982), harvesting (Harrigan, 1980; Porter, 1980; Frost & Joson, 1998) or rationalization/closure (Harrigan, 1980; McKiernan, 1982; O'Neill, 1986). The first task in stabilizing a declining firm is to stop the cash drain to prevent the firm from bleeding to death (Goldstein, 1988).

If a strategic choice is made to revive the firm, it is imperative to generate funds. This may be possible by increasing revenues (Hofer, 1980; Hambrick & Schecter, 1983; Balgobin & Pandit, 2001; Bibeault, 1982), short-term financing (Bibeault, 1982) and developing strong financial controls (Argenti, 1976; Balgobin & Pandit, 2001; Bibeault, 1982; Gopal, 1991; Grinyer, Mayes & McKiernan, 1988, 1990; Slatter, 1984-a). Operating efficiencies will also have to be brought in, which could involve modernizing of facilities (Bibeault, 1982; Schendel Patton & Riggs, 1976; Khandwalla, 1992, 2001), improving quality (Hambrick & Schecter, 1983; Grinyer, Mayes & McKiernan, 1988, 1990; Manimala, 1991; Khandwalla, 1992, 2001), improving R&D (Schendel Patton & Riggs, 1976; Manimala, 1991), reducing costs (Balgobin & Pandit, 2001; Bibeault, 1982; Gopal, 1991; Grinyer, Mayes & McKiernan, 1988, 1990; Hambrick & Schecter, 1983; Hofer, 1980; Manimala, 1991; Khandwalla, 1992, 2001; Slatter, 1984-a; Pandit, 2000), and adopting efficiency measures (Bibeault, 1982; Hambrick & Schecter, 1983; Schendel, Patton & Riggs, 1976; Manimala, 1991; Pandit, 2000; Arogyaswamy, 1995; Eitel, 1995). Associated with this, firms will also have to restructure the organization (Gopal, 1991; McKiernan, 1982; Manimala, 1991; Khandwalla, 1992, 2001; O'Neill, 1986; Pandit, 2000), the assets (Argenti, 1976; Balgobin & Pandit, 2001; Bibeault, 1982; Gopal, 1991; Hambrick & Schecter, 1983; Hofer, 1980; Slatter, 1984-a; Frost & Joson, 1998; Pandit, 2000), the debt (Bibeault, 1982; Gopal, 1991; Grinyer, Mayes & McKiernan, 1988, 1990; Manimala, 1991; Slatter, 1984-a; Frost & Joson, 1998), and may have to go in for some organization change (Gopal, 1991; Manimala, 1991; Slatter, 1984-a; Pandit, 2000; Eitel, 1995).

A review of literature indicates that strategies for rejuvenation/turnaround are internally focused, that is they highlight what internal changes an organization can make to counter situations of decline. This being the case it may be possible to generate some insights by focusing on strategies adopted by firms for countering each of the internal causes of decline.

Top Management and Planning Skills

The strategies identified by research for improving the top management and planning are change the top management (Argenti, 1976; Bibeault, 1982; Gopal, 1991; Grinyer, Mayes & McKiernan, 1988, Khandwalla, 1992, 2001; O'Neill, 1986; Schendel, Patton & Riggs, 1976; Slatter, 1984-a; Frost & Joson, 1998; Pandit, 2000) bring in people who are committed, positive and with a bias for action, who believe in stimulating innovative and entrepreneurial behavior by injecting new values and vision to drive the company; set in organizational change (Gopal, 1991; Slatter, 1984-a; Pandit, 2000; Eitel, 1995; Manimala, 1991) and restructure the organization (Gopal, 1991; McKiernan, 1982; Khandwalla, 1992 & 2001; O'Neill, 1986, Pandit, 2000).

Financial Management and Control Skills

The strategies identified by research for improving the financial management and control are developing strong financial controls (Argenti, 1976; Balgobin & Pandit, 2001; Gopal, 1991; Grinyer, Mayes & McKiernan, 1988 & 1990; Slatter, 1984-a; Bibeault, 1982); reducing assets (Argenti, 1976; Balgobin & Pandit, 2001; Goldstein, 1988; Gopal, 1991; Grinyer, Mayes & McKiernan, 1988 & 1990; Hambrick & Schecter, 1983; Hofer, 1980; Slatter, 1984-a; Bibeault, 1982; Manimala, 1991; Frost & Joson, 1998; Pandit, 1998); debt restructuring (Argenti, 1976; Gopal, 1991; Grinyer, Mayes & McKiernan, 1988 & 1990; Slatter, 1984-a; Bibeault, 1982; Manimala, 1991, Frost & Joson, 1998; Pandit, 1998); and short-term financing (Bibeault, 1982).

Operations Management

The strategies identified by research for improving the Operations Management include modernization (Schendel, Patton & Riggs, 1976; Bibeault, 1982; Manimala, 1991; Khandwalla, 2001); quality improvement (Grinyer, Mayes & McKiernan, 1988 & 1990; Manimala, 1991; Khandwalla, 2000; Hambrick & Schecter, 1983); cost reduction (Balgobin & Pandit, 2001; Goldstein, 1988; Gopal, 1991; Grinyer, Mayes & McKiernan, 1988 & 1990; Hambrick & Schecter, 1983; Hofer, 1980; Slatter, 1984-a; Bibeault, 1982; Manimala, 1991; Frost & Joson, 1998; Pandit, 1998); efficiency measures (Balgobin & Pandit, 2001; Goldstein, 1988; Gopal, 1991; Grinyer, Mayes & McKiernan, 1988 &

1990; Hambrick & Schecter, 1983; Hofer, 1980; Khandwalla, 1992, 2001; Slatter, 1984-a; Bibeault, 1982; Manimala, 1991; Frost & Joson, 1998; Pandit, 1998); and investment in R&D (Schendel, Patton & Riggs, 1976; Manimala, 1991).

Human Resource Management

Human resource-related changes may include reducing employees (Bibeault, 1982; Goldstein, 1988; Manimala, 1991; Gopal, 1991; Khandwalla, 1992, 2001; Frost & Joson, 1998; Pandit, 1998) either by direct labor reductions or overhead reductions or both; training employees (Manimala, 1991; Gopal, 1991; Khandwalla, 1992; Eitel, 1995; Pandit, 1998), providing financial incentives for employees (Manimala, 1991), information dissemination (Manimala, 1991) and culture building (Manimala, 1991). The change process will be facilitated by commitment to employees (Eitel, 1995) and improving employee motivation (Balgobin & Pandit, 2001; Bibeault, 1982 O'Neill, nimala, 1991) to change from a defeatist; attitude to one of confidence by good leadership that people can trust, work responsibility, participation in decision-making, and granting authority and freedom as the firm moves from a crisis stage to a stabilization and growth stage (Bibeault, 1982).

Marketing Management

The firm will also need to increase revenues (Balgobin & Pandit, 2001; Bibeault, 1982; Hambrick & Schecter, 1983; Hofer, 1980) by generating more demand for its output through improved marketing (Bibeault, 1982; Gopal, 1991; Grinyer, Mayes & McKiernan, 1988, 1990; Khandwalla, 1992, 2001; McKiernan, 1982; Manimala, 1991; Slatter, 1984-a; Pandit, 2000) by getting closer to the customer, improving distribution channels, focusing on profitable customers, optimizing after sales service, improved market information, cost effective advertising, rationalizing product range in existing markets and aligning itself with the changing market demands. The firms enter export markets (Grinyer, Mayes & McKiernan, 1988, 1990) via sales subsidiaries, overseas agents or home-based export salesmen (Grinyer, Mayes & McKiernan, 1988), introduce new products (Bibeault, 1982; Schendel Patton & Riggs, 1976; Gopal, 1991; Manimala, 1991) and/or initiate product market reconstitution (Bibeault, 1982; Grinyer, Mayes & McKiernan, 1988, 1990; Hambrick & Schecter, 1983; Slatter, 1984-a;

McKiernan, 1982; Manimala, 1991; Khandwalla, 1992, 2001; Pandit, 2000) by building profitable add-on volume in existing lines that offer high returns at lower risk, aiming at eliminating marginal products, pushing more profitable product mix, exploiting existing products and making product line extensions.

Results

External Causes of Decline

Literature identified six external factors causing decline. The study indicated that most of the external causes of decline identified through literature remained relevant in the post-economic reforms environment of India and at least seven firms out of eight were impacted by all of the factors (Table 3).

Table 3: Impact of External Factors on Firm Performance

External factor	n
Economic Changes	8
Competitive Changes	8
Sociological / demographic Changes	8
Technological Changes	7
Government Constraints	8
General Calamities	7

Legend
n-firms where factor was found relevant.
Total No. of firms (N). 8

From the economic perspective firms felt the impact of inflation, with increase in prices of raw materials and components. On the competitive front, firms witnessed a shift from being in the sellers' market to being in a convergence (sociological factor). With the crumbling of geographic boundaries, technological divide was also disappearing as consumers had access to the most advanced technology globally. Non availability of inputs and lack of adequate infrastructure were some of the problems faced by a few firms.

Internal Causes of Decline

Literature identified 40 internal factors causing decline, including 11 factors relating to top management and planning skills, 11 relating to financial management and control skills, 10 relating to operations management, 5 relating to marketing management and 2 relating to HRM.

Out of the 11 factors relating to top management and planning skills brought out by literature, none of the eight firms indicated conditions of poor management; one-man rule; non-participative board; lack of management depth; dishonest entrepreneurs; and non-responsiveness to change. In 7 out of 8 firms, conditions of poorly conceived schemes; faulty planning/implementation; inappropriate collaborations; bad location; internal conflict and dissension among partners were not observed.

Table 4: Impact of Internal Factors on Firm Performance

Top Management & Planning Skills	**n**	**Financial Management & Control Skills**	**n**
Poor management / One man rule	0	Inadequate control / information systems	0
Non-participative / weak board	0	Lack of inventory & cost control	0
Lack of management depth / bureaucratic management	0	Faulty accounting	0
Ambitious programs/ Poorly conceived schemes	1	Low capital base / high leverage	2
Faulty planning / implementation of	1	Inadequate working capital	0
Inappropriate collaborations	1	Over-expansion diversification, acquisitions	1
Bad location	1	Diversion of funds	0
Dishonesty of entrepreneurs / Corporate Mgt	0	Cost overruns	2
Internal conflict	1	Delayed distribution of profits	2
Dissensions among partners	1	Tardy debtor collections	2
Non responsiveness to change	0	Gearing and overtrading	3
Marketing Management	**n**	**Operations Management**	**n**
Lack of marketing effort	1	High cost structure/cost price disparity	4
Dependence on few buyers	1	Inefficient machines	1
Lack of market research	3	Raw material scarcity	6
Ineffective advertising	1	Shortage of infrastructure including	6
Poor after-sales service	0	Capacity underutilization/surplus workforce	3
Human Resource Management	**n**	Faulty production programs	0
Labour-Related Issues	1	Dependence on few suppliers	3
		Poor quality	0

Contd...

Contd...			
Wage levels	0	Technological obsolescence / non Lack of R&D	3

Legend

Total No. of Firms (N)=8.

No. of firms where the factor was found to be relevant (n).

Out of the 11 factors relating to financial management and control skills brought out by literature, none of the eight firms indicated conditions of inadequate control/information systems; lack of inventory and cost control; faulty accounting; and inadequate working capital and diversion of funds. Only 3 of the 8 firms indicated conditions of gearing and high leverage; cost overruns; delayed distribution of profit; and tardy collection of debts were found to be relevant in only 2 out of 8 firms.

Literature also identified 10 operations management factors causing decline of firms. Out of these, only 2 factors, shortage of infrastructure and raw material scarcity were found to be impacting 6 firms out of 8. High cost structure impacted 4 firms. Lack of R&D, dependence on few suppliers and capacity under-utilization /surplus workforce each impacted 3 firms out of 8. Inefficient machines, faulty production programs, poor quality and technological obsolescence were not found to be relevant factors in any of the firms.

Out of the five marketing management-related factors, only one factor, lack of market research was found to be relevant in 3 firms out of 8. Poor after-sales service was not observed at any of the firms, while lack of marketing effort, dependence on few customers and ineffective advertising were observed at one firm each. Regarding the HRM-related factors, labor-related issues were found to be impacting only one firm out of 8 and wage levels were not found to be relevant in any of the firms (Table 4).

Rejuvenation/Turnaround Strategies

Earlier research identified 21 rejuvenation/turnaround strategies. Ten of these strategies, i.e., increase revenues; strong financial control; modernize; improve quality; reduce cost; efficiency measures; debt restructuring; improve motivation;

improve marketing and export were found to be effective in all 8 firms. Three strategies, employee training; culture building; and introducing new products were relevant in 7 firms. Six firms adopted product-market reconstitution; two used short term financing; organizational change; and employee reduction, while one firm resorted to restructuring. None of the firms changed top management or reduced assets (Table 5).

New Rejuvenation/Turnaround Strategies Identified

In order to identify the rejuvenation strategy adopted by firms, the factors causing decline were listed for each of the companies. Alongside each of these factors, the

Table 5: Rejuvenation/Turnaround Strategies adopted by Firms

Causes of Decline	N	Strategies Adopted To Counter The Causes	
Economic Changes	8	Reduce costs/expenses (8), efficiency measures (8), debt restructuring (8)	Value Added Products / Value for money (4)
Competitive Changes	8	Modernize (8), improve quality (8), reduce cost/expenses (8), employee training (7)	
Sociological or demographic Change	8	Introduce new products (7), culture building (7), employee training (7)	Marketing in emerging segments (3), CRM (3), decommoditiosation (2)
Government constraints	8		Alliances (5)
Increase in input cost	8	Import substitution (5), e-procurement (3), vendor management (2), value engineering (2)	
Changes in fiscal & monetary policies	8		
Import/export policies	8		Alliances (5), Production/ assembly units abroad (1)
Changes in international market conditions	8	Culture Building (7), employee training (7)	Safety Health & Environment (6), Customisation (4)
Technological Changes	7	Employee Training (7)	Recruit & Retain talent (4), IT enabled KM (4), TQM (3)
General calamities	7		Risk Management (1)
Transit from sellers' to buyers' market	7	Introduce new products (7), culture building (7), employee training (7)	

Contd...

Contd...			
Inflation	7		
Raw material Scarcity	6		Real-time information sharing (4), captive resources (4), vendor management (2)
Shortage of infrastructure including power	6		Build own infrastructure (4)
Lack of R&D	5		Reinvest profits (8), recruit & retain talent (4), collaborative R&D (2)
Legend		Old Strategies	New Strategies

organizational response to these factors was listed. The summary of these responses indicate that in response to economic changes, firms reduced costs, restructured debt and adopted efficiency measures in line with factors brought out by earlier research. However, they went further and also ensured supply of value-added products, where customers could perceive value for money in the purchase. In response to competitive changes, firms modernized, improved quality, reduced costs and embarked on training program for employees all of which were strategies brought out by literature. In response to demographic changes, new products suiting changed lifestyles were introduced alongside employee training and culture building. However, some new strategies like tapping markets in emerging segments, de-commoditization of erstwhile commodity products and emphasis on CRM became important dimensions.

With the crumbling of geographic boundaries due to liberalization and deregulation, firms entered alliances which gave them technological prowess and financial strength and also set up production/assembly units overseas. In order to compete in global markets, firms adhered to stringent safety, health and environmental norms and also customized products and services to country-specific needs. To meet the technological upheavals, a lot of emphasis was placed on IT-enabled Knowledge Management, collaborative R&D, recruiting & retaining talent and adopting TQM. Once firms were competing in global markets, supply line had to be maintained, the main stumbling blocks of which were raw material scarcity and lack of infrastructure. Firms sought ways to have captive sources of raw materials, developed vendor management skills and systems for real-time information sharing were put in place. Considering large scale natural calamities in the recent past, firms also developed and upgraded risk management techniques.

New Rejuvenation Process Framework

An integration of the above factors indicates that rejuvenating firms focus on four processes—product development process, market expansion process, cost reduction process and resource generation process.

Product Development

Firms start new product development at the product concept, which includes a study of customer requirement and establishing a target for product quality. With an in-depth understanding of customer requirement, firms design new product prototypes. At this stage supplier involvement is essential to ensure availability of inputs at competitive cost. Supplier feedback is also incorporated at this stage to prevent rework. Use of technology (CAD) facilitates modifications in product design with reduced lead time. With product design in place, firms work on product development with targets set for cost, time and development of production facility. Firms that do not have the technological or financial strength to invest in new product development, often collaborate with research labs, parent company or alliance partners across the globe to provide the necessary support. Quality proving is done inhouse to ensure minimum post-launch problems. Therefore, the following proposition:

Proposition 1: To remain in profit post-economic reforms, firms constantly evolve new products that are developed with an in-depth understanding of customer requirement, at competitive cost and reduced leadtime that provides the first-mover advantage to the firms.

Market Expansion

New products themselves cannot improve the performance of firms unless there is a market for the new products. For developing a market, firms have to ensure an appropriate delivery infrastructure and promotion of the product to the customers. Dealer network is expanded using standardized procedures to ensure wide reach of products. Corporate identity is developed across the markets to build brand image. Dealers are trained in quality management and customer service, and best practices of dealers are shared across the market.

Firms target specific customer segments for different products and have customized promotional packages for each segment. Advertising, incentives, discounts, finance tie-up and developing brand ambassadors are often used to increase sale. Involvement with the customer remains after the sale is made for ensuring referrals and repeats purchase by customers. Customer relationship management has emerged as a useful tool for retaining customers and ensuring replacement/upgrade sale. In an attempt to increase the customer base, firms are redefining markets and changing industry boundaries. Firms in commodity markets are also focusing on de-commoditiosation of products through differentiation and branding initiatives.

Having established their presence in domestic markets, firms are looking at overseas markets to increase their sale. In the initial stages, firms start with exports and/or marketing alliances with global players. This may require customization of product to meet individual country standards and consumer preferences. It may also require compliance to safety, health and environmental policies of the importing country. Gradually, as firms establish their presence overseas, they may consider setting up production or assembly units abroad. Therefore, the following proposition:

Proposition 2: To remain in profit post-economic reforms, firms constantly expand their markets by redefining markets, supplying world-class products, supported by high quality distribution network, appropriate publicity and promotional packages and after sales service.

Cost Reduction

Lowering costs through quality and process improvement and by reducing input costs improves operating efficiency. Setting up quality task forces and adoption of TQM facilitate process improvements, thereby improving efficiency. Trained and motivated employees also bring about improved efficiency. Cost reduction is also achieved by reducing waste, which is done by resource conservation teams. Input cost are reduced through R&D, backward integration, use of by-products, import substitution, real-time information sharing, e-procurement, value engineering and technology transfer to vendors. Therefore, the following proposition:

Proposition 3: To remain in profit post-economic reforms, firms constantly endeavour to reduce costs through manufacturing efficiency and reduction in input cost, which is possible with improved R&D, indigenisation, e-procurement, value engineering and technology transfer to vendors, bringing about lowest cost of production.

Resource Generation

Firms need resources for new product development, market expansion and adopting quality processes. These resources are generated either through divesting non-core assets, short-term financing or internal accruals. Reinvestment is possible only when firms have high internal accruals, which are achieved by increasing turnover (Propositions 1 and 2) and reducing cost (Proposition 3) resulting in higher margins. Alongside, the debt component is reduced to lower the interest burden, giving opportunity for reinvesting profits. Therefore, the following proposition:

Proposition 4: To sustain propositions 1, 2 and 3, firms generate resources through higher operating margins and reducing the debt burden, which facilitates reinvesting internal accruals into the business. The process framework is depicted in Figure 1.

Agenda for Further Research

A study to test the hypothesis on a larger sample size may validate the findings. The study may also be validated in public sector companies and foreign-owned companies. Studies can also be conducted to study control variables like business groups, ownership patterns, firm size and industry. A comparison with successful firms, which were never in loss and with failures that could either not turnaround or could not sustain the turnaround may also contribute to the existing knowledge. A comparative study with other economies undergoing economic reforms may add further insights. The process framework for rejuvenation, used for identification of factors can be tested.

Fig.1 – A Generic Framework for Rejuvenation

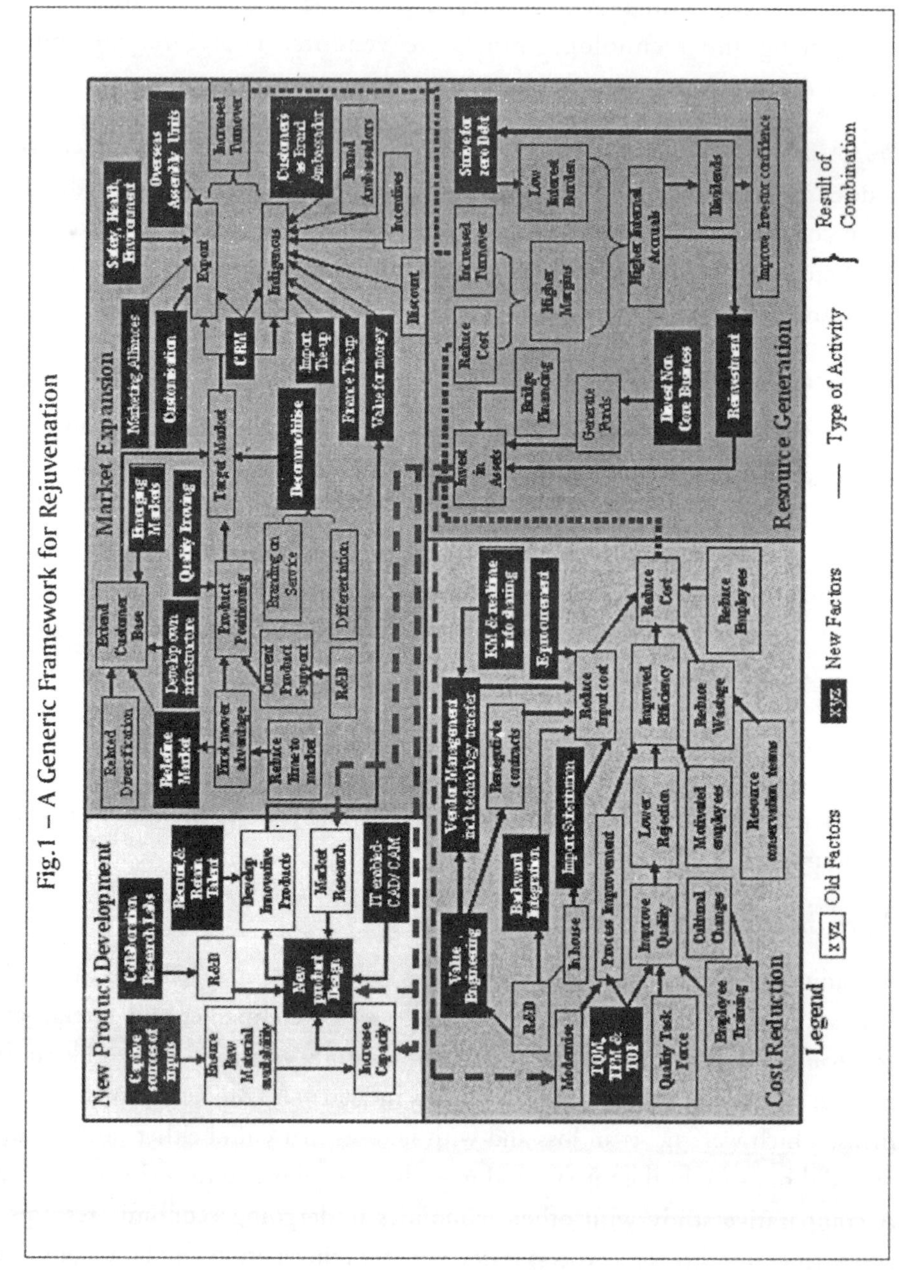

Limitations of the Study

The number of firms used for evolving the rejuvenation process framework was limited to eight, as larger number of firms, though might have added to the robustness of the study, would have posed a problem in terms of standardization. In order to limit the scope of the study, public sector and foreign ownership companies were excluded and the firms for study were taken from the Indian private sector only. A comparison with firms that failed and/or firms that never went into losses may add to the insights of the study. A study of similar size of firms or firms within a single industry might have been useful to study intra-industry characteristics of the firms.

Conclusion

Insights from the study have provided some propositions, which may provide direction for rejuvenation of firms. Apart from this, the study validated the importance of 6 out of 7 external causes of decline identified by earlier research. The study also validated that only 2 operations management factors out of 40 internal causes of decline of firms are relevant post-economic reforms. It indicated the relevance of 15 rejuvenation strategies brought out by earlier research, post-economic reforms and also identified 22 new factors for rejuvenation in the post-economic reforms context, which were not identified by erstwhile research. It outlined product development process, market expansion process, cost reduction process and resource generation process as imperative processes for rejuvenation of firms. Indian firms, facing decline as a fallout of economic reforms, can use the resultant generic framework for rejuvenation to rejuvenate and improve their performance. The process framework has been derived from an in-depth study of eight firms and can be a useful base for testing the new factors of rejuvenation by researchers.

(Dr. Amita Mital, Faculty, Strategic Management Area, Xavier Labour Relations Institute, Jamshedpur, India.)

References

Ahluwalia, Montek S. (1994), India's Business, Spring 94, 29, 1, p.6.

Altman, Edward I. (1983-a), Corporate Financial Distress: A complete guide to predicting, avoiding and dealing with bankruptcy, John Wiley.

Altman, Edward I. and La Fleur, James K., (1981), Managing a return to Financial Health, *The Journal of Business Strategy,* Summer 1981, p.31-38.

Altman, Edward I., (1983-b), Exploring the road to Bankruptcy, *The Journal of Business Strategy,* p.36-41.

Altman, Edward I., (1983-c), Why Businesses Fail, *The Journal of Business Strategy,* p.15-21.

Argenti, John (1976), Corporate Collapse: The Causes and Symptoms, McGraw-Hill, NY.

Arogyaswamy, Kamala, Barker III, Vincent L. and Yasai-Ardekani, Masoud (1995), Firm Turnarounds: an integrative two-stage model, *Journal of Management Studies,*

Balgobin, Rolf and Pandit, Naresh (2001), Stages in the Turnaround process: The case of IBM UK, *European Management Journal,* 19, 3 301-316.

Barker, V. L. III and Duhaime, Irene M. (1997) Strategic Change in the Turnaround Process: Theory and empirical Evidence, *Strategic Management Journal,* 18, 13-38.

Barker, V. L. III and Mone, M. A. (1997), Retrenchment: Cause of turnaround or consequence of decline? *Strategic Management Journal,* 15, 395-405.

Bhagwati, Jagdish (1994), India's economic

Bibeault, Donald B. (1982), Corporate Turnaround: How managers turn losers into Winners, Mc Graw Hill, New York.

Bradley, Jana, (1993), Methodological issues and practices in qualitative research, *The Library Quarterly,* Vol 63, number 4, pg.431-449.

Brewerton, Paul and Lynne, Milward, (2001), Organisational Research Methods – A guide for students and researchers, Sage, London.

Bruton, Garey D, Ahlstrom, David and Wan Johny, C.C. (1995), Turnaround in East Asian Firms: Evidence from ethnic overseas Chinese Countries, *Strategic Management Journal,* Jun 2003, 24, 6, p.519-541.

Bryman, Alan (1984), The debate about quantitative and qualitative research: A question of method or epistemology?, *The British Journal of Sociology,* Vol XXXV Number 1 p.75-92.

Bryman, Alan (1988), Doing Research in Organizations, Routledge, London.

Bryman, Alan (1989), Research Methods and Organization Studies, Routledge, London.

Budget Speech, Government of India Union Budget 2003-04.

Cameron, Kim S. & Zammuto, Raymond F. (1983) Matching Managerial strategies to conditions of decline, in Kim S.Cameron, Robert I Sutton, & David A.Whetten, Readings in Organizational Decline: Frameworks, research and Prescriptions, Ballinger Publishing company, Cambridge, MA.

Chakraborty, S.K. (1980), Towards a National policy framework for combating industrial sickness in S.K. Chakraborty (ed) Industrial sickness and revival in India.

Chowdhury, Shamsud D., Lang, James R. (1993), Crisis, decline, and turnaround: A test of competing hypotheses for short-term performance improvement in small firms, *Journal of Small Business Management,* Oct 93, 31, 4.

Collins, Elaine C., (1992), Qualitative Research as an art: Toward a Holistic process, Theory into Practice, Volume XXXI, number 2, Spring 1992.

Covin, Teresa Joyce and Kilmann, Ralph H, (1988), Critcal Issues in Large-Scale Change, *Journal of Organizational change Management,* Vol.1, Iss.2, 59-72.

Denzin, Norman K. & Lincoln, Yvonna S., (2000), Handbook of Qualitative Research (2nd Ed) pg.3, Sage, California.

Dhuldhoya, N.M. (1993) Reform pace must quicken in *The Hindu Survey of Indian Industry* 1993.

Dutt, B.K. (1980), Industrial sickness in India, some plain truths in S.K. Chakraborty, Industrial sickness and revival in India.

Eisenhardt, Kathleen M. (1989), Building Theories from case study research, *Academy of Management Review,* 14, p 532-550.

Eitel, Charles R. (1998), The ten disciplines of business turnaround, *Management Review,* Dec 98, 87, 11.

Ely, Margot and Anzul, Margaret, (1991), Doing Qualitative Research: Circles within circles, Falmer, London.

Fielding, Nigel G. and Fielding, Jane L., (1986), Linking Data, Sage, California.

Finkin, E.F. (1987). Successful Corporate Turnarounds: A Guide for Board Members, Financial Managers, Financial Institutions, and other Creditors. New York: Quorum Books.

Frost, Frederick A., and Joson, Gerardo R. (1998) Turnaround Strategies of electric utilities in New Zealand and Phillipines, Strategic Change 7, p.289-300.

Glaser, Barney G. and Strauss, Anselm M. (1967), The Discovery of grounded Theory: Strategies for Qualitative Research, Aldine, New York.

Goldstein, Arnold S. (1988) Corporate Comeback: Managing turnarounds and troubled companies, John Wiley, New York.

Goldston, Mark R. (1992), The turnaround prescription: Repositioning troubled companies, Free Press, New York.

Goodman, S. (1982). How to Manage a Turnaround. New York: Free Press.

Gopal, R. (1991), Turning around sick companies – The Indian Experience, Long Range Planning, 24:3, p 79-83.

Goulding, Christina (2002), Grounded Theory – A practical Guide for Management, Business and Market Researchers, Sage, London

Graebner, Mellissa E., (2004), Momentum And Serendipity: How Acquired Leaders Create Value in Integration of Technology firms, *Strategic Management Journal*, 25: 751-777.

Greiner, Larry E. (1972), Evolution and Revolution as Organizations Grow, *Harvard Business Review*, July-August 1972, p.57-66.

Grinyer, Peter H. & McKiernan, Peter (1990), Generating Major Change in stagnating Companies, *Strategic Management Journal* 11, p 131-146.

Grinyer, Peter H. & McKiernan, Peter (1991), The determinants of Corporate Profitability in the UK Electrical engineering Industry, *British Journal of Management*, 2, 17-32.

Grinyer, Peter H., Mayes, David G. & McKiernan, Peter (1988), Sharpbenders: The secrets of unleashing Corporate Potential, Basil Blackwell, Oxford.

Hambrick, Donald C. & Schecter, Steven M. (1983), Turnaround Strategies for Mature Industrial Product Business Units, *Academy of Management Journal*, Vol.26, No.2, 231-248.

Hambrick, Donald C. & D'Aveni, (1988), Large Corporate Failures as downward spirals, *Administrative Science Quarterly*, Vol.33, 1-23.

Harper, Dean, (1994), What problems do you confront? An approach to doing qualitative research, *Qualitative Sociology*, Vol 17., No.1 pg 89-95.

Harrigan, Kathryn Rudie (1980), Strategies for declining industries, in Kim S.Cameron, Robert I Sutton, & David A.Whetten, Readings in Organizational Decline: Frameworks, research and Prescriptions, Ballinger Publishing company, Cambridge, Massachusetts.

Harrigan, Kathryn Rudie and Porter Michael E. (1983), End Game Strategies for declining industries, *Harvard Business Review*, Jul-Aug 1983, 111-120.

Hofer, Charles W. (1980), Turnaround Strategies, *The Journal of Business Strategy*, Summer 80, Vol. 1 Issue 1, p19-31.

Hofer, Charles W. (1980), Strategy Formulation: Analytical concepts, West Publishing, New York.

Janesick, Valerie J., (2000), The Choreography of Qualitative Research Design-Minuets, Improvisation and Crystallization, in Denzin, Norman K. & Lincoln, Yvonna S., (2000), Handbook of Qualitative Research (2nd Ed) pg 379-399, Sage, California.

Kanter, Rosabeth Moss (1983) The Change Masters: Corporate Entrepreneurs at Work, Unwin Paperbacks, London.

Kaveri, V.S. (1983), How to diagnose, prevent and cure industrial Sickness, Sultan Chand & Sons, New Delhi.

Khandwalla, Pradip N. (1992), Innovative Corporate Turnarounds, Sage, New Delhi.

Khandwalla, Pradip N. (2001), Turnaround Excellence: Insights from 120 cases, Sage, New Delhi.

Kilmann, Ralph H, Covin, Teresa Joyce and Associates (1988), Corporate Transformation – Revitalizing Organizations for a Competitive World, Jossey Bass, California.

Kumar, Krishna (1982), Organization and Ownership – A comparative Sectoral Study of General Management Functions, Macmillan, New Delhi.

Kumar, Krishna (2003), Corporate Leaders of India, presented at the 6th Annual Conference of Strategic Management Forum, XLRI, Jamshedpur, April 24-26, 2003.

Kumar, Krishna (2003), Has India Inc. Failed in Playing the Leadership Role, Vikalpa, Vol:28, No.3, Jul-Sep'03 p: 1-13.

Kumar, Krishna (2004), How are the Indian Organizations going to meet the challenge, presented at the 33rd International Federation of Training and Development Organisations, The Ashok Hotel, New Delhi, India November 22-25, 2004.

Lall, Sanjay (1992), Building industrial competitiveness in Developing Countries, Development center of the Organization for Economic Cooperation and Development, Paris.

Lincoln, Yvonna S., and Guba, Egon C., (1985), Naturalistic Inquiry, Sage, California.

Manimala Mathew, (1991), Turnaround Management: Lessons from successful cases, *ASCI Journal of Management,* Vol. 20.

Markides, Constantinos and Stopford, John M. (1995), From Ugly Ducklings to Elegant Swans : Transforming Parochial Firms into World Leaders, *Business Strategy Review,* Summer 1995, Vol. 6, No.2, 1-24.

Marshall, Catherine and Rossman, Gretchen B., (1989), Designing Qualitative Research, Sage, California.

Mathur, Satish B. (1999), Sickness in Small scale sector, Causes and cures, Concept Publishing, New Delhi.

May, Tim, (2002),Qualitative Research in Action, Sage, London.

McKiernan, Peter (1982), Strategies of Growth: Maturity, recovery and internationalization, Routledge, London.

Miles, Matthew B., and Huberman, A.Michael, (1994) Qualitative data Analysis (2nd ed), Sage, California.

O'Neill, Hugh M. (1986), Turnaround Planning, 19, 1 p 80-88.

Pandit, Naresh R (2000), Some Recommendations for improved Research on Corporate Turnaround, Management 3:2, p 31-56.

Pandit, Naresh R. (1998), British Steel Corporation: probably the biggest turnaround story in UK industrial history, Strategic Change 7, p 65-79.

Patton, Michael Quinn, (1990), Qualitative Evaluation and Research Methods (2nd Ed), Sage, California.

Pearce II, J.A. and Robbins, D.Keith (1993), Toward Improved Theory and Research on Business Turnaround, *Journal of Management* Vo.19, No.3, p 613-636.

Pettigrew, Andrew M. (1987), Researching Strategic Change, in Andrew M. Pettigrew (Ed.) The Management of Strategic Change, Blackwell, Oxford.

Pettigrew, Andrew M. (1987), Context and action in the Transformation of the Firm, *Journal of Management Studies,* 24:6 November 1987, 649-670.

Pettigrew, Andrew M. (1992), The character and significance of strategy process research, *Strategic Management Journal,* Vol. 13, 5-16.

Podar, Kantikumar R., (1993), Industry in the Nineties in *The Hindu Survey of Indian Industry* 1993.

Porter, Michael E. (1980), Competitive Strategy: Techniques for Analyzing Industries and Competitors, New York: The Free Press.

Porter, Michael E. (1985) Competitive Advantage. New York: The Free Press.

Rangarajan, C. (1993), New Economic Policy- Genesis, content and significance in *The Hindu Survey of Indian Industry* 1993.

Ray, Sougata (2003), Strategic Adaptation of Firms during Economic Liberalisation: Emerging Issues and a research Agenda, *International Journal of Management,* p 271-281.

Ray, Sougata (2004), Environment-Strategy-Performance Linkages: A study of Indian Firms during Economic Liberalisation, Vikalpa Vol. 20, No. 2, Apr-Jun 2004, pg 9-23.

Ray, Sougata (2004), Performance Implications of Corporate Strategic Behavior of Firms in an Emerging Economy during Economic Liberalization, 2004, pg 246-256.

Robbins, D.Keith and Pearce II, J.A. (1992), Turnaround: Retrenchment & Recovery, *Strategic Management Journal,* 13, p 287-309.

Romanelli, Elaine and Tushman, Michael L.(1994), Organizational Transformation as Punctuated Equilibrium: An empirical test, *Academy of Management Journal,* Oct 94, Vol. 37 Issue 5, p1141-1166.

Schendel, D.E, Patton, G.R & Riggs, J. (1976), Corporate Turnaround Strategies: A study of Profit, Decline and recovery, *Journal of General Management,* 3,3, p 3-11.

Schendel, D.E and Patton, G.R (1976), An empirical study of Corporate Stagnation and Turnaround, Academy of Management Proceedings, 1975, p49-51.

Scholz, Roland W. & Tietje, Olaf (2002), Embedded case study methods-Integrating Quantitative and qualitative Knowledge, Sage, California.

Slatter, Stuart (1984-a), Corporate Recovery: A guide to Turnaround Management, Penguin, London.

Slatter, Stuart (1984-b), The impact of crisis on managerial behavior, *Business Horizons,* May-Jun 84, 64-68.

Smith, Denis and Sipika, Chris (1993), Back from the Brink – Post-crisis management, Long Range Planning, 26, 1 p 28 –38.

Spender, J.C. and Grinyer, P.H., (1996), Organizational Renewal, International Studies of Management and Organization, Spring 96, Vol. 26 Issue 1, p17-40.

Stopford, John M and Baden-Fuller, Charles (1990), Corporate Rejuvenation, Journal of Management Studies Vol: 27 Issue: 4 Date: Jul 1990 p 399-415.

Sull, Donald N. (1999), Why Good Companies go Bad, *Harvard Business Review,* July-August 1999, p 42-52.

Sutton, Brett (1993), The rationale for qualitative research: A review of Principles and Theoretical Foundations, *Library Quarterly,* Vol. 63, No. 4, pg 411-430.

Tranfield, David and Smith, Stuart (1998), The Strategic regeneration of manufacturing by changing routines, *International Journal of Operations & Production Management;* 18:2, p 114-129.

Tushman, Michael, Newman, William & Romanelli, Elaine (1986), Covergence and Upheaval: Managing the unsteady pace of Organization Evolution in Michael L.Tushman, Charles and David Nadler, The Management of Organizations: Strategies, Tactics, Analyses, Harper and Row, New York (1989).

Van de Ven, A.H. (1992) Suggestions for studying strategy process: A research note, *Strategic Management Journal,* Vo.13, 169-188.

World Trade Organization, (2002), Trade Policy Review, India 2002, WTO, Geneva.

Zimmerman, Frederick M (1989), Managing a successful Turnaround, Long Range Planning, 22.3, p 105 –124.

Zimmerman, Frederick M. (1986), Turnaround – A painful learning experience, Long Range Planning, 19.4, p 104 –114.

Zammuto, Raymond F. and Cameron, Kim S. (1982) Environmental Decline and Organizational Response, Academy of Management Proceedings, 1982, p.250-254.

10

Change Management 101: A Primer

Fred Nickols

Organizations frequently survive the people who establish change gracefully. Successful organizations resolve early on the issue of structure, that is, the definition, placement and coordination of functions and people. Skills (Political, Analytical, People, Business and System) and Strategies (Empirical-Rational, Normative-Reeducative, Power-Coercive, Environmental-Adaptive) that are required for managing change are explained and factors which help in choosing the right strategy are also elucidated. This paper provides a broad overview of the concept of "change management" and is mainly written for people who are coming to grips with change management problems for the first time and for more experienced people who wish to reflect upon their experience in a structured way. The process of change has been characterized as having three basic stages: unfreezing, changing, and re-freezing. The change process is also thought about as a problem-solving and problem-finding situation. At the heart of change management lies the change problem. The change problem as "How", "What" and "Why" are also dealt with.

I. Introduction

Purpose and Audience

The purpose of this paper is to provide a broad overview of the concept of "change management." It was written primarily for people who are coming to grips with change management problems for the first time and for more experienced people who wish to reflect upon their experience in a structured way.

II. Change Management Defined

Three Basic Definitions

In thinking about what is meant by "change management," at least four basic definitions come to mind:

1. The task of managing change.
2. An area of professional practice.
3. A body of knowledge.
4. A control mechanism.

The Task of Managing Change

The first and most obvious definition of "change management" means the task of managing change. The obvious is not necessarily unambiguous. Managing change is itself a term that has at least two meanings.

One meaning of "managing change" refers to *the making of changes in a planned and managed or systematic fashion.* The aim is to more effectively implement new methods and systems in an ongoing organization. The changes to be managed lie within and are controlled by the organization.[1] However, these internal changes might have been triggered by events originating outside the organization, in what is usually termed "the environment." Hence, the second meaning of managing change, namely, *the response to changes over which the organization exercises little or no control* (e.g., legislation, social and political upheaval, the actions of competitors, shifting economic tides and currents, and so on). Researchers and

1 Perhaps the most familiar instance of this kind of change is the "change control" aspect of information systems development projects.

practitioners alike typically distinguish between a knee-jerk or reactive response and an anticipative or proactive response.

An Area of Professional Practice

The second definition of change management is "an area of professional practice."

There are dozens, if not hundreds, of independent consultants who will quickly and proudly proclaim that they are engaged in planned change, that they are change agents, that they manage change for their clients, and that their practices are change management practices. There are numerous small consulting firms whose principals would make these same statements about their firms. And, of course, most of the major management consulting firms have a change management practice area.

Some of these change management experts claim to help clients manage the changes they face—the changes happening to them. Others claim to help clients make changes. Still others offer to help by taking on the task of managing changes that must be made. In almost all cases, the process of change is treated separately from the specifics of the situation. It is expertise in this task of managing the general process of change that is laid claim to by professional change agents.

A Body of Knowledge

Stemming from the view of change management as an area of professional practice, there arises yet a third definition of change management: the content or subject matter of change management. This consists chiefly of the models, methods and techniques, tools, skills and other forms of knowledge that go into making up any practice.

The content or subject matter of change management is drawn from psychology, sociology, business administration, economics, industrial engineering, systems engineering and the study of human and organizational behavior. For many practitioners, these component bodies of knowledge are linked and integrated by a set of concepts and principles known as General Systems Theory (GST). It is not clear whether this area of professional practice should be termed as a profession, a discipline, an art, a set of techniques or a technology. For now, suffice it to say that there is a large, reasonably cohesive, albeit somewhat eclectic, body of knowledge underlying the practice and on which most practitioners would agree—even if their application of it does exhibit a high degree of variance.

A Control Mechanism

For many years now, Information Systems groups have tried to rein in and otherwise ride herd on changes to systems and the applications that run on them. For the most part, this is referred to as "version control" and most people in the workplace are familiar with it. In recent years, systems people have begun to refer to this control mechanism as "change management." Moreover, similar control mechanisms exist in other areas. Chemical processing plants, for example, are required by OSHA to satisfy some exacting requirements in the course of making changes. These fall under the heading of Management of Change or MOC.

To recapitulate, there are at least four basic definitions of change management:

1. The *task of managing change* (from a reactive or a proactive posture)
2. An *area of professional practice* (with considerable variation in competency and skill levels among practitioners)
3. A *body of knowledge* (consisting of models, methods, techniques, and other tools)
4. A *control mechanism* (consisting of requirements, standards, processes and procedures).

Content and Process

Organizations are highly specialized systems and there are many different schemes for grouping and classifying them. Some are said to be in the retail business, others are in manufacturing, and still others confine their activities to distribution. Some are profit-oriented and some are not for profit. Some are in the public sector and some are in the private sector. Some are members of the financial services industry, which encompasses banking, insurance, and brokerage houses. Others belong to the automobile industry, where they can be classified as Original Equipment Manufacturers (OEM) or after-market providers. Some belong to the healthcare industry, as providers, as insureds, or as insurers. Many are regulated, some are not. Some face stiff competition, some do not. Some are foreign-owned and some are foreign-based. Some are corporations, some are partnerships, and some are sole proprietorships. Some are publicly held and some are privately held. Some have been around a long time and some are newcomers. Some have been built up over the years, while others have been pieced together through mergers and acquisitions. No two are exactly alike.

The preceding paragraph points out that the problems found in organizations, especially the change problems, have both a content and a process dimension. It is one thing, for instance, to introduce a new claims processing system in a functionally organized health insurer. It is quite another to introduce a similar system in a health insurer that is organized along product lines and market segments. It is yet a different thing altogether to introduce a system of equal size and significance in an educational establishment that relies on a matrix structure. The languages spoken differ. The values differ. The cultures differ. And, at a detailed level, the problems differ. However, the overall processes of change and change management remain pretty much the same, and it is this fundamental similarity of the change processes across organizations, industries, and structures that makes change management a task, a process, and an area of professional practice.

III. The Change Process

The Change Process as "Unfreezing, Changing and Refreezing"

The process of change has been characterized as having three basic stages: unfreezing, changing, and re-freezing. This view draws heavily on Kurt Lewin's adoption of the systems concept of homeostasis or dynamic stability.

What is useful about this framework is that it gives rise to thinking about a staged approach to changing things. Looking before you leap is usually sound practice.

What is not useful about this framework is that it does not allow for change efforts that begin with the organization in extremes, (i.e., already "unfrozen"), nor does it allow for organizations faced with the prospect of having to "hang loose" for extended periods of time (i.e., staying "unfrozen").

In other words, the beginning and ending point of the unfreeze-change-refreeze model is stability—which, for some people and some organizations, is a luxury. For others, internal stability spells disaster. A tortoise on the move can overtake even the fastest hare if that hare stands still.

The Change Process as Problem-Solving and Problem-Finding

A very useful framework for thinking about the change process is problem-solving. Managing change is seen as a matter of moving from one state to another, specifically from the problem state to the solved state. Diagnosis or problem analysis is generally acknowledged as essential. Goals are set and achieved at various levels and in various areas or functions. Ends and means are discussed and related to one another. Careful planning is accompanied by efforts to obtain buy-in, support and commitment. The net effect is a transition from one state to another in a planned, orderly fashion. This is the planned change model.

The word "problem" carries with it connotations that some people prefer to avoid. They choose instead to use the word "opportunity." For such people, a problem is seen as a bad situation, one that shouldn't have been allowed to happen in the first place, and for which someone is likely to be punished—if the guilty party (or a suitable scapegoat) can be identified. For the purposes of this paper, we will set aside any cultural or personal preferences regarding the use of "problem" or "opportunity." From a rational, analytical perspective, a problem is nothing more than a situation requiring action but in which the required action is not known. Hence, there is a requirement to search for a solution, a course of action that will lead to the solved state. This search activity is known as "problem solving."

From the preceding discussion, it follows that "problem finding" is the search for situations requiring action. Whether we choose to call these situations "problems" (because they are troublesome or spell bad news), or whether we choose to call them "opportunities" (either for reasons of political sensitivity or because the time is ripe to exploit a situation) is immaterial. In both cases, the practical matter is one of identifying and settling on a course of action that will bring about some desired and predetermined change in the situation.

The Change Problem

At the heart of change management lies the change problem, that is, some future state to be realized, some current state to be left behind, and some structured, organized process for getting from the one to the other. The change problem might be large or small in scope and scale, and it might focus on individuals or groups, on one or more divisions or departments, the entire organization, or one or on more aspects of the organization's environment.

At a conceptual level, the change problem is a matter of moving from one state (A) to another state (A'). Moving from A to A' is typically accomplished as a result of setting up and achieving three types of goals: *transform*, *reduce*, and *apply*. Transform goals are concerned with identifying differences between the two states. Reduce goals are concerned with determining ways of eliminating these differences. Apply goals are concerned with putting into play operators that actually effect the elimination of these differences (see Newell & Simon).

As the preceding 'goal types' suggest, the analysis of a change problem at various times will focus on defining the outcomes of the change effort, on identifying the changes necessary to produce these outcomes, and on finding and implementing ways and means of making the required changes. In simpler terms, the change problem can be treated as smaller problems having to do with the how, what, and why of change.

Change as a "How" Problem

The change problem is often expressed, at least initially, in the form of a "how" question. How do we get people to be more open, to assume more responsibility, to be more creative? How do we introduce self-managed teams in Department W? How do we change over from System X to System Y in Division Z? How do we move from a mainframe-centered computing environment to one that accommodates and integrates PCs? How do we get this organization to be more innovative, competitive, or productive? How do we raise more effective barriers to market entry by our competitors? How might we more tightly bind our suppliers to us? How do we reduce cycle times? In short, the initial formulation of a change problem is means-centered, with the goal state more or less implied. There is a reason why the initial statement of a problem is so often means-centered and we will touch on it later. For now, let's examine the other two ways in which the problem might be formulated—as "what" or as "why" questions.

Change as a "What" Problem

As was pointed out in the preceding section, to frame the change effort in the form of "how" questions is to focus the effort on means. Diagnosis is assumed or not performed at all. Consequently, the ends sought are not discussed. This might or might not be problematic. To focus on ends requires the posing of "what" questions. What are we trying to accomplish? What changes are necessary? What indicators will signal success? What standards apply? What measures of performance are we trying to affect?

Change as a "Why" Problem

Ends and means are relative notions, not absolutes; that is, something is an end or a means only in relation to something else. Thus, chains and networks of ends-means relationships often have to be traced out before one finds the "true" ends of a change effort. In this regard, "why" questions prove extremely useful.

Consider the following hypothetical dialogue with yourself as an illustration of tracing out ends-means relationships.

1. Why do people need to be more creative?
2. I'll tell you why! Because we have to change the way we do things and we need ideas about how to do that.
3. Why do we have to change the way we do things?
4. Because they cost too much and take too long.
5. Why do they cost too much?
6. Because we pay higher wages than any of our competitors.
7. Why do we pay higher wages than our competitors?

8. Because our productivity used to be higher, too, but now it's not.
9. Eureka! The true aim is to improve productivity!
10. No it isn't; keep going.
11. Why does productivity need to be improved?
12. To increase profits.
13. Why do profits need to be increased?
14. To improve earnings per share.
15. Why do earnings per share need to be improved?
16. To attract additional capital.
17. Why is additional capital needed?
18. We need to fund research aimed at developing the next generation of products.
19. Why do we need a new generation of products?
20. Because our competitors are rolling them out faster than we are and gobbling up marketshare.
21. Oh, so that's why we need to reduce cycle times.
22. Hmm. Why do things take so long?

To ask "why" questions is to get at the ultimate purposes of functions and to open the door to finding new and better ways of performing them. Why do we do what we do? Why do we do it the way we do it? Asking "why" questions also gets at the ultimate purposes of people, but that's a different matter altogether, a "political" matter, and one we'll not go into in this paper.

The Approach taken to Change Management Mirrors Management's Mindset

The emphasis placed on the three types of questions just mentioned reflects the management mindset, that is, the tendency to think along certain lines depending on where one is situated in the organization. A person's placement in the organization typically defines the scope and scale of the kinds of changes with which he or she will become involved, and the nature of the changes with which he or she will be concerned. Thus, the systems people tend to be concerned with technology and technological developments, the marketing people with customer needs and competitive activity, the legal people with legislative and other regulatory actions, and so on. Also, the higher up a person is in the hierarchy, the longer the time perspective and the wider the range of issues with which he or she must be concerned.

For the most part, changes and the change problems they present are problems of adaptation, that is, they require of the organization only that it adjust to an ever-changing set of circumstances. But, either as a result of continued, cumulative compounding of adaptive maneuvers that were nothing more than band-aids, or as the result of sudden changes so significant as to call for a redefinition of the organization, there are times when the changes that must be made are deep and far-reaching. At such times, the design of the organization itself is called into question.

Organizations frequently survive the people who establish them. AT&T and IBM are two ready examples. At some point it becomes the case that such organizations have been designed by one group of people but are being operated or run by another. (It has been said of the United States Navy, for instance, that "It was designed by geniuses to be run by idiots.") Successful organizations resolve early on the issue of structure, that is, the definition, placement and coordination of functions and people. Other people then have to live with this design and, because the ends have already been established, these other people are chiefly concerned with means. This is why so many problem-solving efforts start out focused on means.

Some organizations are designed to buffer their core operations from turbulence in the environment. In such organizations all units fit into one of three categories: core, buffer, and perimeter.

In core units (e.g., systems and operations), coordination is achieved through standardization, that is, adherence to routine. In buffer units (e.g., upper management and staff or support functions), coordination is achieved through planning.

In perimeter units (e.g., sales, marketing, and customer service), coordination is achieved through mutual adjustment (see Thompson).

People in core units, buffered as they are from environmental turbulence and with a history of relying on adherence to standardized procedures, typically focus on "how" questions. People in buffer units, responsible for performance through planning, often ask "what" questions. People in the perimeter units are as accountable as anyone else for performance and frequently for performance of a financial nature. They can be heard asking "what" and "how" questions. "Why" questions are generally asked by people with no direct responsibility for day-to-day operations or results. In the group most will able to take this long-term or strategic view, that is, cadre of senior executives responsible for the continued well-being of the firm: top management. If the design of the firm is to be called into question or, more significantly, if it is actually to be altered, these are the people who must make the decision to do so.

Finally, when organizational redefinition and redesign prove necessary, all people in all units must concern themselves with all three sets of questions or the changes made will not stand the test of time.

To summarize: Problems may be formulated in terms of "how," "what" and "why" questions. What formulation is used depends on where in the organization the person posing the question or formulating the problem is situated, and where the organization is situated in its own life cycle.

- "How" questions tend to cluster in core units.
- "What" questions tend to cluster in buffer units.
- People in perimeter units tend to ask "what" and "how" questions.
- "Why" questions are typically the responsibility of top management.

In turbulent times, everyone must be concerned with everything.

IV. Skills and Strategies

Managing the kinds of changes encountered by and instituted within organizations requires an unusually broad and finely honed set of skills, chief among which are the following.

Political Skills

Organizations are first and foremost social systems. Without people there can be no organization. Lose sight of this fact and any would-be change agent will likely lose his or her head. Organizations are hotly and intensely political. And, as one wag pointed out, the lower the stakes, the more intense the politics. Change agents dare not join in this game but they had better understanding. This is one area where you must make your own judgments and keep your own counsel; no one can do it for you.

Analytical Skills

Make no mistake about it, those who would be change agents had better be very good at something, and that something better be analyzed. Guessing won't do. Insight is nice, even useful, and sometimes shines with brilliance, but it is darned difficult to sell and almost impossible to defend. A lucid, rational, well-argued analysis can be ignored and even suppressed, but not successfully contested and, in most cases, will carry the day. If not, then the political issues haven't been adequately addressed.

Two particular sets of skills are very important here: (1) workflow operations or systems analysis, and (2) financial analysis. Change agents must learn to take apart and reassemble operations and systems in novel ways, and then determine the financial and political impacts of what they have done. Conversely, they must be able to start with some financial measure or indicator or goal, and make their way quickly to those operations and systems that, if reconfigured a certain way, would have the desired financial impact. Those who master these two techniques have learned a trade that will be in demand for the foreseeable future. (This trade, by the way, has a name. It is called "Solution Engineering.")

People Skills

As stated earlier, people are the *sine qua non* of organization. Moreover, they come characterized by all manner of sizes, shapes, colors, intelligence and ability levels, gender, sexual preferences, national origins, first and second languages, religious beliefs, attitudes toward life and work, personalities, and priorities—and these are just a few of the dimensions along which people vary. We have to deal with them all.

The skills most needed in this area are those that typically fall under the heading of communication or interpersonal skills. To be effective, we must be able to listen and listen actively, to restate, to reflect, to clarify without interrogating, to draw out the speaker, to lead or channel a discussion, to plant ideas, and to develop them. All these and more are needed. Not all of us will have to learn Russian, French, or Spanish, but most of us will have to learn to speak Systems, Marketing, Manufacturing, Finance, Personnel, Legal, and a host of other organizational dialects. More important, we have to learn to see things through the eyes of these other inhabitants of the organizational world. A situation viewed from a marketing frame of reference is an entirely different situation when seen through the eyes of a systems person. Part of the job of a change agent is to reconcile and resolve the conflict between and among disparate (and sometimes desperate) points of view. Charm is great if you have it. Courtesy is even better. A well-paid compliment can buy gratitude. A sincere "Thank you" can earn respect.

System Skills

There's much more to this than learning about computers, although most people employed in today's world of work do need to learn about computer-based information systems. For now, let's just say that a system is an arrangement of resources and routines intended to produce specified results. To organize is to arrange. A system reflects organization and, by the same token, an organization is a system.

A word processing equipment is operated from a system. So do computers and the larger information processing systems in which computers are so often embedded. These are generally known as "hard" systems. There are "soft" systems as well: compensation systems, appraisal systems, promotion systems, and reward and incentive systems.

There are two sets of systems skills to be mastered. Many people associate the first set with computers and it is exemplified by "systems analysis." This set of skills, by the way, actually predates the digital computer and is known elsewhere (particularly in the United States Air Force and the aerospace industry) as "systems engineering." For the most part, the kind of system with which this skill set concerns itself is a "closed" system which, for now, we can say is simply a mechanistic or contrived system with no purpose of its own and incapable of altering its own structure. In other words, it cannot learn and it cannot change of its own volition. The second set of system skills associated with a body of knowledge is generally referred to as General Systems Theory (GST) and it deals with people, organizations, industries, economies, and even nations as socio-technical systems—as "open," purposive systems, carrying out transactions with other systems and bent on survival, continuance, prosperity, dominance, plus a host of other goals and objectives.

Business Skills

Simply put, you'd better understand how a business works. In particular, you'd better understand how the business in which and on which you're working works. This entails an understanding of money—where it comes from, where it goes, how to get it, and how to keep it. It also calls into play knowledge of markets and marketing, products and product development, customers, sales, selling, buying, hiring, firing, EEO, AAP, and just about anything else you might think of.

Four Basic Change Management Strategies

(see the Bennis, Benne & Chin reference)

Note: The fourth and last strategy in the table below is not one of those presented by Bennis, Benne and Chin. It is instead the product of the author's own

Strategy	Description
Empirical-Rational	People are rational and will follow their self-interest—once it is revealed to them. Change is based on the communication of information and the proffering of incentives.
Normative-Reeducative	People are social beings and will adhere to cultural norms and values. Change is based on redefining and reinterpreting existing norms and values, and developing commitments to new ones.
Power-Coercive	People are basically compliant and will generally do what they are told or can be made to do. Change is based on the exercise of authority and the imposition of sanctions.
Environmental-Adaptive	People oppose loss and disruption but they adapt readily to new circumstances. Change is based on building a new organization and gradually transferring people from the old one to the new one.

experiences during some 30 years of making and adapting to changes in, to, and on behalf of organizations. An excellent example of this strategy in action, albeit on an accelerated basis, is provided by the way in which Rupert Murdoch handled the printers of Fleet Street. He quietly set about building an entirely new operation in Wapping, some distance away. When it was ready to be occupied and made operational, he informed the employees in the old operation that he had some bad news and some good news. The bad news was that the existing operation was being shut down. Everyone was being fired. The good news was that the new operation had jobs for all of them—but on very different terms. That there are also elements of the Empircal-Rational and Power-Coercive strategies at play here serves to make the point that successful change efforts inevitably involve some mix of these basic change strategies, a point that is elaborated on below.

Factors in Selecting a Change Strategy

Generally speaking, there is no single change strategy. You can adopt a general or what is called a "grand strategy" but, for any given initiative, you are best served by some mix of strategies.

Which of the preceding strategies to use in your mix of strategies is a decision affected by a number of factors. Some of the more important ones follow.

- ***Degree of Resistance.*** Strong resistance argues for a coupling of Power-Coercive and Environmental-Adaptive strategies. Weak resistance or concurrence argues for a combination of Empirical-Rational and Normative-Reeducative strategies.
- ***Target Population.*** Large populations argue for a mix of all four strategies, something for everyone, so to speak.
- ***The Stakes.*** High stakes argue for a mix of all four strategies. When the stakes are high, nothing can be left to chance.
- ***The Time Frame.*** Short time frames argue for a Power-Coercive strategy. Longer time frames argue for a mix of Empirical-Rational, Normative-Reeducative, and Environmental-Adaptive strategies.

- *Expertise.* Having available adequate expertise at making change argues for some mix of the strategies outlined above. Not having it available argues for reliance on the power-coercive strategy.
- *Dependency.* This is a classic double-edged sword. If the organization is dependent on its people, management's ability to command or demand is limited. Conversely, if people are dependent upon the organization, their ability to oppose or resist is limited. (Mutual dependency almost always signals a requirement for some level of negotiation.)

One More Time: How do you Manage Change?

The honest answer is that you manage it pretty much the same way you'd manage anything else of a turbulent, messy, chaotic nature, that is, you don't really manage it, you grapple with it. It's more a matter of leadership ability than management skill.

1. The first thing to do is jump in. You can't do anything about it from the outside.
2. A clear sense of mission or purpose is essential. The simpler the mission statement the better. "Kick ass in the marketplace" is a whole lot more meaningful than "Respond to market needs with a range of products and services that have been carefully designed and developed to compare so favorably in our customers' eyes with the products and services offered by our competitors that the majority of buying decisions will be made in our favor."
3. Build a team. "Lone wolves" have their uses, but managing change isn't one of them. On the other hand, the right kind of lone wolf makes an excellent temporary team leader.
4. Maintain a flat organizational team structure and rely on minimal and informal reporting requirements.
5. Pick people with relevant skills and high energy levels. You'll need both.
6. Toss out the rulebook. Change, by definition, calls for a configured response, not adherence to prefigured routines.

7. Shift to an action-feedback model. Plan and act in short intervals. Do your analysis on the fly. No lengthy up-front studies, please. Remember the hare and the tortoise.

8. Set flexible priorities. You must have the ability to drop what you're doing and tend to something more important.

9. Treat everything as a temporary measure. Don't "lock in" until the last minute, and then insist on the right to change your mind.

10. Ask for volunteers. You'll be surprised at who shows up. You'll be pleasantly surprised by what they can do.

11. Find a good "straw boss" or team leader and stay out of his or her way.

12. Give the team members whatever they ask for—except authority. They'll generally ask only for what they really need in the way of resources. If they start asking for authority, that's a signal they're headed toward some kind of power-based confrontation and that spells trouble. Nip it in the bud!

13. Concentrate dispersed knowledge. Start and maintain an issues logbook. Let anyone go anywhere and talk to anyone about anything. Keep the communications barriers low, widely spaced, and easily hurdled. Initially, if things look chaotic, relax—they are.

Remember, the task of change management is to bring order to a messy situation, not pretend that it's already well organized and disciplined.

(Fred Nickols, Senior Consultant, Distance Consulting. He can be reached at nickols@att.net).

Selected Sources

1. Allen Newell and Herbert A. Simon. *Human Problem Solving*. Prentice-Hall, Englewood Cliffs: 1972.

2. James D. Thompson. *Organizations in Action*. McGraw-Hill, New York: 1967.

3. Warren G. Bennis, Kenneth D. Benne, and Robert Chin (Eds.). *The Planning of Change* (2nd Edition). Holt, Rinehart and Winston, New York: 1969.

11

Conflict During the Changing Process: Human Resources' Role in 2002 and in 2010

A J du Plessis

In the absence of conflict regulation mechanisms or insufficient mechanisms to countervail the influence of aggravators, conflict will escalate in size and intensity. Conflict ensues where parties have high aspirations or unfulfilled perceptions. Aggravating factors include past achievements and unwanted labour legislation. During an organisation's phase of change, traditional norms are weakened giving rise to aspirations and disputes that result in conflict. Conflict needs to be managed. Change is a big challenge facing managers now and more so in the future.

Empirical research was undertaken in 2002, whereby 1,640 questionnaires were distributed and 207 useable responses were received from registered personnel practitioners in South Africa. The results, amongst others, revealed the conflict and change aspects in organisations in terms of the current position (2002) and what would be required in 2010.

Conflict plays an important role globally in managing organisations. It is dependent on how change is approached and managed.

Introduction

One must bear in mind that working conditions in certain sectors differ completely from other economic sectors, depending on size, products, methods and so forth. The recommendations of the Wiehahn commission in 1979 brought about an immense change in the South African labour force. One of the most important recommendations was that blacks could legally become union members. Since labour law became more common for black labourers in South Africa (SA) in 1980, the average expenditure has shown a downward trend annually. Employment relations also deteriorated because SA is losing between 2 and 3 million working days per annum due to strikes (De Lange, 1999:4).

Although some labour laws were promulgated and enforced since 1995, a large number of amendments were promulgated thereafter. With new amendments and new legislation to be promulgated in the near future, the backlog in employment relations and knowledge of labour legislation is still very evident.

The rapid commencement of labour laws forced employers to either attend courses in labour legislation or to get acquainted with the relevant acts by means of studying it. The average employer, thereby leaving them ignorant and increasing the backlog took neither of the two options.

Until the early 1990s farm workers were excluded from legislation regulating working conditions. Employment relations between farmers and farm labourers were determined mainly by common law. The industries, on the other hand, were subjected to different employment relation acts that had to be used as guidelines during changing processes and negotiations.

Labour law and trade union activities have become acknowledged forces in the agricultural sector that contributed to the disappearance of the traditional relationship between the farmers and their employees.

There are several unions who are very active in the agricultural sector in the Brits district. The South African Agricultural, Plantation and Allied Workers Union (SAAPAWU), Food and Allied Workers Union (FAWU) and General Industrial Workers Union of South Africa (GIWUSA) are some of the most active unions on the farms.

Another problem is that, as in any other industry or society, there are some farmers who do not abide by the rules of the game. This can result in a strike, protected or unprotected. If it happens at a critical period, such as during planting or harvesting time, it may have catastrophic results. Therefore, there must be labour legislation to regulate the relation between the farmers and their employees.

The problem lies therefore in the dispute resolution mechanisms as prescribed in the different labour Acts, on the one hand, and in the ignorance and users' unfriendly environment created by these Acts for the modern farmer as the employer, on the other.

Farmers and farm labourers are co-workers of the land, partners on the farm and neighbours in the dwelling place. In 1990 Du Toit (Weiss, 1990:52-53) was already of the opinion that politicians must not damage the good work relations between the employer and their employees for political reasons. They must also not use labour laws against farmers to gain a few extra votes, because the damage thereby caused will be irreparable. Both groups will then be losers and no win-win situation will ensue.

The question can therefore be asked: in what way can the users' unfriendly labour laws be made more users' friendly for the agricultural sector and the modern farmer and how can they implement these laws without causing labour unrest on their farms?

Labour legislation and union activities are a reality in the agricultural sector. It is therefore necessary that the farmers, like their peers in the industrial sector, must get themselves acquainted with the relevant labour Acts, unless they want to find themselves in a dilemma that may cost them thousands of Rands.

In 1999 unemployment increased by 420,000 in SA. Over the past 10 years, more than a million jobs were lost due to downsizing, illegal strikes, etc. By 2000 one out of 20 jobs was filled with a casual worker and this has increased to one out of 12 jobs. This situation is mainly caused by employers who are unsure of the implications of the new amendments, new labour legislation, strikes, threatening labour unrest concomitant with conflict and HIV/AIDS (De Lange, 2000:2).

Theoretical Perspective

Cultural lag is one of the most important issues to be taken into consideration in the process of social change. The actions and reactions of the people in social structures where changes take place, play a tremendous role in that society which has a definite influence on organisations.

Cultural diversity is an empirical premise in SA, also known as ethnicity. Tradition and culture cannot be separated from each other, tradition is the transfer of culture from one generation to the next. Booysen (cited in Nel *et al.,* 2004) is of the opinion that there is a definite lack of cultural awareness in South Africa and that only 24% of the companies have implemented diversity management programmes. He states further that new recruits are expected to assimilate into the organisational culture. One can therefore comprehend that there will be resistance, taking into consideration the recent changes in the South African labour legislation. Although acculturation and assimilation are taking place, neither whites nor Blacks will waive their tradition or culture and the resistance to change is even more severe, sometimes resulting in violence.

Diversity management involves a fundamental change in attitude and behaviour and is seen by more and more organisations as a competitive advantage as well as a strategic necessity to survive in a globally diverse environment. Affirmative action and employment equity are legally enforced in South African organisations to which they might willingly or unwillingly submit. The South African government employed strategies such as affirmative action, employment equity and diversity management to remove all forms of apartheid. Resistance to implement the said legislation lead to conflict not only between employers and government officials, but also to conflict in the workplace.

Jones and George (2003) state very clearly that organisational conflict is an *inevitable part* of organisational life because the goals of different stakeholders are often *incompatible*. Conflict also exists where departments or divisions compete for resources during the changing process. They state further that managers must develop the skills necessary to manage conflict effectively, because it has important implications for performance.

One of the roles of the HR manager, as seen by Nel *et al.* (2004) for the future, is to enhance shareholder value by improving the *communication* and *integrity* of an organisation. They should have multiple channels of communication and should be informed and aligned with the organisation's goals and objectives.

Conflicting *pressures* in the labour market made the role of HR more important and changes in the diverse business environment are affecting nearly every aspect of managing businesses or organisations (Adler, 2000). Therefore conflict will be present in these organisations.

Vago (1999) refers to *social change as change* that rapidly appears in any society. One must be aware of the components of change which is essential to explain and understand what is changing, on what level, how rapidly and in what direction is it that change takes place. It is also the process of unplanned or planned, qualitative or quantitative adaptation in a social phenomenon that can be analysed in terms of identity, level, time, extent and rapidity.

Swingewood (2000) is of the opinion that social change in the modern society, smashes the value system and results in *tension* or *stress,* which results again in disequilibrium and instability.

Change results in conflict. Employee/industrial relations, advance issue identification, job creation/downsizing, equal opportunities, remuneration, employee participation and manager/employee communication are but a few examples where *change can result in conflict* and the results will be referred to in this article. Conflict is therefore a phenomenon present in any organisation, society and at all levels.

Anstey (1999) refers to Thomas (1976) who distinguished between two conflict models, both of which focus on the conflict-handling behaviour of the parties involved. He refers to the *structural model* and the *process model.* The *structural model* attempts to understand conflict phenomenon by studying how underlining conditions shape events, which are relatively fixed or slow changing and are seen as structural in nature. The *process model* focuses on the internal dynamics of conflict episodes studying events and their effects on succeeding events in conflict episodes. Both these models and tactics are necessary for effective managing of conflict and fit in the larger view of conflict structure and process. A full understanding and managing of conflict must therefore give attention to both structural and process aspects of a working relationship in an organisation and how they influence each other.

Deutsch (cited in Anstey, 1999) distinguishes between *destructive* and *constructive* conflict. It was observed that the former has a tendency to expand and escalate as the parties assume increasingly competitive stances, commit their resources to the conflict process and misjudge the situation on a variety of levels.

Conflict Theories

Conflict theorists such as those of Mills, Pierce, James, Dewey and others have made an enormous contribution to conflict studies with their theories. The theories of Ralf Dahrendorf and Karl Marx have similarities with the implementation of the present labour legislation, especially in the agricultural sector and the conflict it generates there.

Conflict Theory of R Dahrendorf

This theory concentrates on the larger social structure. The identification of the different power roles is mainly in the society, whereas Dahrendorf is critical about the identification of conflict on the *individual* level in an organisation (Dahrendorf, 1990).

Power is coupled to position, which always implies subordination and control. Power is not a constant and is vested in position. The groups with power will *strive* after their *own interests* and the groups without power will *look* after their *own interests* (Kinloch, 1977).

He is also interested in the determinants of active conflict and the manner in which social institutional groups with conflicting concerns produce. A further point of interest for Dahrendorf was the circumstances in which the groups will begin to organise and become active. These points can be compared with the present situation in the agricultural sector where trade unions are getting more and more active and labour laws have to be implemented. It makes Dahrendorf's theory therefore even more applicable on this study.

The same theorist also concentrates on macro-social structures. In analyzing conflict, the identification of the different power rolls in society is of dire importance (Dahrendorf, 1990).

Dahrendorf is also of the opinion that *inequity* and *conflicting interests* will result in conflict. Authority is coupled to power, which, in turn, is coupled to a specific roll or position and is supported by sanctions. Persons, who have the authority, give instructions to those who do not have any power, thereby forcing them to carry out the instructions. The hierarchy on the farm is typical of this and is a breeding-ground for conflict.

In this article, the respondents' views on Equal Employment Opportunities will be discussed.

Conflict Theory of Karl Marx

There is a definite resemblance between the conflict models of Dahrendorf and Marx, which relate to the conflict in the South African organisations. Marx regarded the labourers as the proletariat and the capitalists as the bourgeoisie. Conflict will always exist and will have to be managed. Marx is of the opinion that *social change* is to be found in all organisations and societies; they all have conflict based on each person in a certain position of *power* or *authority*. Such a person can force the subordinates to carry out the instructions. There is also conflict between *interests of people* (Tester, 1993). The respondents' opinions in this regard will be discussed in this article.

The capitalistic economy generates conflict that can result in the disequilibrium of the system and its total collapse. The interaction in the society's social activity incorporates positive changes to eliminate the disadvantageous changes. Marx states that the capitalistic system will vanish. A new system will emerge where no exploiting of one class by another class will take place. Marx sees that the proletariat will take the initiative to diminish the capitalistic system and form a new socialistic system where no exploitation will take place and everybody will share in the wealth (Tester, 1993).

Marx's sympathy lies with the underdogs of the masses. Only a revolution can free the masses from exploitation, subordination and alienation. According to him, only a *revolution* (conflict) can free the masses from exploitation, subordination and alienation. He is also of the opinion that *conflict is the dominant process* in society and in an organisation (Marx, 1984), and that the only solution was social ownership of the means of production.

Pettigrew *et al.* (2003) describe four theoretical types in a changing organisation. The first type is *conservative* where the organisation avoids change but uses an exploitive learning style to refine existing practices. The second one is *adaptive* where existing frames of reference focus on incremental change. The next type is *reformative.* Organisations search for inspiration and opportunities outside the organisation by learning from others and the last type is *generative.* In this type organisations are genuinely searching for renewal from internal resources (their own employees). The importance of employee participation, communication and advance issue identification as well as the application of the above four types will be highlighted in this article.

Problem Statement

Labour laws have an immeasurable influence on organisations. The problem lies therefore in the dispute resolution mechanisms as prescribed in the different labour statutes, on the one hand, and in the ignorance and users' unfriendly environment created by these acts for the modern employer, on the other.

There are some employers who do not abide by the rules of the game. This can result in a strike, protected or unprotected with catastrophic results and *conflict.* Therefore there must be labour legislation to regulate the employment relations between the employer and the employees. The question can therefore be asked: in what way can the labour laws be made more user friendly for the 2010 organisations, employers and HR practitioners. How can the necessary changes be made *without causing conflict* and labour unrest in South Africa's diverse labour force? Some *solutions* are identified and presented in this article.

Goal and Objectives of this Study

It is of the utmost importance that HR practitioners, organisations, businesses and managers in South Africa know all about the future changes, to keep and remain globally competitive. In 2002, empirical research was undertaken in South Africa to identify possible answers and solutions to the said changes in organisations, the possibility of conflict during these changing periods, and the role of HR managers in 2010, which is the main objective of this paper.

Methodology

In 1994 a questionnaire was jointly compiled in New Zealand and Australia and used by the Human Resource Institute of New Zealand for a survey to identify the future role and quality of human resources in those countries for the year 2000 (IPMNZ, 1994). The same questionnaire was modified and refined and used again in 2000 to determine a future perspective on human resources in 2010 in New Zealand.

The same questionnaire was used with permission after a minor modification for an identical survey in SA in 2002. It meant that one section concerning human resources information systems of the questionnaire was not used in an attempt to shorten it to increase the response rate in SA. The topics covered in the questionnaire included human resource goals, roles and activities, human resources staffing and implications of changes in the business environment. The final section of the questionnaire sought to obtain demographic information from respondents. The survey was executed in the last quarter of 2002.

Various sections of the SA questionnaire were used to compile the results on conflict, culture, employee/industrial relations, equal opportunity, employee participation in decision-making and change based on the responses with regard to the view of HR practitioners in SA.

Empirical Results

From the replies of the respondents, 67.99% are HR practitioners (officer to director). Therefore, their opinions are very valuable and reliable. It is significant that 83.2% of the respondents are working in organisations with 100 or more employees. For the purpose, of this paper only respondents who replied in the *highly satisfied* group for 2002 and the *top priority* group for 2010 were used and this demarcation will be used to interpret and analyse the results.

It was necessary to do this empirical study to verify certain aspects and problems encountered in the organisations in 2002 and it is anticipated for 2010 in the HR field in SA.

Factual information was obtained through this empirical study and questionnaires were handed out. The completed questionnaires received from respondents were subjected to verification for accuracy before responses were collated and treated statistically using the SPSS program. The statistical analysis was used to obtain responses in terms of the various questions *vis-à-vis* organisation size, occupation of respondent and so on. Furthermore, a comparison of response of the respondents for 2002 and 2010 was also recorded.

Results were recorded to reflect the percentage of all respondents selecting a particular alternative for a particular organisation size or occupation in a particular occupation. Note these must be taken that due to the conference limitation imposed for paper length, only the afore-mentioned possibilities are given. The responses were compared in terms of the 2002 result and the envisaged importance in 2010.

The anticipated changes for 2010, as opposed to the current situation in 2002, are reflected in this paper. The respondents' views of the role of HR during the changing process in an organisation, where conflict will be present and the possible managing thereof, are reflected in the results. Only the six main areas in Table 1 that can cause conflict, as pointed out by the *highly satisfied* and the *top priority group,* are addressed.

Table 1: Respondents' Views on Six Related Roles of HR

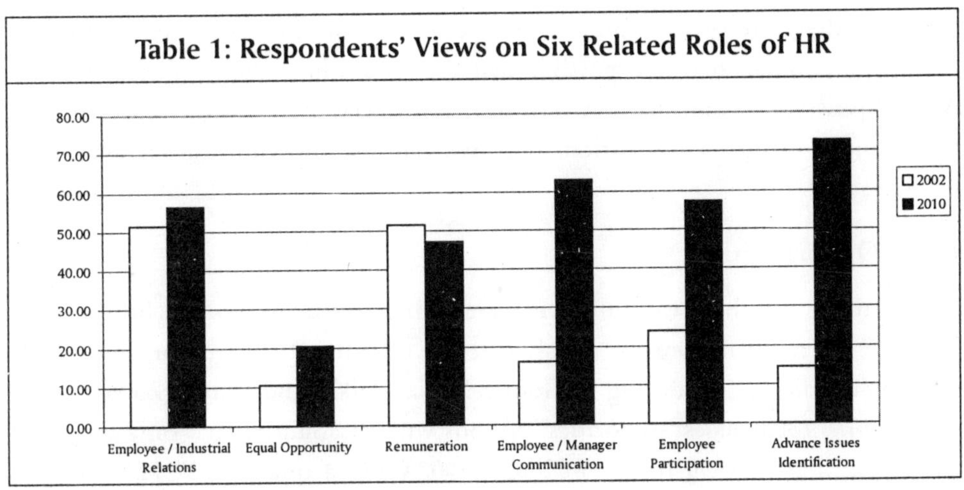

Analysis of the Results

Employee/Industrial relations

Jones and George (2003) are of the opinion that another challenge for managers is to recognise the need to treat human resources in a fair and equitable manner; the diverse workforce present new challenges for managers. Managers must establish procedures and practices that are legal and fair with no discrimination. Nel *et al.* (2004) describe an employment relations policy and advice organisations to have such a policy. It is a declaration of the fundamental values, beliefs, standards and philosophies that underlie the behaviour of the organisation. They say further that such a policy should cover the development of mutual trust and cooperation; prevention of problems and disputes through procedures acceptable to the workforce. Certain issues need to be spelled out precisely such as dispute-handling procedures, collective bargaining, strike-handling and so forth.

There is almost no difference (5.92%) in the 2002 view of the respondents regarding *employee/industrial relations* and the 2010 view (54.19% in 2002 and 60.11% in 2010). The main reason may be that the respondents regard their relationships with the employees currently as excellent with a policy in place and that they would like to keep it that way in future. Alternatively, not many respondents regarded it as a top priority because they were not experiencing any labour unrest or *conflict* at the time when they were completing the questionnaire and were therefore of the opinion that their relationships with their employees were good enough. It is also possible that they could have their policies in place. A third possibility could be that they have good relations with the representative trade unions in their organisations with policies and procedures all in place and working well.

Equal Opportunities

Determining whether two employees are doing the same job can be difficult. Jobs are the same if they are equal in terms of skill, effort, responsibility and working conditions, according to Gomez-Mejia, Balkin and Cardy (2004). *Equal opportunities* for females, minorities, persons with disabilities, etc., only increased in priority by 10.89% from 2002 to 2010. Only a quarter (27.72%) of the respondents regarded it as top priority in 2010, which is very low for a country such as SA that experienced major political changes recently. One could expect that equal opportunities could be a dispute point *resulting in conflict.* A large volume of labour legislation was promulgated and just as many amendments were implemented. It can be deduced that the respondents regarded equal opportunities so low because the employee participation in the workplaces is so high. The response rate was the lowest for this point, which is a clear indication that respondents *do not regard equal opportunities as a dispute that can result in conflict during the changing process.* This can then be seen as *a solution to prevent conflict* in an organisation: to have employees informed, committed and participating in management. Tinarelli (2000) is, however, of the opinion that the Employment Equity Act (no.55 of 1998) does have *the potential of creating conflict* because of the high costs of institutional and cultural changes and the lack of resources to ensure proper compliance. The *solution* for this issue can be, if employers implement equal opportunities gradually, to spread or even out their costs.

Remuneration

Dessler, Griffiths and Lloyd-Walker (2004) describe remuneration as money paid for work done. Total remuneration, according to them, includes pay and all other forms of rewards, both monetary and non-monetary, that employees receive arising from their employment. This can be broken up into two main components: The direct financial payments in the form of wages, incentives, bonuses, etc; and the indirect payments in the form of financial benefits such as holidays, subsidised parking, childcare, i.e., items that cannot easily be exchanged for money. In this article we will regard *remuneration*, therefore, as *total remuneration.*

Although 53.23% of the respondents rated *remuneration* as highly satisfied in 2002, there was a *decrease in priority* of 4.83% to 48.40% anticipated to 2010. The result is surprising since it is expected that remuneration will become increasingly important for employees as the demands for higher wages continue to escalate. Strikes are taking place and millions of working hours were lost over the years for the so-called "living wage". It can be deduced that the respondents foresee remuneration as less important because the workforce is already receiving monetary and non-monetary rewards as total remuneration. A possibility is also that they will rather negotiate for more and better benefits such as better medical schemes or better superannuation funds, as part of their total remuneration. It can therefore be said that *negotiations can prevent conflict.* Alternatively the respondents ruled remuneration out as a factor for conflict as they regarded their workforces highly satisfied with their current remuneration and also future remuneration.

Employee and Manager Communications

Communication starts with a sender encoding a message in words, numbers or digital symbols to the receiver who has to decode the message and understand its true meaning. If the message is filled with technical jargon that makes it difficult to decode, the receiver may misinterpret the sender's motives for sending the message or the message lends itself to multiple interpretations. Therefore, important communication should include opportunities for feedback from the receiver to minimise misinterpretations. This is called two-way communications because interaction is allowed, according to Gomez-Mejia *et al.* (2004). Noise is another serious disrupter of communication that must be taken into consideration during effective communication.

A total of 70.26% of the respondents admitted that *employee and manager communications* would be a high priority in 2010. Only 23.65% of the respondents were highly satisfied with the situation in 2002. This is an enormous increase of 46.61%. It can be deduced that past experiences of HR practitioners (respondents) confirm the importance of good communication channels in an organisation. Past experiences could include conflict that resulted from poor communication or violence/disputes that could have been prevented if there were proper communication channels. Therefore it can be said that the respondents want to *prevent future conflict* by having *good and effective communication* between the employees and management.

Employee Participation

Employee participation in decision-making can take many forms. De Cieri *et al.* (2003) point out that employees may serve on taskforces charged with recommending and designing a pay programme and the communication thereof to employees. This practice is actually rare. More often one will find employee participation in policy-making and assisting management in the implementation thereof but the line manager is normally responsible for making the policies work. A more participative work environment through team-building and joint effort has also effected the structures as organisations seek to develop congruence with a more collaborative workculture. It can be said then that organisations do want employee participation with certain issues and that can be the reason why a substantial number (61.78%) of the respondents see *employee participation* as being important in managing and implementation of changes in an organisation. It can be deduced that the respondents (33.83%) are of the opinion that in 2002 employee participation and empowerment were not so important in an organisation, but because of the anticipated changes in the near future, 27.95% more respondents indicated that employee participation would be more important in 2010. It was pointed out above that employers make use of employees to develop and help with the implementation of these changed policies and procedures. Therefore *employee participation is yet another solution in combating conflict.* The employment relations legislation will undoubtedly contribute to the *managing of conflict* in any organisation because of the guidelines in the Code of Good Practice as envisaged in the Labour Relations Act of 1995 as amended.

Advance Issue Identification

A total of 84.92% of the respondents admitted that *advance issue identification* would be very important in 2010. Only 20.20% of the respondents agreed that it is not feasible for employees, including line management, to be excluded in strategic planning. It is very clear that the respondents have a problem being excluded from strategic planning and that they see themselves more and more as part and parcel of the strategic team. Cascio and Aguinis (2005) support the responses of the respondents by saying that strategies are the means that organisations use to compete through innovation, quality, speed or cost leadership. They also see planning as the heart of management for it helps managers to reduce the uncertainty of the future and thereby do a better job of coping with the future challenges. They are also of the opinion that effective planning leads to success. Successful organisations, through planning, define their objectives and goals and thus provide direction for employees resulting in less conflict. Each and every employee should be well informed in advance of the goals and objectives of the organisation. This can only enhance sound labour relations and *prevent conflict.*

Conclusions

Organisations must take serious note of the most recent labour laws and amendments that came into effect and these laws are to be implemented without any conflict during the changing process. Labour legislation is enforced on employers and more recently on farmers and their resistance to change their practices and procedures can create conflict. Employers need to realise that they, as managers, have to implement new labour laws and amendments. If they do not become acquainted with the labour laws, they can find themselves in an unbearable situation. Employers must take note that, should they contravene by deviation or negligence, it could mean that they are acting procedurally and substantially unfair, which, over time, could have disastrous financial implications.

Burton (2003) explains that employees in the SA workforce are faced with continual and rapid change, economic uncertainty, unrealised expectations and a general feeling of disempowerment, which could be the breeding-ground for conflict.

The problem appears to be in the dispute resolution mechanisms as prescribed in the different labour Acts, on the one hand, and in the ignorance and users' unfriendly environment created by labour legislation for the modern employer in 2010, on the other.

Labour legislation and union activities remain a reality in all organisations in South Afrtica. Sources of conflict behaviour and the perceptions and feelings of the parties involved, require serious attention.

The role of the HR manager of 2010 will be to organise the resources to make them strategic. The future structuring of jobs to ensure the dispersal of key skills among employees and the design of systems by which to capture and routinise otherwise tacit and private information, are central to embedding such human resources to the advantages of the organisation. In the so-called knowledge age, HR has become more important and the challenge is to manage this knowledge in forcing, strategising and organising closer together to combat conflict.

It is evident that change and conflict need to be managed and that this reality should apply to all employers. The conciliation mechanisms as envisaged in the LRA (1995, as amended) are to be followed and the Code of Good Practice is to be kept in mind at all times. To survive, visionary leadership is required.

It is well advised for employers to have a written contract of service with each of their employees. A disciplinary code and procedure, a grievance procedure and relevant policies must also be implemented as soon as possible where it does not exist in a business. If these basic functions are in place, there can be no doubt what the agreement was all about and the risk of conflict is minimised. Moreover, an employer must also have regular meetings with the employees where their problems can be addressed, as this opens channels for better communication. The employers must also ensure that they act procedurally and substantively fair at all times to prevent the possibility of conflict. The capitalistic economy generates conflict that can result in the disequilibrium of the system and also its total collapse.

The interaction in the society's social activity incorporates positive changes to eliminate the disadvantageous changes. Marx states that the capitalistic system will vanish. A new system will emerge where no exploiting of one class by another class will take place. Marx sees that the proletariat will take the initiative to diminish the capitalistic system and form a new socialistic system where no exploitation will take place and everybody will share in the wealth (Tester, 1993:108-109). Marx's sympathy lies with the underdogs of the masses. Only a revolution can free the masses from exploitation, subordination and alienation.

Considering the fact that 70.26% respondents want communication improved, it can be deduced that organisations will have to change their communication and participation practices and procedures *to avoid conflict* in the future.

(Dr. A J du Plessis is associated with School of Management and Entrepreneurship, Auckland, New Zealand, He can be reached at aduplessis@unitec.ac.nz).

References

Anstey, M. 1999. *Managing change: Negotiating conflict.* Cape Town: Creda Press.

Adler, N.J. 1984 as cited in Nel, P. 2003. Acculturation and the Adjustment of the Expatriate Manager and his Spouse. Submitted thesis to the Faculty of Economic and Management Sciences at the University of Pretoria.

Burchell, N. 2001. "2000 to 2010: Future directions for HR in New Zealand". Auckland: New Zealand. UNITEC Institute of Technology.

Burton, L. 2003. "The next big thing". *People Dynamics,* 21(2): 22-23.

Cascio, W. F., Aguinis, H. 2005. *Applied psychology in human resource management* (6th ed). New Yersey. Pearson. Prentice Hall.

Dahrendorf, R. 1990. The modern social conflict: An essay on the politics of liberty. Berkeley, California: University of California Press.

De Cieri, H., Kramar, R., Noe, R. A., Hollenbeck, J. R., Gerhart, B., Wright, P. M. 2003. Human resource management in Australia. Australia. McGraw-Hill Australia Pty Ltd.

De Lange, J. 1999. Arbeidswetgewing kon Suid-Afrika werkers nie help. Sake-Beeld: 4, Nov. 9.

De Lange, J. 2000. Suid-Afrika het verlede jaar 420,000 werkloses gekry.Sake-Beeld: 2, Feb.15.

Dessler, G., Griffiths, J., Lloyd-Walker, B. 2004. Human resource management. (2nd ed). Australia. Pearson Education Australia Pty. Ltd.

Gibson, R. 1998. "Rethinking the future". London. Biddles Ltd.

Gomez-Mejia, L. R., Balkin, D. B., Cardy, R. L. 2004. Managing human resources (4th ed). New Yersey. Pearson. Prentice Hall.

Harigopal, K. 2001. Management of organisational change: Leveraging transformation. New Delhi. Response books.

Institute of Personnel Management New Zealand. 1994. *Human resources priorities for competitive advantage. 1994-2000. The IPM survey report.* Auckland: New Zealand.

Jones, G.R. & George, J.M. 2003. *Contemporary Management.* (3rd ed). New York: McGraw-Hill.

Kinloch, G.C. 1977. Sociological theory. New York: McGraw-Hill.

Lombard, B.U. 1998. Unbundling corporate management. Johannesburg: Lex Patria.

Marx, A. & Nel, P.S. 2003. Human resources management trends and forecasts between 2002 and 2010. Unpulished research report, University of Pretoria, Pretoria.

Marx, K. 1984. *Capital: A critique of political economy,* Vol.1. New York: International Publishers.

Nel, P.S., van Dyk, P.S., Haasbroek, G.D., Schultz, H.B., Sono, T. & Werner, A. 2004. *Human resources management.* (6th ed.) Cape Town: Oxford University Press.

Pettigrew, A.M., Whittington, R., Melin, L., Runde, C.S., van den Bosch, F.A.J., Ruigrok, W., Numagami, T. 2003. *Innovative forms of Organising.* London: Sage Publications.

Swanepoel, B. J. (ed). Erasmus, B.J., Van Wyk, M. & Schenk, H. 2003. *South African human resource management: Theory and practice.* (3rd ed.) Cape Town: Juta & Co. Ltd.

Swingewood, A. 2000. A short history of sociological thought. (3rd ed). London: MacMillan Press.

Tester, K. 1993. The life and times of Post-Modernity. Cornwall: T.J. Press.

Tinarelli, S. 2000. Employers' guide to the Employment Equity Act. Pretoria. Van Schaik Publishers.

Vago, S. 1999. Social change. (4th ed). Upper Saddle River, N.J.: Prentice-Hall.

12

e-HRM: Innovation or Irritation? An Explorative Empirical Study in Five Large Companies on Web-based Human Resource Management

Huub Ruël, Tanya Bondarouk and Jan Kees Looise

This is an explorative empirical study in five large companies on Web-based HRM. The five companies with an employee size of more than 10,000 have been studied: They are Dow Chemicals, ABN AMRO, Ford Motor Company, IBM and Belgacom. All these companies have been on the 'e-HR road'. Amongst other conclusions are the facts that e-HRM is an innovation in terms of the opportunities it creates to put employee-management relationships in the hands of the employees and line managers, and the fast flow of communication. The same is an irritation when goals are neither clear nor realistic to line managers and employees; when that aimed for e-HRM type does not fit the real needs of the line managers, employees and the HR departments.

1. Introduction

Until now, empirically-founded models for e-HRM are scarce, as is research on e-HR in general. The models and approaches available are mostly practical e-HR models and focus on the implementation of the technical system that is supposed to support e-HR. In short, they are very much technology-driven. We think this is a limited view and believe that the phenomenon of e-HRM deserves a closer and more fundamental examination and thus we start from the roots.

This research report aims at demystifying the phenomenon of e-HRM by raising the following questions:

- What actually is e-HRM?
- How to analyze e-HRM theoretically?
- To what extent is it already 'visible' in organizations?
- What types of e-HRM can be distinguished?
- What are the goals?
- And, finally, what are the consequences for HR departments?

We will look for answers to these questions by reviewing the literature and by presenting five case studies. Based upon the literature, an e-HRM research model is developed and, guided by this model, five organizations have been studied that have already been on the 'e-HR road' for a number of years.

Defining e-HRM

e-HRM is a way of implementing HR strategies, policies, and practices in organizations through a conscious and directed support of and/or with the full use of web-technology-based channels. The word 'implementing' in this context has a broad meaning, such as making something work, putting something into practice, or having something realized. e-HRM, therefore, is a concept—a way of 'doing' HRM.

Research Questions

Our conclusion about what is known about e-HRM, and how it is working out in reality, is that it is limited and very much based upon consultancy-based survey material. What are lacking are more explorative, qualitative data-based results. Therefore, our aim is to fill up this gap and, to this end, we pose the following central research question:

To what extent does the management of employee relationships in companies change with the planned use of web tools for HRM purposes, and how does this change occur?

From this basis, we distinguish a number of sub-questions:

1. What are the goals that decision-makers within companies try to achieve when they start with the planned use of web-tools for HRM purposes?
2. What types of e-HRM can be distinguished in companies?
3. What are the consequences, in terms of HR outcomes, of the use of web tools for HRM? Based upon these three questions, we first build a research model and then describe a research strategy to answers these questions.

2. A Research Model

Having laid a basis for e-HRM by defining it, we will now dig deeper by theoretically framing e-HRM guided by the research questions posed at the end of Section One. The ultimate goal of this exercise is to develop an e-HRM model that can function as a frame of reference for our research.

As already explained, we aim to develop a model for e-HRM inspired by the thoughts and ideas expressed above. The steps towards the model, when combined, form a chain of reasoning: the basis for the model. The steps, or parts of the model, will be:

1. The state of HRM in an organization.
2. The e-HRM goals.
3. Types of e-HRM.
4. e-HRM Outcomes.

The State of HRM in an Organization

Organizations do not start with nothing when they step out onto the e-HRM road. For a start, there will be certain implicit or explicit HRM policy assumptions and practices already in use. Further, every management decision contains some HRM component. Beer *et al.*, speak about HRM policy choices. The set of HRM policy choices within an organization can be categorized into one of the three types distinguished by Beer *et al.*: the bureaucratic policy, the market policy, and the clan policy. From the existing state of the HRM in an organization (the frame of reference), the individuals and groups involved (the stakeholders) make choices with regard to e-HRM. As these are made within a certain context, the choices are purpose-driven.

e-HRM Goals

What goals drive stakeholders when deciding about e-HRM? Based upon a scan of professionally-oriented and academic journals, we can draw conclusions about

Figure 1: The Research Model

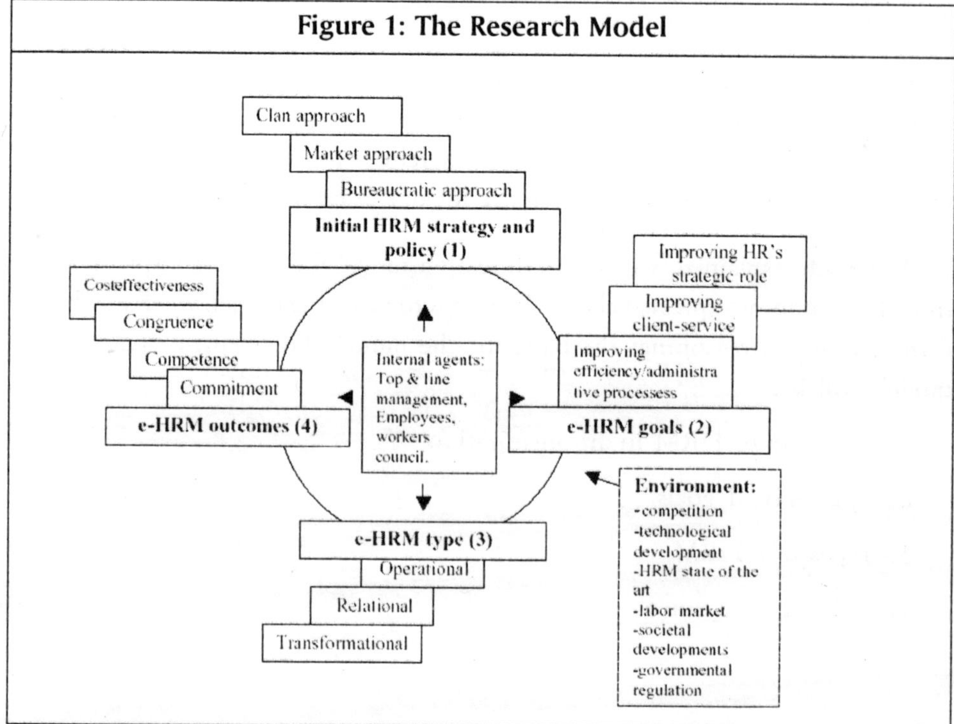

the reasons or goals of organizations making steps towards e-HRM. The four 'pressures' from Lepak and Snell (1998) are a good start, but we think that they can be reduced to three types of goals, namely: 1) Improving the strategic orientation of HRM, 2) Cost reduction/efficiency gains, and 3) Client service improvement/facilitating management and employees.

Types of e-HRM

e-HRM is not a specific stage in the development of HRM, but a choice for an approach to HRM. Wright and Dyer (2000) distinguish three areas of HRM where organizations can choose to 'offer' HR services face-to-face or through an electronic means: transactional HRM, traditional HRM, and transformational HRM. Lepak and Snell (1998) make a similar distinction, namely, operational HRM, relational HRM and transformational HRM.

e-HRM Outcomes

We assume, based upon Beer *et al.*'s ideas about the expected results or outcomes of HRM, that e-HRM also aims to achieve a certain set of outcomes. All HRM activities, and therefore also all e-HRM activities, will implicitly or explicitly be directed towards these 'overall' outcomes. Beer *et al.* (1984) distinguish four possibilities: high commitment, high competence, cost effectiveness, and higher congruence. These outcomes, in turn, may change the state of HRM in an organization, or through individuals and/or groups within an organization, and actually result in a new HRM state. This closes the circle. With the addition of the e-HRM outcomes, the building blocks have been identified that are needed to finalize our e-HRM model (see Figure 1):

After having modeled e-HRM, there is another question for us to answer: what are the consequences of e-HRM for the HR department itself?

Consequences for the HRM Department

The literature seems to be clear: e-HRM will not leave HR departments 'untouched'. Less administrative tasks for the HR department and therefore less administrative positions, and more focus on the strategic goals of the organization and therefore an HRM staff consisting mainly of 'thinkers'; this is, in essence, what HR departments can expect or are already facing and experiencing.

From our definition of, and approach to, e-HRM, the following can be concluded about the consequences of e-HRM for the HR department. e-HRM will assume an active role for line management and employees in implementing HRM strategies, policies, and practices. In terms of the more operational and information processing work, such as administration, registration and information distribution, there will be less demand for HR people. This seems most logical for organizations with an operational e-HRM approach. However, also with a relational e-HRM approach dominating, a smaller HR staff will be necessary if line management and employees pick up and use the HRM instruments provided by the HR intranet. There will be still HR experience necessary for the renewal of instruments and to prepare them for easy intranet-based use. Finally, with a more transformational e-HRM approach, strategic HRM expertise will be necessary in order to formulate adequate strategic HRM plans. The scarce empirical studies on this topic suggest that an investment in e-HRM seems to result in companies reducing the number of HRM employees. Based on the earlier arguments, it is likely that this concerns primarily the operational/administrative HRM workers. At the tactical and strategic levels, HRM staff will remain necessary, but will see a shift in their expertise from face-to-face skills towards intranet and Internet activities. In other words, the web-dimension will be added to the toolkit of HRM professionals.

3. The Research Strategy

In our study we have opted for qualitative research methods. Qualitative research can enhance the credibility of a study. Secondly, results of such studies are often accepted as understandable, believable, and meaningful. Thirdly, qualitative research designs can enhance organizational practices since participants and other organizational members can readily see the implications of the obtained results. An outcome of this is that organizations and organizational members are likely to be more willing to cooperate.

Case Selection

The unit of analysis that is chosen for this study is the organization, meaning that a single organization is considered as a case. It is this approach that studies the goal to say something about e-HRM in organizations, how its starts and the way it works out. In other words, e-HRM in organizations constitutes our empirical domain.

For our study, we have chosen conversational interviews as the dominant technique. The conversational interviews are particularly used to describe the variables in the research model. We have used project participants, who had been able to observe the project, as 'our researchers' and we let them tell us their stories. We included representatives of many relevant parties (employees, project team members, HRM professionals, line managers), and so we have a so-called *multiview* of e-HRM developments in companies, and have been able to describe the variables discerned in our research model.

To get a deeper insight into the practice of e-HRM, we involved five large companies (each with more than 15,000 employees). These five companies were Dow Chemicals, ABN AMRO, Ford Motor Company, IBM, and Belgacom. All of them have been on the 'e-HR road' for a number of years, and in a variety of ways. This case selection procedure is valid and appropriate since it is not these studies intent to generalize in a statistical way across all companies. The intent is to explore and, as a result, make a start with theoretical generalization.

4. Conclusions

Based upon the research questions we can draw conclusions regarding the following three topics: (1) e-HRM goals in the companies, (2) types of e-HRM, and (3) e-HRM outcomes.

e-HRM Goals

First of all, the three types of goals identified in our research model (efficiency/cost reduction; improving client service; improving HR's strategic orientation) were all observed in the case studies. What seems to be new is that, especially in the international companies included in our study, a main goal for introducing e-HRM is the standardization and harmonization of HR policies and practices across all parts of the company. This was explained by the initiators in the companies as being necessary in order to strengthen the company's image as a global entity, not just an internationally dispersed one.

Types of e-HRM

Secondly, we found that there is a 'gap' between e-HRM in a technical sense (the available functionality) and the real use made of web-based HRM tools by employees, line managements, and HR. That means that, technically, e-HRM can have the intention of having a transformational (highly advanced) nature, but in practice (real use of tools) it can be of an operational nature (basic personal data management and use as an information source).

What has shown up clearly is that a company with HRM policies and practices that are of the bureaucratic type cannot just jump to a transformational type of e-HRM: other stages have to be gone through first. The cases in this study clearly suggest that it is impossible to 'jump' immediately to a transformational type of e-HRM without first going through operational and relational e-HRM stages.

e-HRM Outcomes

Thirdly, during the period of our investigation, the overall realized outcomes of e-HRM in the companies studied were primarily a reduction of costs, mainly due to reducing the administrative burden; an improvement in client satisfaction with HR services; and an improvement in the perceived quality of communication within the organization. Changes, let alone improvements, in the competences and commitment of the workforce were very limited.

Alongside these main conclusions, we observed a number of additional aspects:

First e-HRM seems to be providing an important 'push': to put HR responsibility in the hands of the line manager. The introduction of e-HRM is accompanied by the decentralization of HR tasks and by the harmonization and standardization of HR processes. For the HR department, introducing e-HRM shows itself to be a 'push-factor' for changing HRM within an organization: from a bureaucratic approach towards a market/clan approach.

Turning to the employees, the introduction of e-HRM brings changes in the way they experience HRM in their company and in the HR tools and instruments they get offered. They acquire the *opportunity* to get updated in terms of organizational dynamics, take part in online discussions, and choose their career path. However, not all employees are willing to accept full responsibility for their personal career development through the available web-based HR tools. Some (and the case studies suggest a specific group) require their managers to come up with career development initiatives.

Interestingly, in those companies that had an 'industrial' nature, PC availability in all 'corners' of the company and the PC skills of employees was found to be a crucial element in successful switching to e-HRM. Employees in the plants or factory (unlike those in offices) tended not to have access, or at best only limited access to online HR tools because of a lack of PCs or because of cost considerations. Perhaps one can speak of a cyber-division at the organizational level?

The implementation of e-HRM in international and global companies seems to be difficult in the sense that it is hard to convince the local HRM departments to contribute and to collaborate because it is difficult to make the advantages of e-HRM visible and tangible to them in the first place. To make local HRM professionals change their way of working is difficult. When implementing e-HRM globally, it can be difficult to get the support of the relatively small components of the company.

When implementing e-HRM on a global scale, it is not easy to make e-HRM appear advantageous on a local scale. That makes it hard to get local HRM professionals enthusiastic. Guaranteeing the security and confidentiality of input data is an important issue for employees in order that they should feel 'safe' when using web-based HR tools.

Our final observation is that employees and line managers' mindsets need to be changed: they have to realize and accept the usefulness of web-based HR tools. They generally feel that they lack the time and space needed to work quietly and thoughtfully with web-based HR tools and so, if there is no real need, they will not do it.

(Huub Ruël is associated with Utrecht School of Governance.

Tanya Bondarouk and Jan Kees Looise are associated with University of Twente.)

SECTION III

EXPERIENCES

13

Participative Management – A Case Study

Janet M Emmett

There is a great deal of "talk" about participative management these days, particularly in relation to police departments. Community Oriented Policing is flourishing as a way to conduct police business, and if you read articles about Community Oriented Policing, you are bound to come across discussions of participative management. But can it work? And how does it work? This paper will discuss participatory management and look at a case study where it has worked.

Background

Harvard Business School professor Elton Mayo conducted studies at the Western Electric Hawthorne Works in Chicago from 1927 to 1932 in which he studied productivity and working conditions. These studies became known as The Hawthorne Studies. Many theories were developed out of these studies. One portion dwelt with the positive effects of benign supervision and concern for workers that made them feel like part of a team. Over time, these studies evolved

---

into a variety of management forms such as quality circles, team-building, and participatory management. Some of Mayo's conclusions from the Hawthorne Studies included the following:

- Work is a group activity.
- The need for recognition, security and sense of belonging is more important in determining workers' morale and productivity than the physical conditions under which he/she works.
- Group collaboration does not occur by accident; it must be planned and developed.

Out of early studies such as the Hawthorne Studies and many others, there developed an organizational culture within industry to be more collaborative, provide employees with higher levels of decision-making authority over their own work, building teams to harness creativity and increase productivity. In the mid-80s many of us in the private work sector became involved in Total Quality Management and other similar variations on the theme.

Meanwhile, the culture of police departments was also changing over time. Throughout the entire world, police departments began adopting a philosophy of community-oriented policing. Community-oriented policing is about values and reform, empowering officers to work with the community to resolve problems and improve communities. An article on police reform in South Africa included the following:

"...the public service was identified as the key sector requiring transformation. This involved refashioning the types of delivery offered to the public and a complete renovation of the labor relations practices and institutions within public service organizations. The police were expected to dramatically change their labor relations framework and practices to allow for increased 'worker' participation in decision-making processes and enhanced performance management... .Existing legacies of authoritarianism and police disciplinary customs and a lack of directive leadership from management have seriously limited this attempt at transforming police labor relations. This, in turn, has hampered the unit's transition towards operating in accordance with the community policing framework that is supposed to guide the practice of the 'new' South African Police Service."[1]

Change, as we all know, is difficult. Change managers learned that in order to transition to a philosophy of community-oriented policing, changes needed to happen within the very core of the department.

"Two of the greatest dilemmas facing the change manager at the most fundamental level are: 1) *reconciling the needs of the organization with the needs of the individuals who work for it; and* 2) *creating a vision with a set of core values and an implementation strategy for community policing which are congruent with and supported by the structure, systems, and practice of the police organization."*[2]

You may notice a similarity between community-oriented policing and participatory management. Both involve empowerment of the employee to make decisions or provide input at a higher level than the traditional para-militaristic culture of taking orders and following orders. As the two have these similarities, there was an evolution of thought towards the realization that in order to be successful in community-oriented policing, an organization must also be successful in participatory management. The organization must adopt a model of participatory management to empower workers to feel that they are a part of the department team and take that teamwork philosophy with them throughout their day. *"Encouragement of a participatory management style is essential if empowerment is to become a reality."*[3]

Participatory Management in Action

May 1991 found the City of South Lake Tahoe police department in a state of extreme turmoil. Each unit of the police department was at odds with other units. All were suffering from broken trust. Sworn and non-sworn were separated into camps. The environment was bogged down by mistrust, lingering grievances, unforgiveness about past mistreatment, and hopelessness. Both the Police Officers' Association and the Sergeants' Association were pursuing a "no-confidence" vote towards the Chief and a Lieutenant, an action which led the City Council to direct the City Manager and Chief to pursue some sort of team-building process. A month later a meeting was held with a cross-section of the department, including representatives from each bargaining unit and work unit. The group identified desired outcomes of the team-building process, including increased stability in the labor-management relationship. It was decided to hire an outside consulting firm to assist in the process.

The path to participative management started in these early steps to repair the damaged department. The process of selecting the consultant was done with representatives from every unit of the department. All department members had the opportunity to interview potential consultants to ensure there was across-the-board support of the final selection.

Initially the selected consultant had the goal of simply stabilizing the department. They met with small employee groups, with council, with city management. They gained the trust of the officers association and started work on showing management that there were alternative ways to manage employees. They completed 130 hours of executive coaching, confrontation meetings, and personal counseling.

The consultants worked with the initial team (a cross-section of the entire department) to help them understand that the department needed to develop its own participatory management style. Early points of key interest included:

- Representation – parties had to learn that they must represent each other honestly.
- Wholeness – every aspect of the department is important.
- Empowerment – everyone is accountable and responsible.
- Integration – working on the participative management team is a bona fide part of work.

The group formulated rules to govern their team-building process, the most significant of which was the fact that decisions by the group would be made by consensus.

By October 1991 the consultant was conducting training related to trust, behavioral patterns, effective communications, and win-win outcomes. Open doors, building trust through constant communication and participation were already paying off. Committee members and the entire department were beginning to accept the changes and see the potential of this new way of doing things.

In November 1991 a series of meetings were held among work groups to discuss the problems and establish stronger relationships for moving forward. The focus of these meetings was on participative management that would result in increased morale, work satisfaction, employee commitment and accountability, and effective/open communication. The level of participatory management to pursue was discussed: from a simple open door policy to full employee empowerment.

As the year came to a close, the initial committee developed into the first participatory management team (PMT). One of the very first tasks of the team included providing input into the qualities the city should look for in a new Police Chief. This input was included in the job announcement and the PMT was invited to participate in the actual selection process. During this time the PMT also developed itself. A mission statement was written. Sub-committees were established in the areas of design, communication, commitment/planning, and training. In a paper addressing the progress of the team-building process, PMT members wrote, "The following assumption was discussed related to the committee's direction: Successful organizations are learning organizations. Self-confidence is required to learn. Participation is required to have self-confidence. Participation has to be planned and sheltered to work over the long haul."

The PMT also developed a "'Code of Trust", which was distributed with the approval of the acting chief. In addition, confidence in the PMT process was built by the team being able to reach a consensus for a temporary solution to some scheduling issues within the department.

1992 saw a new openness fostered by improved communications, a sense of optimism throughout the department, and improved attitudes at all levels. The consultants declared the department stabilized and moved on to address Phase 2: sustained improvements in morale and operational efficiency.

Concerns regarding how the PMT would operate within the department were addressed. These included: who exactly was in control? All parties agreed that the chief continued to be in control of the department. Decisions made by the PMT would be within guidelines established by the Chief. All members of the department grew to recognize that everyone benefited from this process.

The chief and city management would have greater access to employees and could base decisions on having all the needed information; employees would be able to participate in decisions and feel empowered, which would lead to stronger commitment to the organization and the community; the city would potentially see monetary savings from reduced workers compensation claims, reduced sick leave usage, reduced turnover, and reduced labor litigation/grievance costs; and the public would see a more caring, dedicated, effective department.

Over the next few years, the PMT process flourished and evolved. Early decisions made by the team included manpower adjustments, equipment selection issues, major event staffing decisions, recommendations and involvement in promotional exams, department redesign, and K-9 program expansion.

The PMT history binder kept by the department includes the following statistics for changes between the fiscal year 1990/91 and 1991/92:

- Grievances went from 6 to 0
- Disability retirements went from 4 to 1
- Formal internal affairs investigations went from 24 to 6
- Sick leave usage went from 8,344 hours to 6,533 hours.
- Hours spent in meet and confer negotiations with the Police Officers' Association went from 90.5 hours with no agreement reached, to 12 hours and a satisfactory agreement.

Fourteen Years Later...

Fast forward about fourteen years – where is the PMT today? How does it actually operate?

Each work unit/division of the department elects a representative who serves a one-year term (though one person may serve multiple years). The new term begins in January of each year. The chief represents himself but is just a member like everyone else. At the beginning of the year, the team elects co-leaders. One leader is elected from management and one is elected from line level. The two work as a team to lead the PMT. Over the years, the group has met monthly. Recently they chose to meet bi-monthly with the understanding that if significant issues were raised that needed more regular attention, they would return to monthly.

Prior to a meeting, discussion items are solicited from every member of the department. The only off-limit topic is that of personnel issues. Department members may either come to the meeting to discuss an item they have brought up, or they can ask their area representative to present the issue. Based on the discussion items brought forward, an agenda is prepared prior to the actual meeting.

At the actual meeting, Roberts Rules for meetings is followed. In addition, the group practices consensus decision-making. They never vote. Even though any member of the department may attend the meeting, only the representatives actually partake in the decision process. There is no winner or loser when a decision is made and they try not to compromise. A topic will either be agreed to, shelved for future discussion, or dropped. A particular representative may not totally like a decision that has been made, but they seek agreement that it is at least a decision they can live with.

At the close of each meeting, the chief takes a few minute's to discuss various topics about the department such as budget issues, department direction, etc. The PMT meeting has turned out to be an excellent communication tool. After a meeting, minutes are prepared and distributed to the entire department. All supervisors (sworn and non-sworn) discuss the minutes with their employees as part of their briefings.

Recently the PMT has discussed various topics such as changing the patrol cars, a uniform type of handgun to be issued, changes in uniforms, schedule changes, and detective rotation assignments. Whereas the earlier part of this paper discussed the fact that participatory management is supported as a necessary organizational style for successful community-oriented policing, the City of South Lake Tahoe put the cart before the horse. The PMT process led to a discussion of implementing COPPS philosophy for the department.

Into the Future...

As an early pioneer in implementing participatory management, where is the PMT going from here?

In researching for this paper, I spoke to some long-term participants in this process and gained some very interesting insights into the long-term outlook for the PMT process. In the City of South Lake Tahoe, the PMT arose out of chaos. The early participants became true believers and very committed to participatory management. Even though it is much talked about, only a few police departments embrace the process as thoroughly as South Lake Tahoe. Employees who remember the "old days" continue to have a great deal of commitment to PMT and are protective of it. However, meetings have become poorly attended and fewer issues are being raised. It appears that newer department members see less value in the process. Personally, I have a theory that with the generational changes in the workforce, our newer employees take a participatory culture for granted and accept it as "what is". They have not necessarily worked in a department that is as military in style as police departments used to be. They are learning to be more collaborative in their schooling and academy training, which fosters an expectation that they will be included in department decisions. Long-term employees remember when collaboration and empowerment were foreign concepts. Has participatory management team process run its course in South Lake Tahoe? I don't think so. Even if it is in a slow period at the moment, isn't it of value to know that if the department were to find itself in turmoil again, they have a proven method for airing out their concerns and working together to resolve them?

The lessons learned after fourteen years experience with an active participatory management culture, will always have value—such as those learned in the early Hawthorne Studies on productivity that workers find value in empowerment over their workplace. And empowered workers take that empowerment to the streets; translating it into a greater sense of community as they practice community-oriented policing.

Participatory Management Team Meeting Rules

(As posted proudly in the conference room of the City of South Lake Tahoe Police Department.)

1. Decisions by consensus.
2. For the group to be effective, everyone must participate.

3. Attack the issues, not the individuals.

4. No collusion outside the participative management process.

5. No recriminations.

6. All agreements will be recorded in the minutes.

7. Deadlines will be set for all agreements.

8. Don't re-plow old ground; once an issue is laid to rest, leave it there.

(Janet M Emmett, Human Resources Manager, City of South Lake Tahoe. The author can be reached at jemmett@cityofslt.us).

Endnotes

1 M. Marks and 1. Flemming, "As Unremarkable as the Air They Breathe? Reforming Police Management in South Africa," *Current Sociology,* Vol. 52, No.5, 784-808 (2004).

2 The Police Organization in Transition; Community Policing Consortium; http://www.communitypolicing.org/pforgtrans.secc.html.

3 Ibid.

14

Reform of Top Management Systems in Japan

Aoki, Hidetaka

The paper focuses on the Executive Officer System (EOS), being one of the top management reforms started in Japanese companies during the late 1990s and the reason behind the failure of this system to produce the expected result. The first part of the paper discusses about the characteristics of Japanese type of board of directors such as the large number of directors, the internal hierarchy, low percentage of outsiders, and those promoted within the firm make up the majority. The benefits and problems of such characteristics are explained. An introduction to the situation and the purpose of EOS is explained. The cause of failure of this system is analyzed in detail. Also analyzed are some cases of companies that improved performance with the implementation of EOS.

1. Introduction

With the post-bubble downfall becoming a long-term recession and a succession of business scandals, debate on corporate governance has increased in Japan since

---

the 1990s. Under the Anglo-American governance mechanism of market for corporate control, managers are disciplined by the threat of takeovers. On the other hand, in Japan, while the silent stockholders based on a mutual cross-shareholdings made company managers free from the capital market pressures, the main banks disciplined them. Thus, in the governance mechanism of Japanese companies, the role of a main bank has been conventionally emphasized (Aoki, 1990, 1995; Sheard, 1989, 1994). However, in connection with the financing patterns of companies having shifted from indirect financing to direct financing by the increase in the equity finance from the late 1980s, it is known that the influence of main banks declined. Moreover, the efficiency of a management system centering on a boards of directors was called into question.

With the background of these governance debates, top management reforms, such as introducing the executive officer system, outside director system, stock options, "Company with Committee System" and so on, were briskly attempted during the late 1990s. This paper especially focuses on the executive officer system (EOS), which was to play the leading reform role among these menus. According to the results of previous researches, although the EOS introduction was caused by a low firm performance and a over-sized board of directors (Aoki, 2002), its effect on a performance recovery is limited (Nobeoka and Tanaka, 2002). Therefore, this paper considered the reasons why this system could not produce an expected result. Because the decision-making of introducing the EOS is fundamentally under the discretion of managers, it is important to know the problems concerning the EOS and to provide some implications for a desirable management structure.

This paper is made up as follows. In Section 2, the features of typical Japanese boards of directors are set out, and its benefits and costs are summarized. In Section 3, after understanding the EOS, an introductory situation and its purpose are confirmed. Section 4 considers the reasons why the EOS had not contributed to the effective reform. The last section concludes.

2. Characteristics of Japanese – Types of Boards of Directors

The following features are pointed out as a typical Japanese boards of directors (Keizai Douyuukai,1996; Fukao and Morita,1997). A) With a large number of directors, and there is an internal hierarchy[1]. B) The percentage of outsiders on a board is low and those promoted within the firm make up the majority. C) On a functional level, an overlap in management and execution can be seen because most of directors are the representatives of particular business sections concurrently. The benefits of these characteristics would be as follows. The large and insider-dominated boards had an incentive effect on employees in terms of increasing their chances of promotion. Further, complementally with the characteristics of the Japanese business system such as 'long-term employment' and competition trough 'ranking hierarchy', it also has supplied an incentive to accumulate firm-specific skills. Then, the trait of having an insider-dominant structure and the concurrent post holding between directors and section chiefs generated the benefit of decision-making based on the information from work arena. This was regarded as one of the strengths of former Japanese business. However, a variety of problems related to each feature of Japanese-style boards were pointed out (Japan Productivity Center for Socio-Economic Development, Productivity Research Laboratory, 1998). These criticisms can be essentially summarized in terms of the following two points. One is the problem of the quality of the decision-making. Board members who concurrently hold positions as section chiefs tend to prioritize the benefits for their own areas of responsibility, and the decision-making rooted in a whole-company perspective becomes difficult. Besides, it is difficult to carry out an active debate with oversized boards of directors. Accordingly, actual decision-making occurs in the operating committee or the management strategy meetings made up of a few senior managers. The board merely exists to ratify them. The other is the problem of the effectiveness of monitoring. Because the monitor (evaluator) and the executor being one, an objective evaluation for one's own results becomes difficult. Further, the fact that a board hierarchy, in which the president has authority over personnel affairs, weakens checks on the top management has come under criticism (Kondo *et al.*, 1999).

3. Executive Officer System – An Introductory Situation and the Purpose

It was the EOS on which expectations came to be placed as a way of alleviating problems mentioned above. When the EOS is adopted, the new position executive officer is created, and as a result, management and execution would be divided. Here management defines as strategic decision-making rooted in a whole company

of introduction of the EOS has the average number of directors at 10.32, the average number of executive officers at 15.29, and the average number of directors concurrently holding the post of executive officers at 1.54. Thus the ratio of concurrent post-holding is 16.7% (1.54/10.32). Looking at only this figure, the level of concurrent post-holding of directors and executive officers is not so high. However, there are a considerable number of directors who in reality work as section chiefs of specific projects, even if there is no entry on the list of the company's directors concerning a concurrence of positions with that of executive officer. Then, modifying the cases where, in real terms, they could be considered as being responsible for an executive function, and re-estimating the actual numbers of concurrent position-holders, the figure becomes 7.9 and the ratio of concurrent position holding becomes 80.6% for the whole sample (Table 2). This fact means that the EOS does not contribute to separate management from execution. Although the ratio of concurrent post-holding is higher for B-group than G-group, it would be difficult to assert that this is the direct reason why the EOS has not achieved expected results. Because it would rather say that the separation has not progressed in both groups.

The result here means that the interests of sections still have been brought into the place where the strategic decision-making based on a whole company perspective should be made. Nobeoka and Tanaka (2002) also pointed out that a perfunctory adoption of the EOS does not necessarily improve the capability of

Table 2: Comparison of Board Structure

	Full sample	ROA		Sales Growth	
	53 companies	G-group(26)	B-group(26)	G-group(26)	B-group(26)
Nunber of directors	10.3	10.8	9.9	10.5	10.2
	(3.4)	(4.1)	(2.7)	(4.1)	(2.8)
Number of executive officers	15.3	15.2	15.3	17.0	13.8
	(7.6)	(8.6)	(6.7)	(7.9)	(7.3)
Number of directors who has	7.9	7.7	8.1	7.0	8.8
positions of executive officer	(2.8)	(2.6)	(3.2)	(2.1)	(3.0)
Ratio of concurrently	80.6%	78.9%	82.0%	75.6%	85.9%
post-holding	(16.1%)	(18.1%)	(14.2%)	(19.3%)	(10.0%)

Note: ( ) shows std. dev.

strategic decision-making[6]. In addition, the result here also means that the directors still monitor and evaluate the results of their own responsibilities. Therefore, when looked at in the light of the reform objectives of the strengthening of the strategic decision-making and the monitoring functions, one has to admit that problems still remain in the implementation of the EOS.

4.2. Firm Characteristic Compatibility

Although there are many negative opinions about the EOS, there are companies such as Nissan and Hitachi that improved performance. What is the difference between successful companies and unsuccessful companies? The next point is the matching between the EOS and the characteristics of a company. In other words, the EOS is not necessarily the best remedy for reform of top management at all companies, rather that the use of the EOS is more rational at some companies than at others. What kinds of characteristics at a company have a high level of compatibility with the EOS? Here focuses on the degree of diversification as an internal condition and shareholding by foreigners as an external condition.

Concerning the strategic decision-making, there is a cost of bringing the divisional interests into the boardroom where the whole company's decision-making should be made. And this cost would be larger for a diversified company compared to a single-business company, because the conflicts among sections would be more serious for the former. Therefore, the following possibility was tested:

H1: the more diversified business structure a company has, the bigger the benefit of separating management from execution by adopting the EOS.

On the other hand, concerning the monitoring function, there remains the problem of 'who monitors the monitor?', even if the monitors (directors) and the executors (executive officers) are separated as a result of adopting the EOS. Therefore, some kinds of disciplinary mechanism over the monitors should be established. Because the foreign shareholders are famous for active investor using 'voice', Here considers the following possibility:

H2: the higher the ratio of shareholding by foreign investors, the better the results of adopting the EOS.

Table 3: Comparison of Firm Characteristics

	ROA				Sales Growth			
	G-group	B-group	Difference	t-value	G-group	B-group	Difference	t-value
Number of directors	10.77	9.88	0.88	0.83	10.54	10.19	0.35	0.41
	(4.09)	(2.75)			(4.05)	(2.83)		
Diversification	0.11	0.03	0.08*	2.01	0.07	0.07	0.00	0.02
	(0.20)	(0.19)			(0.23)	(0.16)		
Shareholding by	19.42	11.97	7.44*	1.94	16.95	13.96	3.00	0.84
foreigners	(16.16)	(8.42)			(15.79)	(10.73)		
Investment ratio	0.13	0.25	-0.12	-1.33	0.22	0.15	0.07	0.80
	(0.09)	(0.44)			(0.43)	(0.13)		

Note: ( ) shows std.dev.
diversification was measured by entropy index.
investment ratio = capital investment figure/fixed assets.
*:$p<0.10$.

Table 3 shows the results of a comparison between G and B groups. In relation to sales growth (DS), no significant differences can be confirmed between the two groups, but in terms of ROA, it was shown that both the degree of diversification and the shareholding by foreigners are higher in G-group than in B-group.[7]

First, the result of diversification indicates that the separation of management and execution by using the EOS would be more important for the diversified companies. For this kind of companies, the coordination among each business section is relatively important, and the needs of releasing the decision-making rooted in a whole company perspective from the interests of each section would be larger. On the other hand, for the companies having nearly single-business structure, the decision-making based on the work-arena information would be more important. For this kind of companies, the separation of management and execution may not have significant meaning.

Second, the result concerning the foreign shareholders indicates that the incentive issue for the monitor is important. In other words, in order for a supervisor (director) to monitor strictly, the condition being exposed to some kinds of pressure should be needed. Accordingly, it was suggested that an independent monitoring function of the boards of directors (two-layers structure) and the pressure from an external stockholder complementally contribute to strengthen the monitoring function.

5. Summary

The top management reforms in Japan have been activated since the 1990s. If the costs of the J-type boards of directors are emphasized too much, easy imitation of the A-type boards may be promoted. Conversely, if the benefits are emphasized too much, companies that really need reforms would remain unchanged. This paper focuses on the EOS, which aims to ease the problems concerning both the strategic decision-making and self-monitoring in J-type board, by separating management from execution, and considering the reasons why it has had little effect so far.

One possibility is the implementation of the system. Even if the EOS was adopted, the degree of concurrent post-holding between directors and executive officers in real terms was as high as approximately 80%. It means that the separation of management and execution is not substantial. However, according to the result of a comparison between successful and unsuccessful groups, the degrees of this separation did not show a significant difference. Then, the compatibility between the EOS and the firm's characteristics was considered. Again, according to a comparison between above two groups, it would be more rational to introduce the EOS for the following types of companies. A) Companies that have diversified business structure. For this type of companies, because the conflicts among business sections would be larger, it is important to separate the decision-making based on a whole company perspective from the decision-making based on a divisional perspective. B) Companies that are exposed to a high level of capital market pressure. For this type of companies, the disciplinary mechanism over the monitors would be established.

The discussion concerning corporate governance has been conventionally carried out on a macro (country) level. For example, does the Japanese governance system converge on Anglo-America type or not? However, the results of this research indicates that the discussion on a micro (company) level is needed. For example, what kinds of firm's characteristics are compatible with a certain governance system?

(Aoki, Hidetaka, Faculty of Commerce and Economics, Chiba University of Commerce. The author can be reached at hidetaka@cuc.ac.jp).

Endnotes

1 Typically, it consists of chairman, president, vice-president, senior managing director, junior managing director and director.

2 Questionnaire survey. Questioning 2,103 listed companies, of which 1,363 replied in November, 2002.

3 Furthermore, in terms of what was considered important for the strengthening of corporate governance, strengthening the prevention of illegal actions (80.9%), strengthening disclosure and the obligation for explanation to shareholders (75.35), and strengthening the function of the board (69.9%) were the highest answers.

4 Questionnaire survey by the company law division, targeting 2,445 listed companies of which 951 replied in February 2000.

5 Setting the year of the EOS introduction as t, the following nine increments were calculated over industry-adjusted ROA and sales growth (DS) for each company. ① from t-1 to t+1, ② from t-2 to t+1, ③ from an average of , t-1 and, t-2 to , t+1, ④ from , t-1 to , t+2, ⑤ from t-2 to t+2, ⑥ from an average of t-1 and t-2 to t+2, ⑦ from t-1 to an average of t+1 and t+2, ⑧ from, t-2 to an average of t+1 and, t+2, and ⑨ from an average of t-1 and t-2 to an average of t+1 and , t+2. Ranking was compiled of the combined those nine results for the both of performance indicates, then classified those higher in the rankings as G-group and those lower in the rankings as B-group.

6 Concretely, comparing the EOS introduction companies to non-introduction companies, they pointed out that the EOS contributed to downsizing the boards and activation of discussion, but the nature of top or the formal meeting have not changed.

7 This trend concerning the shareholding by foreigner is even more marked in the case of comparisons between the top 13 and the bottom 13 companies.

References

Aoki, H. 2002. Torishimariyakukai no Kaikaku to Kouporeito Gabanansu: Shikkouyakuinseido Dounyuu no Youin Bunseki, (Board reform and corporate governance: Analysis of factors leading to introduction of the executive officer system), *Nihon Keiei Gakkaishi* 8: 3-14.

Aoki, M. 1990. "Towards an economic model of the Japanese firm." *Journal of Economic Litelature* 28: 1-27.

Aoki, M. 1995. *Keizai Shisutemu no Shinka to Tagensei,* (Evolution and pluralism in economic systems), Touyou Keizai Shinpousha.

Fukao, M. and Morita,Y. 1997. *Kigyou Gabanansu Kouzou no Kokusai Hikaku,* (International comparison of corporate governance structures), Nihon Keizai Shinbunsha.

Hatada, K. 1998. Shikkouyakuin no Houteki Chii to Sekinin, (The legal position and responsibilities of executive officers), *Shouji Houmu* 1505:49-60.

Japan Productivity Center for Socio-Economic Development, Productivity Research Laboratory. 1998. *Nihon-gata Kouporeito Gabanansu Kouchiku ni muketeno Toppu Manejimento Kinou no Kadai: Toppu Manejimento Kinouno Kakushin to Kouporeito Gabanansu ni kansuru Chosa Houkoku,* (Themes on top management in terms of Japanese-style corporate governance structure: Reform of top management and survey reports on corporate governance).

Keizai Douyuukai. 1996. *Kigyou Hakusho, 12:.Nihon Kigyou no Keiei: Kouporeito Gabanansu no Shiten wo fumaeta Torishimariyakukai to Kansayakukai no Arikata,* (Japanese business management: The shape of boards of directors and auditors from a corporate governance perspective).

Kondo, M.,Ushimaru, Y., Tamura, U., Kawaguchi, Y., Kuronuma, E. and Yukizawa, K. 1999. Shikkouyakuinseido ni kansuru Houteki Kentou, (Legal investigation on the executive officer system), *Shouji Houmu* 1542:4-13, *Shouji Homu* 1543:17-27.

Miyajima, H. and Inagaki, K. 2003. *Shinten suru Kouporeito Gabanansu Kaikaku to Nihon Kigyou no Saisei,* (A progressing corporate governance reform and the revival of Japanese companies), Ministry of Finance, Policy Research Institute.

Nobeoka, K. and Tanaka,K. 2002. Toppu Manejimennto no Senryaku teki Ishikettei Nouryoku, (The ability for strategic decision-making of top management), Itoh, H.(eds.). *Nihonkigyou Henkakuki no Sentaku,* Touyou Keizai Shinpousha.

Sheard, P. 1989. "The main bank system and corporate monitoring and control in Japan". *Journal of Economic Behaviour and Organization* 11:399-422.

Sheard, P. 1994. Main Banks and the Governance of Financial Distress. Aoki, M. and Patrick, H.(eds.). *The Japanese Main Bank System.* Oxford University Press.

Tokyo Bar Association,Company Law Division. 2001. *Bessatsu Shouji Houmu (243): Shikkouyakuin, Shagai Torishimariyaku no Jittai: Shouhou Kaisei no Houkou wo fukumete* (The real body of the executive officer and the outside directors).

Tokyo Stock Exchange. 2003. *Kouporeito Gabanansu ni kansuru Ankeito no Chousa Kekka ni tsuite* (Questionnaire survey results on corporate governance).

15

People Management in IT Industry: Issues and Imperatives

Ravi Dasari

On the global map, India enjoys an enviable position which is very recent. However, it employs young and highly skilled software professionals. The IT companies are encouraging various HR practices to enable this group of people to work effectively towards the organizational goals. The professionals working in this industry are unique in their capabilities and different background. The major issue in managing them is to win their loyalty towards the company. It is necessary for the firms to regularly screen software employees for computer-related injuries by hiring services of medical professionals concerned. The article analyses the HR trends and issues in the Indian IT industry by conducting a survey of the software and HR professionals working in the various software companies.

The Indian Information Technology (IT) industry, though relatively young, has made India proud with its spectacular performance in recent times. This industry has grown at a frenetic pace in the last decade, creating high demand for

Source: HRM Review, August 2006.

software professionals. India's comparative advantage in software industry development is primarily based on the easy availability of trained and quality manpower at a relatively low cost. Although India traditionally has had surplus of highly qualified engineering and technical manpower, with the rapid growth of the global IT industry over the past decade, demand has outstripped supply for several years in a row. The worsening drain of trained manpower from India to other countries has further aggravated the situation. With growing shortfall of trained IT manpower, a large number of countries and companies from the Western world are turning their sights towards India to bridge the gap. A number of large multinational IT companies regularly recruit engineers and managerial manpower from India to meet their worldwide requirements.

Due to the high demand, companies have been continually developing novel and innovative methods in managing the human resources. Despite treating software professionals like associates and partners rather than employees, paying lucrative salaries, offering employee stock options, attractive perks and a host of other benefits, the IT companies continue to face problems of high turnover, unrealistic employee expectations, stress generated by the targets and deadline-bound assignments and massive layoffs of employees.

Unlike traditional industries, IT industry, which is a part of 'new economy', employs highly educated personnel better known as knowledge workers and gold-collared workers, who are very young, ambitious, mobile and having multiple expectations. Indian IT companies are using various HR initiatives like Employee Stock Options (ESOPs), flexible working hours and concepts, considering employees as associates and partners to attract and retain the talent. Since the IT industry has come to play a significant role in the national economy, in general and the New Economy, in particular, and since this industry is particularly people-critical, there is a need for studying the employee dimension of this industry.

Unique Features of the IT Industry

The IT industry which is a part of the 'new economy', besides being new is unique in several ways. Unless this uniqueness is understood it may not be possible to develop sustainable HR strategies to manage IT professionals, who constitute the core of the industry. The unique features of IT industry are:

i. Knowledge and skills of people can become obsolete very soon, and hence, they need continuous updating.

ii. Most companies are young and are operating in a highly competitive and turbulent business environment. They do not have advantage of tradition or precedent to guide them as is the case with the industries in the 'old economy'.

iii. It is a people-critical industry, wherein the most significant input and output is knowledge. Further, knowledge has somewhat assumed the place of capital as a factor of production and propeller of growth.

iv. Large number of employees in the industry are highly qualified professionals having degrees in engineering, sciences and other related areas of knowledge and rare skills.

v. Employees are very young with an age averaging mid-twenties.

vi. It is a glamorous industry with exotic and unrealistic expectations among the new entrants.

vii. There is an intense and at times cut-throat competition among firms for skilled personnel assuming forms such as head hunting, poaching and consequently employee turnover rates are rather high.

viii. The IT professionals are non-unionized and their salaries are determined by individual bargaining rather than by collective bargaining.

ix. Candidates with good English medium background and communication skills are greatly preferred over those with education in vernacular medium for IT jobs.

x. Software professionals are relatively highly paid and their compensation packages are increasing rapidly.

A survey was conducted by the author by interviewing software and HR professionals working in various software companies located in Hyderabad. The following findings were unfolded by the survey.

First, the IT Industry, which is a part of the new economy, is also a young industry. As is evident from the background of its workforce that is very young in age, this youthful profile has two implications, both positive and negative. On the positive side, it can be said that its employees are energetic and enthusiastic and at a dynamic peak of their career. Being younger they are in a learnable age, since people learn more while younger than when old. This portends well for the industry too.

The flip side of this age profile is that the software companies are devoid of experienced hands who generally tend to have a long-term and mature view. Because of the global competition the experienced professionals are continuously leaving the companies for more lucrative offers. The software companies in India are operating in an environment of constant threat of losing their experienced personnel on account of relatively lower salaries they pay. This problem will hopefully be partly mitigated by the current trend of business process outsourcing, which is bringing more software jobs from the developed world to India. As a result, new jobs hitherto generated in high paying developed countries will come down and the above-mentioned threat may somewhat mitigate. Yet this is going to be a big challenge to Indian software industry. The software firms have to device more and more innovative strategies like ESOPs, Venture Capital Fund, etc., to retain experienced hands. The Indian firms also need to increase their pay levels to attract and retain their best professionals.

Secondly, the software professionals hail from a rather narrow demographic background (mostly young male and unmarried) and apparently from urban middle class moorings. As the author was discouraged by the company executives from rural-urban and caste dimension in the questionnaire administered to software professionals, he cannot say for certain about the rural-urban as well as caste background. From discrete enquiries and knowledgeable sources, however, he is driven to the view that they are coming overwhelmingly from higher social strata and middle or higher economic strata. Software employment has resulted in a new social class, which Kenneth Keniston calls as "digirati". The big money that the employment in this industry brings in will help subaltern classes to gain socially as well as economically. The background homogeneity of the software professionals is a favorable factor for team-building, interpersonal communication, and cultural harmony.

Thirdly, one of the major issues in the management of software professionals is that of winning the employee loyalty, which is obviously very important for organizational productivity. The rate of employee turnover in the IT industry shows that the software professionals are currently birds of passage having little organizational loyalty. The software computer companies are vying with one another to rob the experienced and talented and most software employees are leaving organizations for greener pastures without any qualms. Most software professionals interviewed for the study have said that they are not very happy with their salary levels. This indicates that they are only waiting for a good opportunity to change their employer.

The author has many friends among software professionals. If what he has gathered in casual discussions with them is an indication that most of them are very ambitious, they would say that "I should be crorepati before I get hooked", "I have to own a decent house", "I have to buy a limousine" and so on and so forth. Most of them would say that they are willing to quit their jobs if another one offers more money. All this is indicative of the challenge that HR mangers have to face. The challenge is basically that of sustaining the employees' loyalty. This is also a problem for the software professionals themselves. The way they resort to job-hopping has harmed them by not allowing them to strike roots anywhere. This rootlessness will have a telling effect on their sociocultural and spiritual life.

Fourthly, one more major conclusion is that most software professionals being unmarried, they give tremendous advantage to industry. They will be available for longer hours of service with little botheration of family intruding into their professional time. This way the Indian software industry seems to be enjoying a distinctive competitive edge. It has a decided advantage over the software industry in the West, wherein, in all likelihood, the percentage of the married software professionals is comparatively higher. At an average age of 26.5 years, most of the software professionals remaining unmarried is (as evident from the survey data) in sharp contrast, to much lower marriage age in the general population.

Discussions with respondents revealed that most of them postponing marriages in several cases even in the face of parental pressure due to their ambitions like going abroad, acquiring valuable assets and uncertainties of employment market (the recent downturn being fresh in memory) and compulsions of supporting parents and other relatives. In fact, a few software professionals opined that their career is short much like that of sports persons or film stars and hence they would like to make as much money as possible in the short run. In some cases this postponement is due to not getting partners of their choice and in the case of boys not getting an offer of a 'satisfactory' dowry. Being single is professionally helping software professionals to improve their qualifications and learn new languages.

Fifthly, the percentage of women among software professionals is lower than their male counterparts. However, it is fairly high as compared to women's percentage in other sectors of economy. There is a general feeling that software profession is a 'soft profession' and it is suitable for women, as it does not involve outdoor work or hard physical labor. Women work in secure environment in this industry. For certain kinds of employment like the call center jobs women are particularly preferred on account of their sweeter and appealing voices and patient, pleasing demeanor. Whatever the reasons, women getting into software profession in big numbers is a welcome sign.

Given the elite nature of software jobs and the software industry, it is good that women are increasing their share here. However, there are bound to be problems associated with employment of women. In a matriarchal social setup as that of India, these problems may not be special to software profession.

The problems that software employees are facing include working in odd or night shifts particularly in call centers, marital discords due to men's suspicion about their working spouses, problem in securing a work-life balance, and carrying employers' displeasure for prolonged leave due to post-natal problems. Therefore, the industry has to make special efforts to make women's stay in workplaces secure, convenient, and nondiscriminatory.

Lastly, the software professionals are, by and large, happy with the HR practices of the software industry. This is a favorable factor, which augurs well for the productivity of the software industry. However, the software professionals feel that in three areas, there is need for more efforts on the part of the industry: One, increased compensation; two, more training; and three, more attention for prevention and cure of computer-related injuries. Regarding the last, it is necessary for the firms to regularly screen software employees for computer related injuries by hiring services of medical professionals.

(Ravi Dasari, Consulting Editor, HRM Review, Faculty and Program Coordinator, Icfai School of HRD. He can be reached at ravidasari_2000@yahoo.com).

16

From People Success to Business Success

Julie J Gebauer and Andrew S Cherkas

A comprehensive global study by Towers Perrin study of 86,000 workers across 16 countries worldwide provides insights into the issues of what insurance employees want. The article highlights the major elements that attract, engage and retain employees in the insurance industry. The best practices in people management in the industry would help in developing a road map for success.

"By focusing on workforce engagement, insurance companies can strengthen their ability to compete—for people and customers."

Demands on the insurance industry have never been greater—from customers, shareholders, regulators and employees alike. Customers want increasingly diverse products, better pricing, greater protection and outstanding service. Regulators require greater transparency and tighter controls. Shareholders are insisting on less volatility and higher returns. In combination, the nature of the business and the business model itself are being stretched to a point beyond any in the past.

Some organizations will go beyond merely dealing with the challenges; they will stand out by exceeding performance expectations. Not only will they make

Source: Emphasis Magazine, August 2006. © Towers Perrin's 2006. Reprinted with permission.

good directional decisions for their business, but these organizations will also gain competitive advantage through their people. Having better motivated, more talented and effectively retained staff is increasingly becoming a source of significant competitive advantage. For example:

- Commoditization of core products in many markets is shifting the basis of competition to aspects of customer service, distribution support and better customer segmentation and targeting. These require innovation in service and support propositions and flawless delivery—and these are areas where superior, sustained, multilevel workforce performance can make a real difference to business success.
- Insurers have played second fiddle to retail and investment banks and other financial institutions in attracting talent that can, for example, quantify and manage complex risks, create hedging strategies, produce new risk transfer solutions and optimize capital deployment. Arguably, the insurance companies that bring in the best and brightest in this arena will more readily win in the market.

But attracting, retaining and engaging employees is also becoming more difficult as baby boomers retire and talent shortages emerge for companies in all industries. Insurance companies need to ask themselves now where the next generation of employees will come from, what specific skills they will need, what those employees will want and what kind of competition they'll face in this labor market.

What Insurance Employees Want

A comprehensive Towers Perrin study of 86,000 workers across 16 countries worldwide provides insights into some of these issues (see Box I). In particular, through an analysis of employee respondents working for insurers, the study highlights what aspects of the work experience are important in attracting employees to join a company, keep them at the company and engage them to put in discretionary effort to help the company succeed. The study also measures how well employers are doing in these areas.

Broadly, the Towers Perrin Global Workforce Study shows disappointing results. While insurance companies do better than most other industries with which

Box 1: A Comprehensive Global Study

The *Towers Perrin Global Workforce Study*, the largest of its kind to date, provides a comprehensive examination of employee attitudes toward reward programs and the work experience at corporations around the world. It is based on a random survey, conducted on the Web last year, of 86,000 individuals working full-time for mid-size to large organizations in 16 countries.

In addition to examining specific elements of the work experience that attract, retain and engage employees, as well as various reward practices, the survey collected information on how employees view their company, leadership and managers. The insurance sector data are drawn from nearly 2,200 employees working for US life, property/casualty and health insurance organizations.

Source: www.towersperrin.com

they compete for labor, only 24% of employees are highly engaged. The study shows that employees in the insurance industry do not rate their employers highly in a number of crucial workplace areas, with significant implications for their retention and engagement. This is also true for virtually all the countries and industries included in the study. Put simply, few employers anywhere appear to be building and sustaining a work environment that will improve workforce performance and generate competitive advantage.

The good news is that the study points the way toward solutions. Specifically, it identifies the attributes of the workplace that do make a difference in engaging people and focusing them on higher levels of performance. Insurance companies that are willing to explore these attributes and better understand the drivers of attraction, retention and engagement can develop workplace strategies that not only meet their staffing and productivity needs, but do so at a more affordable cost.

Employees on the Move

Insurance company employees, like employees everywhere, are restless. Some 40% said they had no plans to leave their current employer. But an equally large number are "passive job seekers," meaning they are open to considering other job offers at virtually any time. The remaining 20% are either actively looking for another job (11%), readying to move (3%) or planning to retire in the next few years (6%). Overall, more than half are active or passive job seekers.

These statistics underscore the fact that insurers have a large group of people who might be willing to "bail out." Companies can mitigate this risk with a work experience that delivers an appealing return to employees who stay and invest their energy and expertise in the organization.

What does that experience look like? More than ever, it is based on a comprehensive blend of monetary and non-monetary rewards in four broad

Exhibit 1: Top 10 Elements that Attract, Retain and Engage Employees in the Insurance Industry

	Attraction Drivers	Retention Drivers	Engagement Drivers
1.	Competitive base pay	Organization retains employees with needed skills*	Senior management interest in employee well-being*
2.	Salary increases linked to individual performance	My manager understands what motivates me*	Improved my skills and capabilities over the last year**
3.	Work/life balance*	Organization creates appealing culture*	Organization creates appealing culture*
4.	Career advancement opportunities**	Fairly compensated compared to others doing similar work in my organization	Salary criteria are fair and consistent
5.	Competitive healthcare benefits	Opportunities to learn and develop new skills**	Appropriate amount of decision-making authority to do my job well*
6.	Challenging work*	Organization is able to hire people with needed skills*	Organization focuses on customer satisfaction*
7.	Competitive retirement benefits	Performance goals challenging but achievable*	People in my unit work well together as a team*
8.	Reputation of the organization as a good employer*	Salary criteria are fair and consistent	Senior management acts to ensure the organization's long-term success*
9.	Organization's financial health*	Reputation of the organization as a good employer*	Input into decision-making in my department*
10	Caliber of co-workers*	Low- or no-stress work environment*	Reputation of the organization as a good employer*

* Work environment rewards ** Learning and development rewards.

categories: Pay, benefits, learning and development, and the work environment (e.g., work/life balance, culture, quality of supervision).

Exhibit 1 shows precisely what insurance employees value in these categories at different stages of the employment life cycle. In this industry, as in virtually all others, the elements that attract people to a job differ considerably from those that help retain and engage people. Savvy insurers must understand these differences and design and deliver their work experience and reward packages accordingly.

As shown, competitive pay and benefits remain critical "needed to play" components in the recruiting phase of the life cycle, and make up three of the top five attraction drivers. But once employees are in the door, the non-monetary elements take on far more importance. Here the focus needs to shift to intangibles, such as the quality of supervisory skills, leadership visibility and accessibility, an appealing culture, the ability to enhance skills and so on.

Interestingly, these are aspects of the work experience that don't necessarily require significant financial investment and where insurers can make improvements at a comparatively modest cost. But make no mistake, building up these areas is difficult and requires dedicated focus and personal commitment from leadership, typically involving increased and more open communication, training for managers in coaching and mentoring, innovative learning experiences, and so on. This is one reason why, traditionally, many companies have preferred to invest dollars instead.

But as our survey results conclusively show, investments in pay and benefits, while critical, will only take a company so far. Assuming they are reasonable, competitive and perceived as fair, they become a needed-to-play element from the employee's perspective—not a needed-to-win ingredient in securing true engagement.

Focusing on non-traditional rewards also offers a way for insurers to distinguish themselves from competitors for talent. It's relatively easy for companies to copy each other's pay or benefit programs. It is far harder to try to emulate innovations in performance management, autonomous decision-making, creative online learning and an open flow of communication.

For companies that have had to modify their health and retirement benefits, or that will modify them in the near future, rebalancing the mix of rewards offers a way to position change positively and give employees something they truly value. Use of sophisticated optimization modeling techniques gives employers the ability to identify the point at which the cost of a particular reward element exceeds its perceived value and the steps available to bring the cost and value equation into alignment.

Retaining Critical Talent

When it comes to retention, there are even more opportunities to adapt reward practices to better meet needs. Eight of the 10 top retention drivers fall into the work environment and learning and development categories, and most concentrate on the ability to create an attractive environment that brings together dynamic people who are recognized appropriately for their contributions.

Given the importance of these elements, how well are insurers delivering on them today? Based on how respondents scored their companies in these areas, the record is mixed.

Insurance industry employees feel a lot of stress in the work environment. Only 29% agreed their work environment was characterized by little or no stress. And in a related area of inquiry, only 41% gave a favorable response when asked whether they were satisfied that they could balance work and personal life. These results speak to a sense that employees feel overwhelmed at work and may well contribute to their relatively negative view about the top retention driver: The organization's overall ability to retain key people. If people believe the company is not keeping a sufficient number of skilled people, whether intentionally or unintentionally, their own frustration at having to pick-up the additional work and try to keep everything afloat can damage their own willingness to stay and place them under increasing amounts of stress. Equally disturbing, fewer than half of the insurance employees surveyed feel their manager knows how to motivate them or believe the criteria used to determine their salaries are fair and consistent.

On the other hand, almost three-quarters agreed their company has a reputation as a good employer, which may well be a legacy of the industry's long-standing focus on paternalism and relatively rich rewards. Whether and how that view may change over time remains to be seen. But having this kind of reputation is, interestingly enough, one of the most important attributes to employees everywhere in determining where they work, how long they stay and how much they engage. It was, in fact, the only attribute that showed up consistently across all the three areas of the employment life cycle in virtually every country surveyed. Finding ways to sustain and even further enhance their reputation as good employers may be one of the most critical steps insurance companies can take going forward.

Engaging for Peak Performance

When it comes to engaging employees (see Box 2), the insurance industry achieves slightly better results than most other sectors analyzed in the survey—but only by a small margin. Overall, 24% of insurance industry respondents are highly engaged, compared to 21% for the US overall. And 13% are disengaged, compared to 16% for the US overall. The remainder—63% in both cases—are moderately engaged.

Clearly, insurers face a challenge in this area. What will it take for them to move the needle on engagement? Exhibit 2 shows the elements of the work experience that are critical to pushing engagement levels up, as well as how employees currently rate their companies in these areas.

As with the retention drivers, the picture is mixed. On the positive side, approximately three-quarters or more of employees gave favorable ratings to several

Box 2: Defining Engagement

Towers Perrin defines employee engagement as employees' willingness and ability to contribute to the company's success or, put another way, the extent to which employees are willing to put discretionary effort into their work. Engagement is measured using nine factors that reflect both the emotional and rational connections workers have to their work. Full engagement demands, and depends on, both types of connections. If people are emotionally but not rationally engaged, they bring great energy and commitment to the job, but may be doing the wrong things or investing their time poorly. If people are rationally but not emotionally engaged, they know what to do, but may limit their time and energy to purely what's required and give no extra effort, time or thought to their work.

Source: www.towersperrin.com

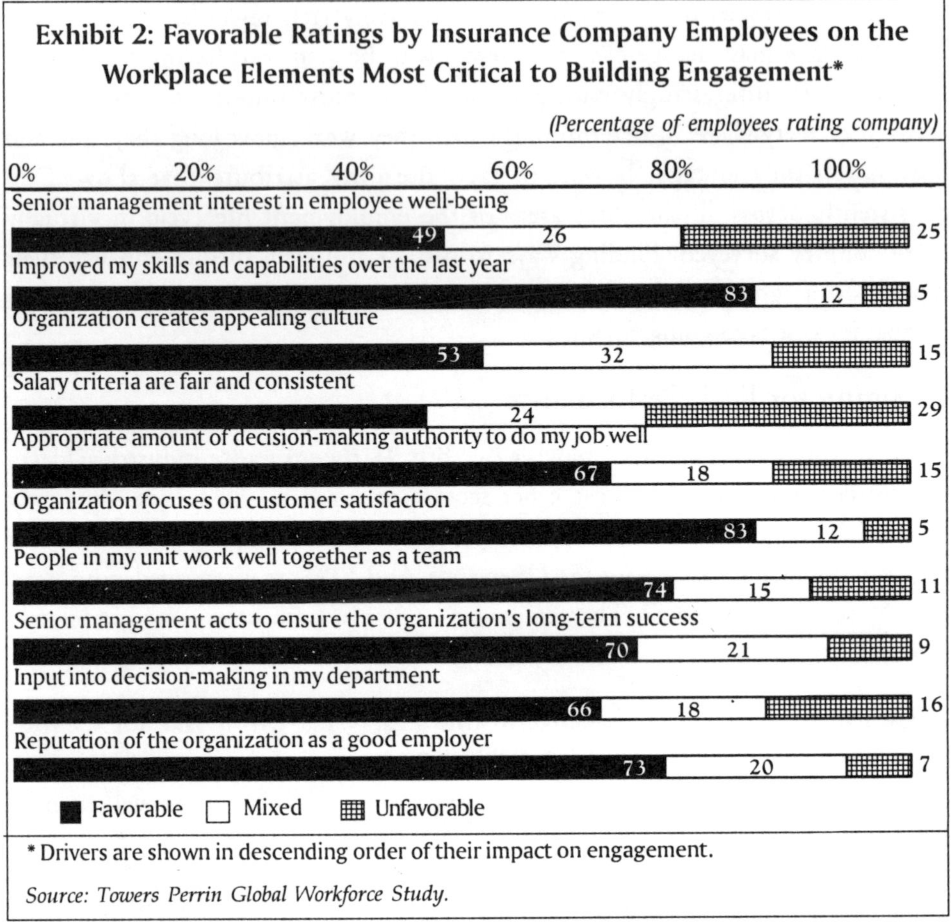

Exhibit 2: Favorable Ratings by Insurance Company Employees on the Workplace Elements Most Critical to Building Engagement*

* Drivers are shown in descending order of their impact on engagement.

Source: Towers Perrin Global Workforce Study.

important attributes, from having input into decision-making to effective teamwork to skill building. These are attributes insurers should continue to emphasize and nurture.

But three areas also stand out as particular challenges. And two of these, significantly, link back to the most intangible elements of the work experience—the organization's culture and the level of interest employees perceive from senior management, which are usually inextricably linked.

Why does engagement matter? Because it affects employees' behavior and actions in very critical ways. For one thing, higher levels of engagement lead to higher retention levels, helping address concerns about a revolving door of people and skills. Even more critically, higher levels of engagement contribute to better individual and, ultimately, better corporate performance. Highly engaged employees are far more likely than their less engaged counterparts to focus on satisfying customers, thus ensuring the quality of their work product and reducing costs in areas where they have such control (see Exhibit 3).

It doesn't take much imagination to consider the combined effect on performance in a large workforce if significant numbers of people put their energies into these areas on a consistent basis.

Exhibit 3: Links between Insurance Employees' Engagement Levels and Key Business Objectives

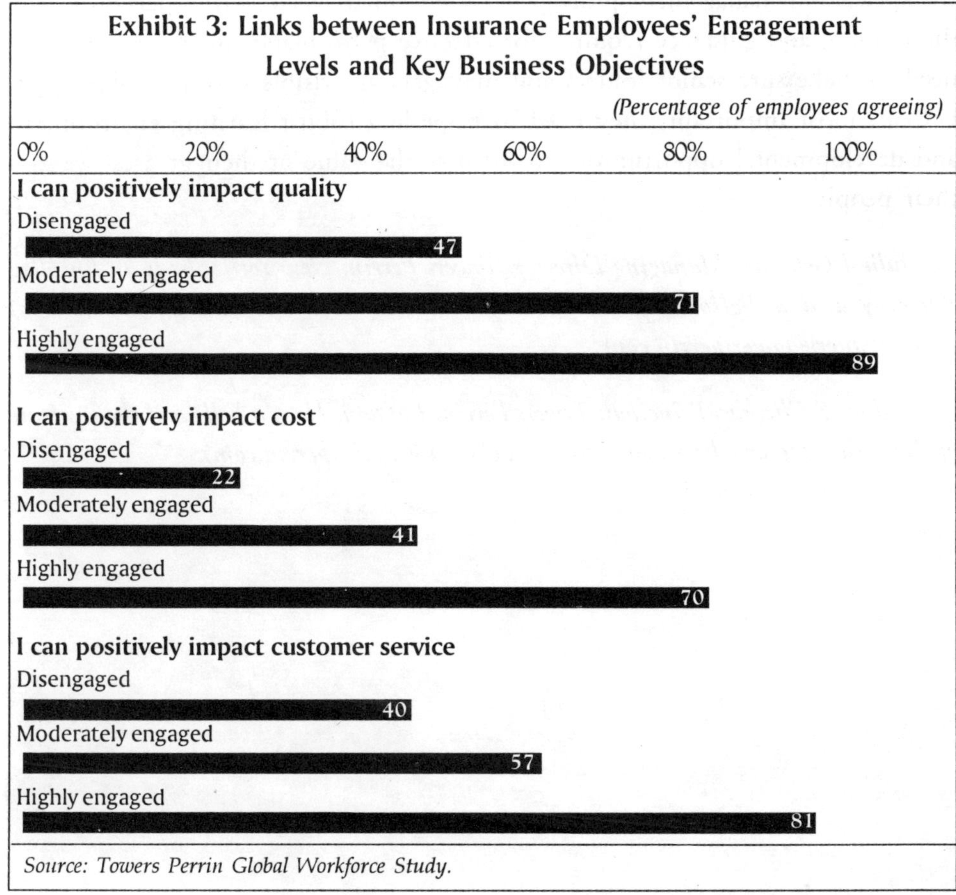

Source: Towers Perrin Global Workforce Study.

Road Map for Success

Our workforce data lay out a road map that insurance companies can follow as they craft employment deals that can serve both their needs and those of their employees—current and future. The starting point is understanding the workforce implications of the business plan and analyzing the composition of the workforce to understand how talent needs are evolving. With a clear picture of the head count and skills required to meet objectives over a specified time horizon, and knowing what the labor market challenges will be, insurance companies will be in a far better position to fashion an optimal deal for key segments of the workforce.

Along the way, insurance companies also need to build on their current workplace and management processes. They need to make sure supervisors have the training and guidance required for effective performance management. They need to make sure senior leaders and managers are visible and accessible. And, perhaps most important, they need to provide a robust learning environment and developmental opportunities to increase the value of their greatest asset—their people.

(Julie J Gebauer, Managing Director, Towers Perrin, New York. She is an Enrolled Actuary and a Fellow of the Society of Actuaries. She can be reached at julie.gebauer@towersperrin.com

Andrew S Cherkas, Principal, Towers Perrin, London. He is a Fellow of the Institute of Actuaries. He can be reached at andy.cherkas@towersperrin.com).

INDEX

R

S

T

U

V